ABOUT THE AUTHOR

Born in Fethard on Sea where his Father was a fisherman, Brendan Power has always had a love of the sea.

In 1952 his family became part of the Irish diaspora, moving to the UK when his Father joined the Merchant Navy. Aged 21, after managing various pop groups, he joined Radio 270, one of the so-called Pirate Radio stations, based on a converted trawler three miles off the coast of Yorkshire. This led to five years with Radio Antilles on Montserrat, the Emerald Isle of the Caribbean, as news editor, disc jockey and, latterly, sales manager. He was also a free-lance journalist for Associated Press and the London Daily Mirror. Returning to the UK for the launch of commercial radio he headed up the commercial production unit of BRMB Radio in Birmingham.

In the mid-seventies he underwent a change of career, spending the next thirty years as a financial adviser during which time he published two books, wrote numerous articles and established himself as a professional speaker, addressing audiences in more than a dozen countries. He is a former director of the Life Insurance Association and a founder and past President of the Professional Speakers Association.

Following his retirement, he returned to Fethard on Sea where he became involved in a community project to build a replica of the *Helen Blake*. Research surrounding this led to the production of this book.

....

"As a young boy, I lived next door to James Morrissey's old house and just six houses away from John Mac, who would often spend time talking to me when I went to the pump for water. Walking to the beach at Grange we would pass the house of Garry Handrick who always had a smile and a wave for us as we went by. Sadly, I had no idea then of their incredible courage, or what they had been through. I hope this book will help to keep their extraordinary story alive."

Brendan Power

Heroes of the Helen Blake

*The true story of an amazing
lifeboat disaster and rescue –
and the mysterious benefactor*

First Edition 2019
ISBN 978-1905597-86-4

A CIP catalogue record for this book is available
from the British Library.

Published by
Hibernia Heritage
HelenBlake@HiberniaHeritage.com

ILLUSTRATIONS

Current photographs of locations are by
Steve Meyler, and remain his copyright.

Paintings of the *Wreck of the Mexico*, and
Mexico are included by kind permission of
maritime artist Brian Cleare from Co Waterford.

Portraits are by various talented artists who worked
from very old, very often indistinct, photographs, and
in three cases from nothing more than vague descriptions
handed down through the generations over the past century.

Book design and layout by David Cronin, Moyhill Publishing
Cover design by Raymond Foley
Image: stylised detail from Brian Cleare's Wreck of the Mexico

Throughout the book I have used the Imperial measurements that were in general use at the time, and were used in the various reports.

1 gallon = 4.55 litres

1 pound = 454 grams

1 ton = 1016 kilograms

1 foot = 30 centimetres

1 yard = 0.91 metres

1 mile = 1609 metres

12 pennies = 1 shilling

20 shillings = one pound (£)

CONTENTS

Helen Blake – The Mysterious Benefactor

FOREWORD

In 2014, Liam Bates, a noted composer who had previously worked with artistes as diverse as Bon Jovi and Pavarotti, created a five movement seascape for orchestra and large choir, which was performed by the Wexford Sinfonia in the National Concert Hall in Dublin. The name chosen for this piece, written to honour volunteers of the RNLI (Royal National Lifeboat Institution) throughout Ireland and the UK, was, *The Heroes of the Helen Blake*.

Since its foundation in 1824 as the National Institution for the Preservation of Life from Shipwreck, the RNLI has relied on volunteers to crew its lifeboats, with virtually every occupation and profession represented at some time or another on one of their boats. It was no different on that fateful day in 1914 when the farmers and fishermen who made up the crew of *Helen Blake*, set out from the tiny village of Fethard on a rescue mission that, tragically, would make history.

That day resulted in one of the biggest losses of life ever suffered by the RNLI in Ireland, and left a village devastated. This book is dedicated to the memory of the fourteen men who put their own lives at risk by launching their lifeboat – a thirty-five foot rowing boat – into the teeth of a gale on an errand of mercy, to save the lives of people they didn't even know.

The **HELEN BLAKE**
LIFEBOAT PROJECT

www.TheHelenBlake.com

HOME FROM THE SEA

On a cold winters night
With the storm at its height
The lifeboat answered the call.
They pitched and they tossed
Till we thought they were lost
As we watched from the harbour wall.
Tho' the night was pitch black,
There was no turning back,
For somcone was waiting out there,
But each volunteer
Had to live with his fear
As they joined in a silent prayer

– *Phil Coulter*

1

Anybody can pilot a ship when the sea is calm.
– Navjot Singh Sidhu

Isla del Carmen on the Yucatán Peninsula in the South East of Mexico is little more than a thin strip of land twenty-five miles long, four or five miles wide and a maximum of ten feet above sea level; together with the neighbouring Isla Aguada it provides a barrier between the ocean and the six hundred square mile Laguna del Términos. At one end of the island is the pre-Hispanic city of Ciudad del Carmen and at the other end stands the port of Laguna, which in the early part of the twentieth century was an important port for Mexico's timber trade.

The busiest time was the dry season from January to May and in preparation for this, thousands of enormous mahogany and cedar logs would be stacked in great piles during the rest of the year, having been brought from the interior by horse drawn carts before being floated across the lagoon to the island, towed by a variety of small boats.

Tuesday 4th November 1913 was a comparatively quiet day for the port with four ships in various stages of loading tied up

alongside the quay; two American, one British and one flying
the flag of Norway. A mile or so offshore a couple of other ships
were at anchor waiting patiently for a space that would allow
them to load their cargoes.

Standing out from the drab steamships surrounding it at the
quayside, and displaying the Norwegian flag, was the sleek
white hull of a regular visitor to the port, the hundred-and-
eighty feet, five-hundred-and- thirty ton three-masted schooner
Mexico. Around the same size as many modern day trawlers,
she had arrived from England with a cargo of coal at a quiet
time almost a week earlier and had been fortunate to find a
berth alongside without having to anchor offshore. Bobbing
gently in the water and attracting admiring looks from those
on board the steamships, there was no indication that the
schooner's imminent voyage would be anything but routine,
or that within a few months her name, and her fate, would be
known around the world.

Mexico had been specially built for the timber trade with a
number of innovative design features. The hull, unusually, was flat
and was fitted with an eleven foot long keel that could be lowered
or lifted to suit the circumstances. Many of the timber ports were
situated in or near river deltas so, to avoid grounding, most ships
had to anchor anything up to three miles offshore where cargo
would be floated out to them on barges and loaded manually. When
Mexico's twelve feet deep keel was raised it reduced the draught
to just nine feet, allowing her to anchor in comparatively shallow
water, much closer to shore, thereby reducing loading time.

It was normal practice at that time to load gravel or soil into
the hold of a ship as ballast to provide stability when it was not
carrying any cargo. The big drawback with this method was that

it took a good deal of back breaking and time consuming work to load it, and even longer to clear the hold before cargo could be brought on board. Such work could very easily add two or three days, or more, to the time spent in port, adding significantly to ship owner's operating costs.

It was with this in mind that the shipbuilders in Fredrikstad had designed *Mexico* with a double hull. Such arrangements are commonplace now with the space between the two hulls being divided into a number of ballast tanks, but when *Mexico* was built it was ground-breaking. The space between the hulls would be filled with water to provide the necessary stability and could then be quickly pumped out using a steam powered donkey engine, which was on deck, to work the pumps – another innovation the original owner, Rolf Seeberg, had included when the ship was built almost nine years earlier.

Weighing anything up to seven tons each, the logs had to be very carefully stowed and packed tightly in the hold to prevent any movement during the voyage. Once again, this was heavy, time consuming work, especially in the hot and humid conditions prevalent in most of the ports. To overcome this problem the powerful little engine was used to drive winches connected to two ten-ton derricks.

The main cargo hatch was longer than normal (a feature that would cause a great deal of concern during the forthcoming voyage) allowing the logs to be swung in with minimum effort, and further reduce the time required for loading. Without the help of the engine, it would have been a struggle to load fifty tons in a day. *Mexico* had just tripled that figure.

The cargo was now loaded and carefully stowed in the hold, the fresh water tanks had been filled and the last of the provisions for the trip were being stored safely below decks, together with a few personal items the crew had picked up on shore. Everybody was in good spirits, they knew the reputation of the captain and they liked the ship; she was fast, handled well in heavy seas and was quick to answer the helm.

Captain Ole Edvin Eriksen assigned twenty-two year old First Mate Sigurd Lie to secure the hatches and prepare the ship for sea whilst he dealt with the last of the paperwork in the offices of Bolnes, Hermanos & Co. Despite his young age, Eriksen had complete confidence in Lie who had served with him for the past twelve months during which time he had proved to be a first class sailor, and leader.

Lie was from Tønsberg, a former capital of Norway, and generally regarded as its oldest town, founded by the Vikings in the ninth century. It was also recognised as 'the cradle of modern whaling' and was home to a huge fleet of sailing ships. It was on one of those that the young Lie had first gone to sea and he had already accumulated over six years' experience before his twenty-first birthday.

Four hundred and eighty one tons of mahogany and cedar logs had been loaded for this trip to Liverpool. On arrival they would be transferred to barges on the Manchester ship canal for delivery to David Midgley & Sons.

As can still be the case today, sailors on merchant ships were not classed as permanent employees, instead working on a trip-by-trip or ship-by-ship basis. This meant they signed on to a ship for a specific period, often just one voyage at a time (today it is more likely to be for twelve months) and because of this there would invariably be a pool of sailors of varying abilities in most ports looking for a ship to join. This was not always the case, however, and very often a ship's crew could be below its normal complement.

Such was the situation with the *Mexico* today; three Mexican sailors had signed off when they reached Laguna and with only one suitable replacement available – a Russian who had arrived in the port a few weeks earlier as a stoker on a British steamship – she would sail this time with a crew of eight instead of the usual ten. The extra hands would be sorely missed in the weeks ahead.

Sixty-four year old Eriksen had sailed this route many times on different ships and always enjoyed the company of shipping agent Luis Bolnes, with whom he had established a very good relationship. This was to be his final voyage; he had joined the ship when Alf Rød bought it a year ago and had informed the owner of his decision to retire when he reached Liverpool, where he would hand her over to a new captain.

At the conclusion of their business, as was usual, the two men drank coffee together, but this time they were joined by masters from the other vessels in port; some of them knew Eriksen personally and all of them knew him by reputation. Five-feet-seven tall and weighing in at one hundred and thirty pounds, sporting almost white hair with a trim beard the same colour and the typical blue eyes of his countrymen, he was not a physically imposing figure, perhaps being better described as distinguished, but in a group of fellow seafarers his presence was immense.

Having qualified as a master at the age of twenty-five and with almost half a century in sailing ships, there were very few people afloat who knew more about the sea – something his crew would be very grateful for on the upcoming voyage – and even fewer who were happy to share their knowledge.

The group spent a pleasant hour or so sharing stories before the theme of the conversation inevitably switched to the weather prospects for the various voyages ahead of them. It was less than a week since what was to be the final tropical storm of the year had developed in the Caribbean Sea, about four hundred miles from Laguna on the other side of the Yucatán Peninsula, but it had only lasted for forty-eight hours before weakening over Cuba and reasonable weather was anticipated for *Mexico's* voyage.

With an experienced, if slightly under strength, crew on board one of the fastest schooners afloat – she was as much a racehorse as a workhorse – Eriksen had no concerns about what lay ahead. The cargo was more than three hundred tons below their capacity, on a route for which the ship had been specifically built, and which it had negotiated many times before. It was anticipated that crossing the Atlantic would take them somewhere in the region of six or seven weeks, putting them in Liverpool a few days before Christmas or, with favourable winds, perhaps even earlier, enabling Eriksen to be home in Norway for Christmas.

From the start things did not go according to plan, however, and the multi-national crew spent an uncomfortable and frustrating first month becalmed in the deepest part of the Gulf of Mexico. As they drifted aimlessly back and forth at the whim of the currents, in temperatures over thirty degrees and relative humidity over eighty percent, the men were forced to sleep on deck to avoid the stifling heat in their cramped quarters.

The Gulf was not a happy place for the *Mexico*; five years earlier she was docked in Pensacola when Norwegian crew member Kurt Jacobsen died after being assaulted by Greek restauranteur John Apostle, who two days previously had been acquitted of a charge of selling liquor on a Sunday. He was charged with Jacobsen's murder but found not guilty and cause of death was later declared as acute meningitis.

The crew were kept busy for much of the day with routine maintenance work but as the sun approached its zenith they had to take shelter from its burning rays. With an abundance of fresh fish to be caught they ate well, but their fresh water needed to be carefully rationed so the only way to cool off was in the sea. By lowering the ship's lifeboat it could be used as a platform where even the non- swimmers could immerse themselves in the cool water as they clung on – in some cases, tied themselves on – to the gunwales. Sparkling in the sunshine the calm blue sea looked very inviting but knowing that a sudden gust of wind could take the ship out of reach in minutes, and with two miles of water beneath them, they were taking no chances.

The sense of relief throughout the ship when the wind did eventually start to pick up was almost overpowering. Monotony had caused boredom to set in during the past few weeks but now, as they could feel the coolness of the breeze on their cheeks, they had a purpose again. It was all hands on deck as the sails were raised to take full advantage of the northerly currents of the Gulf Stream. The Stream would be their companion for the next couple of weeks or so taking them through the Straits of Florida and seven hundred miles along the Eastern Seaboard of America.

Throughout this section of the voyage a bucket of seawater was hauled on board twice a day to check the temperature of the sea. As long ago as 1770, Benjamin Franklin had written, *"A stranger may know when he is in the Gulph* (sic) *Stream, by the warmth of the water, which is much greater than that of the water each side of it"*. Sixty miles wide and varying between two-and-a-half and four thousand feet deep, the Gulf Stream is in the region of five to ten degrees warmer than the surrounding sea and the captain wanted to ensure they stayed in it as the current would add almost an extra five knots to their speed. Twenty-three year old Sebastian Riley who had joined the ship at the start of its outward voyage to Laguna a few months earlier had impressed Eriksen with his enthusiasm and his intelligence, and was given the responsibility for this task.

Riley's father was a successful corn merchant in Manchester who had sent his son to be educated in that city's Victoria University in anticipation of him joining the business. The only thing Sebastian had ever wanted, however, was to go to sea so three years earlier, at the age of twenty-one he signed on as a deckhand with the Irish registered *Cymric*, also a three masted schooner but at two hundred and thirty tons, less than half the size of the *Mexico*. He had decided that at the end of this trip he would be going back to college to study for his first mate's ticket.

Spirits were high after their enforced inactivity and they made good time all the way up the coast. On Monday 22nd December, for the first time since leaving Laguna, there was a slight chill in the air. Perhaps this was an indication of what lay in store for them but for now everything was fine with a good wind and just a slight swell on the sea. With the weather crisp and clear, visibility was almost unlimited throughout the day, and as darkness approached the light from the candy striped Cape Hatteras lighthouse situated on the Outer Banks reached out towards them. The Banks are a string of small islands which act as a buffer between the ocean and the coast of North

MEXICO

Painting by Brian Cleare

Photo courtesy of the State archives of North Carolina

CAPE HATTERAS LIGHTHOUSE

In 1999 the entire 210 foot tower, plus two houses and various associated structures were moved half-a-mile Inland to offset the effects of coastal erosion

Carolina, and where, two hundred years earlier, the notorious pirate Blackbeard (Edward Teach) met his death.

Continuing to sail north easterly the weather changed dramatically and the crew had to break out their oilskins and cold weather clothing to counteract the temperature which had dropped to around half of those experienced off the Florida coast. It would be some time before they were warm again.

One hundred miles off Cape Cod, as they skirted the shallow waters of Georges Bank, Riley spent some time fishing off the stern and landed a few large Cod which were eagerly devoured in the evening. Fifty years earlier this part of the ocean, as little as twenty feet deep in places, would have been crowded with anything up to a hundred fishing schooners from ports along the New England coastline, but today there were no other boats in sight.

Their course took them southeast of the Grand Banks, a volatile and unpredictable area where fifteen years later an earthquake caused a tsunami which killed twenty-seven people. They were now at the point off the coast of Nova Scotia where the Gulf Stream becomes the North Atlantic Drift and takes the great circle route across the ocean all the way to Europe. This was also where the cold waters of the Labrador Current meet up with the Gulf Stream causing one of the densest concentrations of fog in the world. Today was not too bad, with visibility around three hundred feet, but no chances were taken and Eriksen posted four lookouts to scan the area for ships entering or exiting the St Lawrence River. Unusually, there were none to be seen.

Turning to starboard Eriksen pointed the ship towards Europe for an easterly crossing of the North Atlantic. By now they were well behind schedule but it was a well-travelled route they had all been on before, and one that had been used by seafarers for hundreds of years. With the prevailing winds coming from astern, Eriksen estimated that if lady luck was on their side for the rest of the voyage they could still be in Liverpool around the middle of January.

As they sailed out of the fog, they entered the choppy waters of the Flemish Cap, made famous in later years by Sebastian Junger's book, *The Perfect Storm*. By now the crew had returned to their normal routine, working like a well-oiled machine in an effort to make up some of the lost time, ceaselessly trimming the sails to take advantage of every shift in the wind and every run of the sea. Everything went well for the first twenty-four hours but then the swells started to increase in size as the ocean warned them what to expect.

By the third day, instead of celebrating Christmas Day in Liverpool as they had originally anticipated, they were hanging on for dear life as a low pressure system materialised causing a rapid deterioration in the weather. Menacing storms suddenly emerged from the northwest throwing the little ship around in gale force winds and pounding it with waves that were described as being almost as 'high as a house'.

The stinging rain was constantly peppering their faces and as ice cold water from the ocean engulfed the schooner it numbed the men's feet and poured into their oilskins making even routine tasks a laborious chore. On deck the helmsman had to apply the brake to the helm, without which the ferocious action of the sea would have caused it to spin so violently it could have thrown him overboard.

They had little choice now, the wind and the sea had taken command of the ship and they had to go wherever the elements took them. It was not long before they were blown off course as they faced the full fury of a North Atlantic storm that was to become their constant companion during the next few weeks.

2

Be happy for this moment. This moment is your life.
– Omar Khayyham

Three thousand miles east of *Mexico's* position, the community of farmers and fishermen in the tiny village of Fethard, on the south-east coast of Ireland, normally had their lives ruled by the weather but today they had put all thoughts of it to one side as they celebrated Christmas with their families in traditional fashion.

Children had written their letters to Santa Claus a few weeks earlier and had posted them up the chimney where the draught from the fire sped them on their way to the North Pole. Just about everybody in the parish had been to Midnight Mass where they remembered and celebrated the meaning of Christmas as well as taking the opportunity to talk with friends they had not seen since the previous Sunday.

The Church of Ireland congregation gathered in the eighteenth century church of St Mogue's on the edge of village where Rev Ellison took the service. The Catholics had a little farther to travel to the quaint little cruciform style church of

St Aidan's, built a mile away in an isolated wooded hollow in Poulfur during the early nineteenth century when the penal laws against Catholics were in force. Here, Father Daniel Lyne tailored his sermon especially for the children and Christmas carols, many of them in Latin, were sung with enthusiasm by the entire congregation.

Patrick Cullen lived with his wife, Margaret, and their large family in a small, completely exposed, cliff top cottage at the appropriately named Windy Gap. Mary and Bridget were the most popular names in the country at that time and most families had at least one daughter with one of those names. This could easily lead to confusion so it was common practice to give them pet names. Nowhere was this more true that in the Cullen family where they had christened four of their daughters Mary Margaret (Cissie), Mary Bridget (Dolly), Bridget (Bridie) and Mary Kate (Cathy). Less than three weeks earlier they had celebrated the first birthday of Cathy, their youngest child, and now wanted to do something for their other eight children. As a special treat for them Patrick borrowed an ass and cart from his landlord, local farmer Denis Foley, so they could all ride the two miles to church, instead of walking as they normally did. They arrived early to make sure the family would be able to sit together, in the same pew; tonight the church would be full and for the latecomers it would be standing room only.

People spilled out of the Churches when the services were over, gathering together in small groups on the road. Whilst Margaret and the children stopped to admire the crib that had been built in the vestibule, Patrick joined a few of his friends who, like him, were volunteer members of the local lifeboat crew. An early morning frost made it too cold to stand around

WINDY GAP

Patrick Cullen's house was at the end of the small lane in the centre.
The Keeragh Islands can be seen just below the horizon.

Photo by Steve Meyler

for long and this, coupled with the excitement of the children, meant many of the little groups started to disperse almost as soon as they had formed. Two members of the lifeboat crew, John 'Mac' McNamara and Garrett 'Garry' Handrick, decided to walk home together.

The fact that Garry's sister, Mary Bridget, was there may have had something to do with Mac's decision – during the past few months the two of them had spent a great deal of time in each other's company. At five foot five she was a good three inches shorter than Mac, slender with a natural beauty and bright blue eyes in a face framed by light brown shoulder length hair and to Mac, the most beautiful girl he had ever seen.

When they reached Grange crossroads at the top of the village they said their goodbyes with the siblings turning left for their house a quarter of a mile away, close to Grange beach. Mac continued straight on to the bottom of the street where he lived with his youngest brother Patrick, the local postman, opposite the village pump in one of a terrace of seven small houses built as part of the Ely estate half a century earlier.

On Christmas morning children throughout the area woke early, eager to see what was in the stockings that had been hung on the end of the bed the previous evening. The combination of large families and small incomes meant presents were thin on the ground and for most children it would have been a piece of fruit, a few sweets, a home-made toy and perhaps a new jumper or a pair of socks that had been knitted by their mother. For the majority of families money was always scarce and there was little to spare on luxuries but that in no way affected their excitement or enjoyment.

JOHN McNAMARA'S HOUSE

POULFUR CHURCH

Photos by Steve Meyler

In many cases, there was no father to join the celebrations; they were away at sea earning money to keep the family and their only contact for a year or more would be the monthly postal order sent by the shipping company.

The children spent most of the morning playing with their new toys whilst the home grown Christmas dinner was being prepared; a goose that had been reared especially for that day, accompanied by fresh vegetables from the garden, would be followed by the highlight of the day – home-made Christmas pudding with coins wrapped in greaseproof paper hidden inside, there were always enough to make sure each child got one. The evening was spent in front of an open fire playing games, telling stories and singing Christmas songs.

Fethard was, in many ways still is, and hopefully always will be, an idyllic, sleepy, village. Like so many villages in Ireland during the early part of the twentieth century, it consisted of just one street, with a couple of small lanes running off it. What distinguished it from many of the other villages, however, was the varied and surprising array of buildings and businesses. At one end of the street was a church and a fifteenth century castle, and at the other end John Ryan's farmhouse, the main source of milk and meat for the population, and the all-important village pump which provided fresh water for over half of the village. In between was the Royal Irish Constabulary (RIC) barracks, a Wesleyan chapel, a Coast Guard station, a coal yard, a fresh water well, a blacksmith, a saddler, a shoemaker, a doctor's surgery & dispensary, a rectory, a sawmill, a school, two shops, a hotel and two public houses.

The population of just one hundred and seventy lived in forty five houses, mainly simple terraced cottages, some pebble dashed and some whitewashed, each one with a garden where every square inch was used to grow vegetables, and soft fruit for jam making. Flowers were less common on the basis that you cannot eat flowers.

Behind the rectory, Rev William Ellison, a keen astronomer, had built his own observatory which provided entertainment and education in equal measures for many of the young people in the village. Scattered around the immediate vicinity were a few small farms, a sprinkling of cottages, two more churches, three schools, a fishing harbour and a couple more pubs.

Seventeen miles away is New Ross, the nearest town, and it was from here the *Washington Irving* sailed in April 1849. Amongst the almost three hundred passengers who were fleeing the Great Famine to start a new life in America was John F Kennedy's great grandfather, twenty-nine year old Patrick, who boarded the ship at Passage East, half way down the river.

The county town of Wexford is twenty-five miles away and Ireland's capital city of Dublin is a further hundred but that was not enough to stop a number of men from around the county making the journey on their bicycles (sleeping in barns along the way) earlier in the month to see the Wexford team take on Kerry in the first All- Ireland Gaelic football championship to be played at the newly named Croke Park, which would go on to become a symbol of Irish nationalism. Wexford lost the match but turned the tables on Kerry a couple of years later and followed that up by winning the next three finals in a row.

Being at the top of the Hook Peninsula meant it was necessarily something of an insular community. Nobody passes through

Fethard on their way to anywhere else, it is a cul-de-sac and the only visitors are those for whom it is their destination. Situated in the aptly named 'sunny south-east' of Ireland and with fourteen beaches within easy reach around the area, it has always attracted, and welcomed, a number of holidaymakers from the towns and cities during the summer months. In the past they were referred to locally as 'bathers' because whilst very few of the local adults ever went swimming, or bathing as it was called, the visitors, understandably, spent the majority of their time on the beach enjoying the clear waters. When September arrived the holidaymakers went home, the village again retreated into itself and things returned to normal.

This was a village where everybody really did know everybody else, where you could rely on your neighbours, and where you never needed to lock your front door; crime was unheard of. Self- sufficiency was a way of life, something children learned and participated in almost as soon as they could walk and talk, doing naturally what in the twenty-first century has become an upmarket industry; foraging. An early morning walk in the meadows would provide plenty of wild mushrooms during the summer, the hedgerows were full of blackberries and sloes in the autumn and there were even a few apple trees scattered around.

There was an abundance of cockles waiting to be picked on the Little Burrow, plenty of mussels to be found below the lifeboat house, and with miles of coastline between Windy Gap and Bag-in-Bun head, there was no scarcity of barnacles or periwinkles on the rocks at any time of the year.

To put meat on the table, rabbits could be snared in the sand dunes of the Big Burrow and there was never any shortage of fish to be caught from the rocks, on occasions there would be such an abundance of mackerel that they could be scooped up by hand and thrown onto the beach. Behind the Little Burrow, close to the boathouse, children would catch small dabs (a sweet flat fish) by walking barefoot through channels in the silt and reaching down to pick them up when they felt them move beneath their feet. On the edge of the village was a solid bridge with a small sluice gate and for those who liked eels, they could be caught here by baiting a bent pin with a worm and securing it to a length of string by a small piece of fishing line, referred to locally as 'cat-gut'.

Though the terms 'free-range' and 'organic' had yet to enter their vocabulary, they were terms that described their food perfectly. Protein was obtained from the fresh milk, seafood, eggs from the chickens and geese kept in the back yard, and eventually from the poultry itself. Omega 3 came from mackerel, herrings and salmon, and there was an abundance of carbohydrates from fruit, porridge, home- made bread and the ubiquitous potato. When an animal was slaughtered the menu would often include offal such as liver, kidney and tongue, which are packed with minerals and vitamins.

It was wholesome and healthy food with very little fat, an omission that was more than compensated for when crubeens (pigs feet), a favourite with nearly everybody, were served. Many people kept bees to provide honey and children would wait eagerly for a piece of the honeycomb when they were removed from the hives.

All through the year, men, women and children would scour the beaches engaged in what they called wreck hunting, an activity we now know as beachcombing. All kinds of things would end up on the beach from shipwrecks or deck cargo that had been washed overboard. The most plentiful find would be armfuls of driftwood, which was dried out to fuel the fire at home, or to make furniture. Amongst the most prized finds were coloured glass balls which were used as buoys by fishermen in Europe and had broken away from their nets or lobster pots.

At the bottom of the cliff just twenty feet below their cottage was an abundance of driftwood, especially after a storm, and young Jimmy and Patsy Cullen would turn a chore into a game, competing with each other to see who could collect most, even though it was an unfair contest with Jimmy being four years older than seven year old Patsy. Sometimes there would be a piece so big they had to share the load and occasionally one that took two or three men to lift; these specimen pieces would be put to one side and brought out when furniture was being made or a new house was being built. Michael, known as Mikie, was almost fourteen and would be leaving school soon so he was excused wood collection on most days as he was already helping his father on the fishing boat.

Life was simple and life was tough, but for children the whole area was one big playground where they made their own enter-tainment. Schools closed for almost three months during the summer, allowing children to help their parents with the harvest or the fishing and in the warm weather they ran barefoot in the street (boots and shoes were reserved for cold weather and for attending Church) making the soles of their feet as tough as leather. There would not be tarmac on the village street until the late nineteen fifties, for now it was just a combination of mud and stones.

FETHARD 1914

The three men with the bicycle are policemen outside the RIC barracks

The GAA (Gaelic Athletic Association) sports invoked fierce inter parish rivalry. Every village had a Gaelic Football and Hurling team, and in the absence of a purpose built 'ball alley', handball could be played wherever there was a wall to knock a ball against.

At harvest time the children would watch what looked like choreographed moves by the men cutting corn with their scythes, and then help to tie up the sheaves, which were left to dry awaiting the arrival of one of the huge steam engines that would roam the countryside, moving from one farm to another, ready to power the threshing machines.

Down on the dock they would watch the lobsters being unloaded by the fishermen who might sometimes give them a few crabs to take home. There was no market for crabs at that time and any that were caught in the lobster pots were seen as pests. There was an abundance of mackerel and pollock, and while much of the catch was used to bait the lobster pots, there would always be some left over for the table.

During the winter months fishing nets were set in the bay outside the dock and would produce boxes of choice herrings. Children would help the fishermen to unload, or tie up, or wash the deck, or anything else to earn half a dozen of the fish to take home for dinner. Some of the boats spent the winter in the comparative shelter of the river, moving to neighbouring Duncannon where they fished for wild salmon.

Living an outdoor life on the coast, and with pollution a term for the future, the children of Fethard breathed the freshest of fresh air.

On most days during the week the village looked deserted with rarely more than two or three people on the street. The children were at school, the men were working in the fields or on the sea, the women were busy in the house and, of course, there were only two or three cars. There was no reason to be on the street unless you were going to the pump for water, to the farm for milk or, very occasionally, to buy something from the shop.

Weekends were different. Almost from first light on Saturday children would be playing, throughout the day people from the outlying areas would arrive to do their shopping and the men would gather on the corner at the top of the Sluice Lane (also, for some mysterious reason, known as College Street), a few doors away from Matt Finn's blacksmiths workshop. It was here they would exchange gossip, discuss the highs and lows of their week farming or fishing, and generally pass the time of day as they chewed tobacco.

On Sunday morning the village was back to being like a ghost town as everybody went to church, but that all changed around midday when they returned and gathered in the street to talk with their neighbours.

In the absence of electricity, life revolved around the hours of daylight and when it got dark the dim light of lamps and candles could be seen flickering in the windows as the street emptied. In wintertime, the occasional glow could be seen from the heavy oil lights used on bicycles or, very infrequently, the lights of a car. It was May 1952 before Fethard and the surrounding areas known as townlands became the one hundred and ninety ninth rural area in Ireland to be connected to the electricity grid. That was the signal for major changes, typified by a comment from Minister for Industry Seán Lemass who is recorded as saying, *"I hope to see the day when a girl gets a proposal from a farmer*

she will enquire not so much about the number of cows but ...
the electrical appliances she will require ..."

Running water was a novelty when it was first plumbed into the houses in 1957, but in 1913 sanitation was very basic and brides- to-be were still asking about the number of cows. Fresh water for drinking, cooking and washing was provided by the village pump and carried home in a bucket.

Most people collected rain water in barrels and used this to wash clothes or clean the chamber pot, which was kept under the bed at night. Toilet facilities were at their most basic, usually consisting of a large bucket underneath a home-made seat in an outhouse. Taking a bath was a major operation as buckets of water were transferred to large pots to be heated on the stove before being poured into the tin bath, which would be brought out and placed in front of the fire.

The throw away culture of the twenty-first century would have been incomprehensible to people at that time; few of them had more than one spare set of clothing, and some did not even have that. Clothes were frequently home-made, and for children hand-me-downs were normal. It was surely in communities like this that maxims such as 'make do and mend' and 'a stitch in time saves nine' first saw the light of day. Despite all the privations, house proud wives and mothers ensured there were always clean clothes for the family, there was food on the table and the house was kept neat and tidy.

For the people of Fethard on that Christmas Day, there was no hint that what was happening in Mid-Atlantic would, just eight weeks later, have a profound and lasting effect on the village, changing the lives of many of the families forever.

chapter

3

And behold, there arose a great storm on the sea, so that the
boat was being swamped by the waves.
– Matthew 8:24

During the evening of what the Norwegians call the third
day of Christmas – 27th December – a loud crack on
board *Mexico* brought everyone rushing on to the deck
to discover the rudder had been torn away by the storm, putting
the ship at the mercy of the ocean as it was pushed and pulled
in every direction by the wind and waves.

Howling and shrieking through the rigging, the wind raged
as the sea cascaded over the deck, finding its way through
every little gap in the woodwork. One brutal wave ripped the
small lifeboat from the deck and carried it away in a matter of
seconds; if anything happened now, there was no safety net and
the pitiless depths of the Atlantic were just waiting for them if
something went wrong.

It is possible they had been hit by a rogue wave. Rogue waves
are just that, rogues. They can be anything from twice as high as
the average wave and there is no way of knowing when they will

come or where they will come from. If you were fortunate, and visibility was good, you might see them a few minutes before they struck, if visibility was poor there would be no warning before hundreds, perhaps thousands, of tons of angry sea crashed into the hull and onto the deck. In 1861 a rogue wave smashed windows two-hundred-and-twenty feet above sea level at the top of Eagle Island lighthouse off the coast of Mayo in the West of Ireland, and twenty years after *Mexico's* voyage, a wave that must have been close to a hundred feet high broke over the bridge of *RMS Majestic*, the biggest ship in the world, during an Atlantic crossing; in recent years they have even been known to knock helicopters from the sky.

Below deck on *Mexico* clothing and bedding was drenched and anything not locked away was flung around the cabins as the ship rolled and plunged out of control in the mountainous seas. Every man was both physically and mentally exhausted but it was impossible to sit or lie down; all they could do through-out the night was hold on tight to avoid being thrown around and injured.

Experiencing the full fury of a mid-Atlantic depression there was little they could do to help themselves, or the ship. Bilge pumps had to be worked continuously to prevent flooding while on deck the sailors were in danger of being swept off their feet and slammed against the gunwales by the gushing water. As they came close to capsizing on more than one occasion the fate of their sister ship, *Laguna*, must surely have crossed their minds.

Towards the end of September 1905, on the maiden voyages of both vessels they were docked together in Pascagoula, Mississippi when the *Laguna's* captain, Lauritz Melsom, was rushed in to hospital with jaundice. In his absence thirty-three year old first mate Otto Grueneberg took over command of the ship and set sail for Colón in Panama through the Gulf of Mexico, which was shaking off the tail end of a tropical storm.

From there, with a thousand miles to go, she would have sailed through the Yucatán Channel between Cuba and Cancún, Mexico, and into the Caribbean Sea, where a major hurricane developed four days later. The schooner never reached her destination, tragically disappearing without trace and with the loss of all ten men on board.

By some twist of fate, two of Captain Melsom's other ships were also lost at sea when he was not on board – *Prince Eugen* a year earlier when he was hospitalised in Christiania (Oslo) with beriberi and appendicitis, and the barque *Alta Vela* some years later when he was on leave.

As they sailed into what should have been sunrise on Sunday 28th December, there were even more worries for *Mexico's* crew when they were able to see the full extent of the damage to the steering gear and quickly realised the problem was a lot more serious than they had originally believed. The ship was now in dire peril. Every ounce of experience from Captain Eriksen and all the skills and seamanship of his depleted crew, were needed to carry out temporary repairs and make it possible for them to regain command of the vessel. Their labours took most of the day leaving each of them weak and tired from their exertions.

The captain now had an important decision to make; one which could determine whether they lived or died. The ship was no longer in a seaworthy condition, there was no way of knowing how long the repairs to the rudder would last, the storm was still raging and it was vital they sought shelter in a harbour where permanent repairs could be carried out.

Surrounded by tens of thousands of square miles of ostensibly empty ocean and with almost two and a half miles of water beneath them, precarious seems an inadequate word to describe their situation. Nobody else knew where they were, and even if they did it would make no difference, there was no help available.

The nearest ports were New York, five hundred miles to the west and Bermuda, three hundred miles south west. To reach either of these would mean turning into the wind which, even if it was possible, would be an extremely dangerous, and foolhardy, manoeuvre. Wave height was averaging well over twenty feet and Eriksen knew that every eight to nine hours he could expect a wave that would be at least twice that height. In the ship's current state that could be fatal. This was not the first, or the worst, storm the captain had encountered during his almost half a century at sea – five years earlier his ship had been lifted clear out of the water and dumped on land during a cyclone in Australia – and he knew the most important thing was not to panic but to retain discipline amongst the crew.

With the closest ports being unreachable he dismissed them from his mind and searched for alternatives, eventually making a decision to run for the Azores, eighteen hundred miles away to the east.

The schooner's myriad of sails would normally offer countless permutations but with many of them ripped to shreds by the storm, options were limited. It was now more important than ever for the right combination to be chosen and once again everybody on board had reason to be grateful for the Captain's many years of experience. By shortening the sails to the minimum they managed to catch enough wind to limp into 1914, through the continuing bad weather, without putting the ship in any further danger.

On the sixth day, Saturday 3rd January, the wind was in an angry mood again and about an hour before dawn, the ship spun violently, throwing men from their bunks onto decks that were littered with pots and pans from the galley, clothes from cupboards that had swung open and debris washed down along with the flood of water pouring from the deck.

Fearful for their lives, the men scurried across the cabin and bounded up the few steps of the companionway. Even though they could barely make out shapes on the deck in the grey light between night and day, it took less than a minute for them to realise there was nobody at the helm. Mikhail, the Russian deck-hand, rushed across the flooded deck to grab the helm but it just spun freely in his hands. The rudder had gone again.

It was only then they spotted helmsman Hilmar Paulsen lying on the deck, semi-conscious with blood pouring from his cheek. His safety line fixed to the mast was at full stretch but had mercifully saved his life by preventing him being washed overboard. Unable to walk, he was carried below decks where his cuts were tended to by one of the crew while first mate Lie tied a line around his waist and gingerly made his way toward the stern to investigate the problem.

It looked like the temporary rudder had broken away causing the ship to spin around and, caught unawares, the helmsman had been thrown to the deck. The steering gear was on the end of a rope trailing in the wake of the schooner, but with the ship rolling erratically and dangerously it took almost three hours just to get it back on board.

Sporting a very impressive moustache of which Pancho Villa would have been proud, Jorge Hernández, a stocky thirty year old Mexican, was responsible for maintenance of the machinery on board. Without hesitation he took charge of fastening the rudder to the hull. With the waves behind them taking on the appearance of towering black mountains, he climbed over the stern with two safety ropes attached to the mast.

It took a great deal of nerve to continue working in such an exposed position when, every ten minutes or so, there was a huge roar as a big sea broke behind the ship. After almost an hour of being battered by the following seas and with his fingers too numb to continue he was hauled back on deck and taken below to find dry clothes. Before the captain had time to issue new orders, Sebastian Riley made his way across the deck, secured the safety lines around his waist and climbed over the stern to finish the job.

The rest of the day was taken up getting everything working again and by the time they had finished darkness was rapidly descending and visibility disappearing. Everybody on board was now showing signs of extreme fatigue and to avoid over tiredness, which could have led to even more problems, the captain reduced each watch to just two hours instead of the usual four. Not for the last time during the voyage, Eriksen regretted having to leave port with an under strength crew.

High winds, even higher seas and a jury rigged rudder meant the next three weeks were fraught with danger but fortunately they passed without any further complications. As the schooner skirted the high pressure area which would later become known

Photo courtesy of Rupert Parker (www.PlanetAppetite.com)

PONTA DELGADA
SÃO MIGUEL, THE AZORES

*In the twenty-first century the Azores have undergone
a transformation from lonely outpost to tourist destination and
regular stopping point for Transatlantic yachtsmen and women.*

as the Azores High there was a noticeable drop in the ferocity of the wind, at last allowing them to loosen up a little and breathe easier.

At one point everybody stopped what they were doing when a strange calm swept over the ship. Gone was the howling of the wind and the thunder of the sea to be replaced by an unnerving silence. It only lasted a few minutes before being supplanted by rain hitting their oilskins like the sound of a rattling drum but it was enough to rekindle their apprehension.

On the morning of Saturday 24th January there was a real sense of relief. As the sky began to lighten in the east, there was a shout from the lookout. On the horizon he had spotted the welcome sight of the Azores, an archipelago of nine volcanic islands over two and a half thousand miles from Cape Hatteras and almost a thousand miles from the coast of Portugal.

Nobody was more relieved than Eriksen. The sun had stayed hidden for much of the voyage preventing him from taking regular sightings with his sextant and, though he kept his concerns hidden from his crew, he had not been totally confident they were on course and was concerned they might bypass the islands.

From the harbour wall in Ponta Delgada, on the main island of São Miguel, their approach had been carefully monitored for about an hour or so before they reached the entrance where a steam tug was waiting for them. Surrounded by disappointed seagulls who had been hoping for some scraps of fish, *Mexico* lowered her sails and was towed under bare poles to a pier where they at last had some respite from the relentless weather and where they would have access to men and materials to carry out the vital repairs.

Within minutes of tying up alongside and stowing the sails, the crew fell into their bunks. They were cold, they were wet, they were exhausted, but they were relieved. Sleep came easily and quickly with most of them dead to the world for the majority of the next twenty four hours.

The following day, after existing on a diet of tinned food and dry stores, tainted with salt water, the men enjoyed their first hot meal for almost a month. Two hundred yards from the port the captain attended mass in the sixteenth century Igreja Matriz de São Sebastião where he offered his thanks for their safe deliverance, and then made a simple entry in the ship's log: *Sunday 25 January, Observed the holy day.*

Dawn on Monday found the deck a hive of activity as the work began in earnest. Salt encrusted clothing and bedding was washed in fresh water and with pleasant temperatures in the mid-fifties, they were hung on the rigging to dry. Sails that had been torn during the voyage were repaired or replaced and engineers were brought on board to overhaul the donkey engine and the pumps.

A new lifeboat was acquired to replace the original that had been washed overboard, and a dory was purchased to replace the barge used for ferrying cargoes at low tide, which had been damaged beyond repair.

Essential maintenance and general repairs were carried out below decks by the crew and already three months into their voyage with their stores severely depleted and ruined by the salt water, they took the opportunity to re-provision with fresh supplies of food.

Work proceeded well and with the ship back to its old self, the captain rewarded the crew with some shore leave. A few hours on dry land, combined with regular sleep and meals during the time they had been tied up alongside meant the crew were now refreshed and rejuvenated as they eagerly prepared to put to sea again.

They would not have been so eager had they been aware of what lay ahead of them.

chapter
4

Oh her stern was foul and the voyage was long
The winds was bad and the gales was strong
– Leave Her, Johnny (Sea Shanty)

orale was good during the morning of Friday 6th February when ships chandlers delivered two tons of charcoal for the donkey engine and five tons (a little over eleven hundred gallons) of fresh water as the crew prepared to get under way. At three o'clock in the afternoon, after thirteen days in port, and with the ship now fully seaworthy again, Captain Eriksen called for the tug to take them out of the harbour.

Just as the moorings were about to be released, the ship's agent came on board with a telegram from owner Alf Rød in Fredrikshald instructing the captain to *"Proceed as fast as possible sailing directly to Liverpool"*. There is no record of Eriksen's reaction to the message.

There were two new crew members on board when they sailed. Steward Robert Andersen, from Stockholm, had signed off from his previous ship a few weeks earlier and had been waiting for a vessel that would take him closer to home. Together with a new Portuguese deckhand this brought the existing Norwegian, Mexican, Panamanian, Russian, Dutch and British crew up to its full complement of ten.

Twenty-two year old fisherman António Luis da Cunha had apparently been in poor health and was told by his doctor that he should go to sea in order to improve it. Taking his advice he spent four days working as a deckhand on a two-masted inter-island schooner in exchange for his passage from tiny Graciosa Island (where the population is still only around four and a half thousand), crossing some two hundred and fifty miles of the Atlantic Ocean looking for a ship to join.

It was common practice at that time for doctors to recommend people, in particular those with respiratory problems in polluted towns and cities, to 'take the air' by spending time at sea or in the mountains. It seems strange, however, that this should have been suggested to a young fisherman who lived and worked on an island in the middle of the Atlantic where there was certainly no shortage of clean, fresh air.

At six o'clock, as evening slowly surrendered to nightfall, they passed the Ponta da Garça lighthouse farther along the coast and the captain ordered the topsail to be raised to take advantage of the freshening westerly wind as he set an initial course to the southeast.

The wind filled the sails, the schooner picked up speed and with everybody feeling re-energised after their time in port, spirits were high. All that changed however when less than four hours into the second leg of the voyage their problems returned as a new storm erupted with a savage ferocity. The deck was awash with giant waves breaking over the stern as they sailed into more bad weather in the form of gale force winds and heavy snow from the northwest.

Ship's log: Saturday 7 February, Gales and storm with violent showers. The deck is constantly covered in water, and also in the cabin. Water has to be bailed out all the time. Rolls a lot.

That same evening the exhaust for the donkey engine was snapped off by the sea and one of the jig booms was broken.

Changing course to sail north easterly, Eriksen attempted to take sightings of the sun each day but it was being kept well hidden by the heavy rain and hazy skies. Because of the shifting winds and currents such sightings were essential to establish their position, but on most days this was unachievable.

Like the screeching of a banshee the wind raced through the rigging and sails were once again ripped apart causing the ship to slow down, putting them even further behind their schedule. That, however, was the least of their worries.

Ship's log: Monday 9 February, General storm with high breaking seas. The deck is covered in water. Some rigs have been lost overboard. Provisions and equipment ruined by water. The sea is constantly over the cargo hatch.

As usual, the log entry is brief, simply recording facts, and does little to reflect the seriousness of their position. Colossal swells towered above the ship tossing it around like a matchstick as tons of water came crashing on to the deck threatening to sweep everybody into the ocean.

The most immediate problem they faced was whether the hatch cover would remain secure in the face of the raging seas.

If that went the result would be that too much of the Atlantic, which should be on the outside, would be on the inside, leaving no way of saving the ship.

An inspection confirmed their worst fears when they discovered water had been finding its way in and the level in the hold was getting dangerously high. Eriksen instantly recognised the gravity of the problem and realised this could be the beginning of the end. With the pump damaged during the storm, two crew members had to be lowered in to the hold where they stood waist deep filling buckets to be hauled up and emptied into the sea. Every time a wave crashed on deck more water poured in making it a never ending race to keep ahead. Not for the last time during the voyage, Eriksen regretted having to leave port with an under strength crew.

The work was hindered by everyone having to constantly cling on for their lives as the ship swung around to the north and heeled over at seemingly impossible angles. At times it was difficult to see the demarcation between the deck and the sea as the gunwales dipped below the surface. There was a constant struggle to adjust the sails in order to keep heading into the oncoming sea, whilst at the same time the water in the hold was causing poor stability making the schooner ever more difficult to control.

Mexico was now on a roller coaster ride as she slowly climbed up each wave before plunging down the other side. Often, she would ride the crest of a wave with no water beneath her bow and then go into freefall hurtling down at breakneck speed and burying her bow in the trough. At other times she would plough straight into the waves and force her way through with the deck awash.

It was a worrying time and as buoyancy brought her back up, the sea rushed along the full length of the deck seeking out the scuppers where it could escape back to the ocean. Their concern was that the next wave would be too steep to climb, or descend, or that it would arrive before she was ready for it causing the ship to flood and sink. This onslaught continued for almost forty-eight hours during which time nobody had time to sleep. On Wednesday things got even worse when a sudden gust of wind raced through the rigging ripping the mainsail and rendering it useless.

The torn sails were lashing violently against the ropes and the sound of the groaning mast could be clearly heard above the noise of the storm. They were once again in the lap of the gods.

Thursday 12th February. All through the night the storm had been building in intensity and when morning arrived dark clouds were hiding any light that might have been in the sky. The barometer had now dropped almost an inch (30 millibars) in the past twenty four hours giving even more cause for concern. Visibility was extremely poor, the horizon had vanished and it continued to be impossible for the captain to take a sighting of the sun to establish their position.

Ship's log: Increasing wind, gale and storm with rain and hail. Jib and mizzen fastened.

Below decks provisions and clothes had again been damaged by the sea and the cabins were awash. A herculean effort was required from everybody on board to keep the ship upright and moving forward as massive waves appeared to be striking them from every side.

Ship's log: Hurricane like storm with big seas. The ship is laying over in the water up to the middle of the hatch. The ship will not respond.

With water still in the cargo hold the ship was unwieldly and difficult to handle. The pumps were struggling to cope and the donkey engine was continually cutting out as it was covered with water. Every time the ship heeled over it seemed to be taking longer to right itself. Their only hope was that with the wind and sea coming from astern she would straighten up before it was too late.

Since the mainsail had gone, the jib had been taking the brunt of the gale and now that went the same way. The situation had become critical and this was reflected in Captain Eriksen's next entry in the ship's log.

Lowered the jib, unable to fasten it. When the wind filled it, it broke the port ventilation funnel. All the portholes in the galley are broken. Every man is on deck. The canvas for the main hatch has broken loose. To reclose the hatch is not possible, nor can we turn the ship away from the wind. Expecting every moment that the hatch will break loose and the ship will fill with water.

The crew were literally fighting for their lives. The sea is a hard master, unyielding and unforgiving, and they all knew that if the hatch cover gave way their life expectancy would be measured in minutes. There would be no way to prevent the ship sinking, and far from land without any method of communication, there would be no possibility of rescue.

Ship's log: Fitted a new jib in order to save the ship. Got the ship on a starboard tack and got the hatch reclosed.

The new jib made a big difference and enabled them to get the ship around. With slightly less movement on deck, and with dusk rapidly approaching, the crew were now able to secure a new tarpaulin over the hatch cover, preventing any more water from entering the hold. It was very much a case of one step forward two steps back, however, and almost as soon as one problem was resolved another materialised.

Ship's log: The jib has blown to pieces Port side is now totally submerged. Mizzen is torn. Five feet of water in the hold.

The crew could sense looming disaster; from sunset to sunrise everybody was on tenterhooks and preparing for the worst as *Mexico* was again in imminent danger of sinking. There was no further action that could be taken to rectify the situation. All they could do now was pray.

The next day brought some minor relief as the wind moved to the northeast allowing them to re-set the sails in an attempt to get back on course. At this point the schooner was listing more than ever and gigantic waves arriving every five or six seconds were still hammering it on the port side. Once again the fear now was that they would encounter a rogue wave which could rip the tarpaulin from the hatch cover in an instant.

There was still no possibility of an accurate observation to determine exactly where they were.

Ship's log: Saturday 14 February. At eight o'clock this morning put the ship to starboard side in order to put a tarpaulin on this side of the main hatch. Tarpaulin was made of the jib that had blown to pieces. At ten o'clock the

SEXTANT
of the type used by Captain Eriksen

starboard side of the hatch was closed and we turned the ship to port side to get the other side closed and covered. By nightfall the hatch was secured with three tarpaulins and a new four-inch manila hawser to replace the broken ones. Three and a half feet of water in the hold.

Captain Eriksen had his sextant constantly within reach and grabbed it as the sun briefly broke through around mid-morning, managing to get a reasonable observation. With the ship pitching and rolling, two men had to hold on to him to keep him steady.

The mirrors on the instrument were caked in salt spray and the reading was not quite as accurate as he would have wished for, though it did show they were slowly moving in the right direction as indicated by an entry made by the Captain at midday.

Ship's log: General course north 20 degrees east, sailed distance 62 miles.

This meant they had averaged just over two and a half knots an hour since midday on Friday. Storm force winds continued to cause problems for the next few days and the crew were kept busy changing the sails whenever it changed direction.

At one point they were in danger of losing a mast when the port chainplate, to which the mast was secured, was ripped from the deck. Quick thinking and skilful rope work saved the day thanks to the deckhands who secured the mast with a series of ropes and pulleys.

Sailing ships were notoriously dangerous places to work with drowning seen as an occupational hazard for those who plied their trade on the hostile oceans of the world. Every man on board knew of at least one friend or former crew mate who had been lost to the sea and with over a century of experience between them, their focus now was on ensuring they did not join them.

Toilet facilities had long since ceased to exist adding to their problems as they took their life in their hands using the open deck. Sleep was difficult to come by for any of them as they anxiously listened to the groaning of the schooner, waiting for the next catastrophe to happen. In the middle of a storm, in the darkness of night, with thirty foot high waves battering your ship, life is anything but pleasant, and even experienced sailors feel the fear, especially when they know there is no escape route.

Everybody was thankful on more than one occasion that the crew had been brought up to full strength before leaving the Azores. António, the young Portuguese, was eager to please and worked hard, proving his worth time and again. Andersen, the steward, was working miracles in the galley and produced at least one hot meal every day.

Water in the hold was still their biggest problem and they worried that the cargo would break loose and move around, altering the centre of gravity, which would almost certainly cause the schooner to capsize.

5

Out of sight of land the sailor feels safe.
It is the beach that worries him.
– Charles G Davis

On Wednesday 18th February the sky had been heavy, dull and threatening when a lookout spotted smoke on the horizon. Within minutes the first ship they had seen in a total of ninety three days at sea hove into view, coming towards them on a southerly course.

Using signal flags to communicate, the new sighting identified itself as *SS Oldfield Grange* en route to Buenos Aires. The entire crew were on deck as the ships closed on each other and were near enough to wave to the men on the steamship as it passed by before disappearing almost as quickly as it had appeared.

There was no logical reason for it but the sighting had somehow boosted the confidence of the crew, even bringing a smile to their faces for the first time since leaving the Azores. Perhaps it was just the knowledge that they were not alone on the sea and there were others facing the same dangers.

Oldfield Grange was a 4,653 ton steamship built the previous year for Houlder Brothers of Hartlepool that went on to serve with distinction as an armed merchantman during the First World War. She was torpedoed and damaged in June 1917 by German submarine U40 but after repairs was back in the Atlantic convoys within a few months. Nearing the end of a voyage from New York to Cardiff she was torpedoed and sunk by U62 on 11 December 1917, thirty miles off Tory Island in County Donegal (scene of the Royal Navy's victory over the French six weeks after the battle of Castlebar in 1798).

Through a combination of skill and luck, everybody had somehow managed to survive the previous twelve days, since leaving port, without any serious injuries and they breathed a collective sigh of relief when the weather eased enough to allow the captain to take an accurate noon sighting.

Eriksen set a course for the *Coningbeg* lightship anchored nine miles off the Irish coast; from there he would continue to sail east taking them through St George's Channel, into the comparative shelter of the Irish Sea and, finally, onwards to their destination of Liverpool.

A sounding showed they were in over sixty five fathoms of water and even though there was some deterioration in the weather during the afternoon, it looked like the worst was behind them.

Thursday passed without any major problems but poor visibility prevented any meaningful observations and Eriksen was concerned that the wind could have pushed them off course again. Late in the afternoon he ordered another sounding and once more the lead line dropped to sixty five fathoms without touching the bottom.

With a number of strong currents in the area, a northwest gale still blowing, and their position being uncertain, an extra watch was maintained throughout the night and at four in the morning another sounding was taken, producing the same results as the previous day.

On the morning of Friday 20th February, exactly two weeks after leaving Ponta Delgada they woke to a nightmare situation. The heavy rain and sleet had combined with spray from the huge waves to form an impenetrable mist, reducing visibility to zero. They were, effectively, sailing blind, and unable to make a sighting that would verify their position.

The Meteorological Office report for the month gives some indication of the weather they were facing that day. *By the 20th a large and deep depression was advancing towards these Islands from the westward, and before 7 a.m. on the 21st gales from the Southward and South-Westward had become general over Ireland and Great Britain. On the morning of the 21st the core of the depression lay some distance to the north-westward of Ireland, whence it travelled away northward. Before the gale had subsided another, and still more intense, depression approached these Islands from the south-westward. It proved to be the last of the month.*

Heavy rain from the west had been striking the ship for most of the night but during the past hour the wind had moved to the south and they were sailing into it. In the confusion, Eriksen initially assumed they had passed the *Coningbeg* lightship during the hours of darkness but to be certain he needed a clear sight-ing in the absence of which he had no choice but to use dead reckoning – a complicated process of determining where you currently are by using a compass, your ground speed, a clock and a previously known position. He estimated that they were about twenty to twenty five miles southwest of Hook Head lighthouse, which meant they should soon sight land on the port side.

The barometer had again been falling over the past twenty four hours indicating that a big storm was on the way and it was very important for him to know their exact position before it materialised.

Minimum sails were hoisted as they proceeded slowly and carefully with everybody on deck staring into the distance in the hope of sighting land. At around one o'clock there was a moment's relief when a shout came from one of the crew.

"Land ahead!"

Relief soon turned to apprehension however, the land was on the starboard side and they quickly realised something was wrong. They had missed the *Coningbeg* by about three miles and *Mexico* was now in a very perilous position in a channel between the Saltee Islands and the mainland with the wind behind them pushing them ever closer to the coast.

They were by no means the first ship to have been caught up in this situation. In January 1847 the *Niobe* sailing from New York with a cargo of Maize was wrecked on the islands. Reportedly the cargo was salvaged by local fishermen and it went a long way to saving the area the worst effects of the Potato Famine.

During the winter of 1805/06 no fewer than seventeen ships were reported to have gone ashore and fourteen years later seventeen bodies were washed up on Cullenstown strand following the grounding of the *Demerary* (often referred to as the *Demerara*), which was also a three masted ship sailing from

South America to Liverpool. There was later an unconfirmed story of fourteen Norwegian sailors being buried on the Burrow at Ballyteigue Bay,

Samuel Lewis in his Topographical Dictionary of Ireland, first published in 1837, gave the following description: "... *the intermediate space is a large bay with a continual in-draught and heavy sea setting in toward the shore, and dangerous from rocks and shallows, known only to persons well acquainted with this coast. Numerous vessels have been wrecked here, should a vessel get too far into the bay, it is impossible to beat out, and there is no place of refuge except Fethard, which, though it has a small pier, can afford little shelter, from the shallowness of its water and its exposed situation"*.

Beyond the islands the crew spotted signal flags being raised but were unable to determine what they were. In response they raised the Norwegian ensign.

To clear the coast and avoid shallow water, they needed to turn back into the wind. With only a few sails up, Eriksen knew such a manoeuvre would be impossible, if they were to have any chance they would need to increase the number of sails. With the mainsail front rigging tightened and the rudder laid hard over everybody held their breath. It seemed to take forever but slowly the schooner started turning.

Again it was a situation where as soon as one problem was solved another materialised. This time they lost speed and started drifting towards land. Captain Eriksen was not finished yet, more sails would produce more speed and he immediately ordered a double reefed foresail and full mizzen in an attempt to save the ship.

THE SISTERS

KILMORE LIFEBOAT CREW

John Kehoe (Coxswain), Peter Brien, John Walsh, Nicholas Wickham, Matthew Wickham, Richard Wickham, Richard Rochford, Philip Walsh, James O'Flaherty, James Hayes, Nicholas Cousins, William Blake, Walter Power

The storm they had feared earlier in the day was now upon them and unhappily, like those other vessels before him, all their struggles were to no avail. Despite the best efforts of his crew, a combination of strong currents, heavy seas and ferocious winds pushed the ship farther and farther into the bay.

The haze lifted momentarily to reveal low lying land on the starboard side. They were in serious trouble and there was nothing more they could do now except brace themselves for the inevitable as they were hurled towards the Keeragh Islands. Within minutes a sickening shudder went through the whole length of the ship as she went aground on the jagged Demerara rock (named after the 1819 shipwreck) which penetrated the steel hull, opening it up to the sea.

Three miles away in Fethard, a crowd had gathered earlier in the day at the lifeboat house on the Quay Road, about three quarters of a mile outside the village. Built from granite in 1886, it had become an integral part of the community over the years and everybody was there today to prepare it for a dance being held later in the evening by the Young Farmers organisation.

To make room, as in previous years, the *Helen Blake* lifeboat was taken out on its carriage – the difference this year, though nobody knew it at the time, was that it would never be put back.

The weather was appalling with strong winds ensuring the constant deluge of rain and sleet, coming down in sheets, soaked anybody who was exposed to it for even a few minutes. Inside the boathouse, the floor was swept and washed, the walls brushed down, paraffin lamps hung from the rafters, a little makeshift stage for the band was built at one end and hastily made wooden benches provided the seating.

One of those helping out was second coxswain of the lifeboat, thirty-nine year old John Mac. He was a very active man with thick black curly hair and a neatly trimmed moustache. A few years earlier he was one of the first people in the village to join the 'Pioneers' – the Pioneer Total Abstinence Association – which had been founded just before the turn of the century by Dublin priest James Cullen.

Mac was employed as a gardener by Godfrey Lovelace Taylor, the seventy-four year old local land agent who was also honorary president of the lifeboat committee. Although an employee himself, Taylor's life mirrored that of the landed gentry, living in Grangeville, one of the 'grand' houses of the area. It had been built by the third Marquess of Ely and completed in 1857, the year of his death. His son, the fourth Marquess, lived there during the construction of Loftus Hall.

Sporting a neat beard to match his silver hair, which was normally hidden beneath his trilby hat, Taylor was always immaculately dressed, rarely seen without collar and tie and reputed to be the only man in the area who owned an overcoat. As the owner of one of the very few cars in the area he drove to St Mogue's church every Sunday where he and his family occupied a favoured pew.

The entrance to Grangeville's sweeping driveway was no more than twenty yards from Garry Handrick's cottage and Mac would call in to see him – and his sister, Mary Bridget – on most days. Today he had his own special reason for wanting to ensure everything was spick and span in the boathouse. He had not told anybody about his relationship with his friend's sister, which had been very low key so far but he had invited her to the dance and it was to be the first time they would be out together in public.

The Young Farmers dance was one of the highlights of the year, always great *craic* and Mac was looking forward to spending an enjoyable evening. What none of them knew, however, was that this year fate had determined otherwise. There would be no dance tonight, and for Mac and his lifeboat colleagues, the evening would be anything but enjoyable.

Supervising the proceedings was fifty-two year old Christopher 'Christy' Bird who, as coxswain of the lifeboat, was not only the skipper, but was responsible for maintaining the boat and ensuring it was always ready to go to sea at a moment's notice. It was a responsibility he took very seriously and there was rarely a day went by without him, at the very least, making a visual check of the boat and the equipment. Once a month the boat would be taken outside where he would wash it from bow to stern so that in addition to being in first class condition, it looked like the proverbial new pin.

His professionalism in this area was confirmed by RNLI District Inspector Lieutenant Commander Walter Rigg RN, who stated in a letter to the Chief Inspector of Lifeboats, "… on every occasion of my visits I found everything appertaining to the station in excellent order". He went on to say "I always found the coxswain, Christopher Burd (sic), a good and competent seaman, and he always handled the boat in a seamanlike manner. I do not think there was a station on the coast where a coxswain paid greater attention to having everything always in the most efficient condition".

His attention to detail and his preparedness for sea was about to be tested.

Heading up the watch team in the Bar O' Lough Coast Guard station close to Cullenstown strand (beach) was Walter Parvin, who had been there since first light. His notes record that the morning was rainy and foggy with a force four to five south-westerly wind and limited visibility. After midday, he wrote, the weather cleared slightly to reveal the sight of heavy seas break-ing on the Keeraghs (variously pronounced as Key-ricks and Key-rocks), just south of their position, and all along the coast.

The team continually scanned the area with binoculars until around three o'clock when they spotted the masts of a sailing ship coming through the haze between the Saltee Islands and the Keeraghs. As the ship hove into sight Parvin saw it was on a port tack and it was obvious to him that it was in trouble. He straightaway raised the signal flags J.D. ("You are standing into danger") and C.S. ("Do you need assistance?"). There was no response from the vessel.

Farther down the coast at Bannow where the Coast Guards had a better view of the Keeraghs, Thomas Reeves was in charge and his team had also spotted the sails. Like their colleagues they raised the signal flags J.D. and C.S. This time they saw the ship hoist the Norwegian ensign in return.

Both stations were in constant touch by telephone and a decision was taken to advise their main office in Wexford of the potential problem.

Checking on the well-being of some cows in a field on the cliffs just a short distance from the boathouse, thirty-three year old lifeboat volunteer Bill Banville spotted the ship approach-ing the Keeraghs. He knew the waters well and after watching for a few minutes it became clear to him there was a problem. He straightaway made his way on foot to Fethard where he informed lifeboat committee secretary George Bassett of the situation.

FETHARD DOCK

The boathouse is in the centre of the photo, the dock is jutting out on the left, the Saltee Islands (right) and the Keeragh Islands (left) are on the horizon.

Photo by Steve Meyler

THE BOATHOUSE IN 2018

Photos by Steve Meyler

BAR OF LOUGH

Recognising the danger, Basset ordered the lifeboat to be launched and a signal maroon was fired from the 'rocket field' behind the doctor's surgery and dispensary to alert the crew. The sound was loud enough to be heard throughout the village, and beyond, and it was not just the crew who responded.

In a small fishing village everybody knows how dangerous the sea can be but what they did not know yet was what had happened; perhaps one of the local fishermen had taken a chance and gone out in the bad weather. Within minutes virtually every-one in the village had left their houses and gathered outside the dispensary waiting to find out what the emergency was.

Every piece of clothing Banville was wearing was soaked through to his skin so he planned to call at his house on the way to the boathouse and get changed into dry clothes before joining the rest of the crew. Having taken his only other pair of boots to shoemaker Peter Foley, beside Nolan's pub, earlier in the week for repair, he collected those before leaving the village.

The men who formed the lifeboat crew were spread around Fethard and its environs engaged in their various everyday tasks but when they saw, and heard, the signal they dropped everything and made their way to the boathouse, joining Christy Bird and John Mac who were already there.

The two men donned their wet weather gear and, although he had been over it himself only a few hours earlier, Bird ordered Mac to check all the equipment on the lifeboat to make sure it was ready to launch. He was leaving nothing to chance; he knew that today each one of his crew would face the toughest test of his life.

Bird had every confidence in his crew; they had been called out on two previous occasions and on one of these they brought four people safely ashore from a ketch during a gale. They had also come through a training exercise six weeks ago with flying colours. In less than an hour they would place their trust in him on the sea and he had no intention of letting them down.

CHAPTER

6

Go they must, drown they may.
– Jem Wickham

Farthest from the boathouse was Patrick Cullen whose weather beaten face was testament to his outdoor life, and made him look much older than his thirty-nine years. His isolated cottage was about two and a half miles from the village, accessed from the road via a short boreen (lane). Built with stone collected from the beach, bound together with a mortar made from mud and boasting a slated roof on joists made from driftwood, it was a robust little house that would put many modern houses to shame, completely exposed to the sea and the wind, and standing up year after year to gales and storms.

With no more than three hundred square feet of floor space there were no frills, just a family room and bedroom downstairs and a space upstairs, accessed by a set of rough-and-ready stairs and barely high enough to stand up, where the children slept. Heavy rain and strong winds outside meant all nine children, aged between fifteen months and fifteen years, were packed inside today leaving very little room to move around. A heavy

Portrait by Leanne Mullen

PATRICK CULLEN
1874 – 1914

iron pot hung over the fire in the little inglenook fireplace and the combined smell of food and smoke permeated the area.

When he heard the maroon, Patrick grabbed his coat from the bedroom and said a hurried goodbye to Margaret and the children before mounting his bicycle, little knowing they would never see each other again.

His ungainly old Triumph was kept in the little shed where he made sure it was well maintained with the tyres always pumped up and moving parts regularly oiled. The heavy steel frame and the one and a half inch wide tyres were designed to cope with the poor roads, the steel chain guard and mudguards kept the dirt and rain at bay, and the spring loaded carrier doubled up as a seat for the children. Even the Brooks saddle with its heavy protruding springs weighed nearly five pounds, almost ten times that of a modern day mountain bike saddle.

There was also another bicycle in the shed, an old children's bike he had been repairing and renovating as a present for his youngest son, Patsy, whose seventh birthday was the following weekend. It was a present the young boy would keep for many years, even after he had grown out of it. The foul weather meant there were very few people out on the roads that day but just after leaving home he met his young friend Martin Foley and only had time for a quick 'Hello' as he continued his ride in the wind and rain.

Perhaps they had a premonition, but not a word was spoken during that fateful afternoon as the entire Cullen family stood outside their front door overlooking Fethard Bay, watching as the lifeboat pulled away from the shore, heading for the Keeraghs on its errand of mercy. A few of them just caught a glimpse of 'Daddy' without realising it was the last time they would ever see him.

In the days before mechanisation, his forty plus acres made Fred Lewis one of the biggest farmers in the area and on that Friday afternoon he was with the youngest member of the crew, thirty-one year old Garry Handrick, in Walsh's shop next door to Garry's little thatched cottage. He was a genial character with a mischievous smile, of average height with a receding hairline and a bushy moustache that did nothing to hide his youthful looks.

Garry was talking to Lewis about a few days work for the following week when twenty-one year old Simon Power, who worked for neighbouring farming twins Peter and Michael Ryan, ran in and interrupted the conversation to tell them the rocket had been fired.

Garry rushed home and was at the gate when Patrick Cullen rode past calling out with a laugh to *"get a move on young lad, or we'll go without you"*. Getting his bicycle from the shed, he brought it back through the house where his sixty-nine year old mother, Mary, always concerned for his well-being when he was on the lifeboat, made the sign of the cross and knelt to say a prayer for his safe return.

As he left the house Garry shouted to his sister to say he would be back in time to go to the dance with her.

Mary Bridget waved him off and smiled as she started preparing for the evening; this would be her first big night out with Mac and she could hardly contain her excitement at the thought of it. There was very little time spent on deciding what to wear; money was not available for clothes to be a fashion item, they just needed to be warm and hard wearing. In addition to a couple of utilitarian dresses and a slightly better one for going to Mass on Sundays, there was also her pride and joy which she now laid out on the bed in readiness.

She worked at Grangeville, cleaning, cooking and sewing, and before Christmas the lady of the house, sixty-two year old Dorothea Marie, who coincidentally was Norwegian, had given her a present of some pale grey material which she skilfully turned into a beautiful skirt. Beside it was a new shirt-blouse bought especially for the occasion. She had been saving her money and sent a postal order for four shilling and eleven pence to Walpole Brothers in Dublin who sent the blouse within a week.

The lightweight material would be more suitable for mid-summer than a cold and wet February evening but that made no difference. The outfit had been hung in the wardrobe waiting for tonight and she thought a few hours in the open should be enough to lose the smell of moth balls.

Practicality was everything and normal footwear for men, women and children were heavy leather boots – what today we would call working boots – but Mary Bridget also had a pair of shoes that had been discarded by her employer's thirty year old daughter Helen, repaired in the village by Peter Foley and polished to a high shine waiting for just such a special occasion as this.

Tonight she would be the belle of the ball and her only concern at that time was whether she would be able to keep her clothes dry during the walk to the boathouse. Before the day was out her concerns would change dramatically.

Known as a bit of a joker, Garry rode through the village where he met up with his namesake Thomas 'Tom' Handrick, who was bowman on the *Helen Blake*. The two friends completed the journey together laughing and joking as they rode through the foul weather.

Portrait by Jason O'Ceannobháin

THOMAS 'TOM' HANDRICK

Bowman, Helen Blake lifeboat
1874 – 1914

Tom had little formal schooling having always been more interested in working than learning and was the only member of the crew unable to read. He was, however, 'as bright as a button' so it is possible he was dyslexic, a term that had been coined some thirty years earlier but a condition which was yet to be universally recognised.

He was a well-built man who never shirked from any task; if you needed something doing, you could rely on him to get the job done. Tom had worked on boats bringing coal from Wales for a few years before marrying a Welsh girl and settling down in Treharris, in the Taff valley, where he worked in the Deep Navigation Colliery. Shortly after the birth of their daughter, Bridget Mary (known affectionately as Dolly) in 1901 his wife died and finding it impossible to bring the little girl up alone, he returned to Fethard.

Prepared to work wherever he could find a day's employment there was no shortage of takers for his labours and even after a hard day in the fields many of his evenings were spent serving in the bar at Foley's Hotel. Because of this Dolly spent the majority of her time staying with Tom's sister Bridget and his brother, Michael (Mikey).

The previous Sunday had been Tom's fortieth birthday and with the law at that time reflecting the Church's ruling that all bars should be closed on Sundays, he was able to spend the day with Dolly, a precious day that she would remember for many years to come.

In 2002 Dolly's son, Tommy Roche, who had been named in honour of the Grandfather he never knew, singlehandedly saved the lives of five people when he pulled them from the water after a fishing boat had sunk less than two miles from the Keeragh islands; his grandfather would have been proud of him.

Two doors away from Tom on Sluice Lane lived another crewman, George Crumpton, who was working in the coal yard that day and was busy weighing out coal when the signal was fired.

Forty-four year old George was a quiet, mild mannered man who could easily have been mistaken for an accountant or a bank manager. He would do anything to help people and felt it was his civic duty to volunteer for the lifeboat. Like all the others, he dropped everything to respond to the alarm. His wife, Rebecca, had just got their eighteen month old son, Tom, (named in honour of both his grandfathers, Tom Crumpton and Tom Cruise) off to sleep when she heard the signal. Leaving him in his cot she ran across the street with George's coat and boots before he joined the exodus of volunteers and lookers-on ignoring the wind and rain as they made their way across the bridge and up a short hill before turning left on to the Quay Road.

Thirty-eight year old James Morrissey lived just four doors away from John Mac on Sunny Row. When he married fifteen years earlier it was a real life boat occasion; his wife-to-be, Mary-Anne Ryan, had worked for lifeboat president Taylor in Grangeville, Mary Bridget Handrick was one of the witnesses and some of his current crew mates were amongst the guests.

James was a skilled carpenter who had made every piece of furniture in the house, mostly from driftwood; it was simple and functional but made so well that much of it was still in use up to half a century later.

Portrait by Ivana Lavelle

JAMES MORRISSEY
1875 – 1914

Most of his time was spent working for the Ely estate, which owned the lion's share of the properties in Fethard, and for the previous four days he had been busy at Loftus Hall, a magnificent nineteenth century structure that completely dominated the landscape of the Hook Peninsula. Built in 1870 by the fourth Marquess of Ely, it was a three storey house designed to impress. Amongst its many features was a magnificent enclosed portico and over one hundred windows, with twice as many shutters, all of which James was responsible for maintaining and, occasionally, replacing. Even the roof was impressive, completely encircled by an intricate balustrade and featuring two imposing stone eagles keeping watch over the entrance.

Outside was a gate house, walled garden, coach house and enclosed deer park, whilst inside it boasted such features as ornate marble fireplaces, a magnificent oak staircase hand carved and installed by Italian craftsmen and exquisite crystal chandeliers.

The thirty room mansion was, without doubt, the finest house for miles around and now had just one occupant, seventy-one year old Caroline Loftus, the Marchioness of Ely, the last of the family to occupy it. After her death in 1917 the hall spent many years as a convent before becoming a hotel and, latterly, a tourist attraction claiming to be Ireland's most haunted house.

James made the journey every day on his old bicycle with his tool box strapped on the back but the weather today was too bad and he decided to stay at home. It was only five miles outside the village so we might find it difficult now to understand how the weather could be so bad it would prevent him making such a short journey, one that would take ten minutes or less in a car. Conditions in 1914 however were very different. The journey involved a hilly, dirt road, peppered with potholes and open to the elements from both sides of the peninsula. Added to this, the rain was coming down like stair rods in a gale force wind. He would have done well just to remain upright on his bike.

His two-year old daughter, Mamie, was overjoyed that Daddy was staying home; he could now use his free time to fulfil a long standing promise to make her a stool. She sat patiently and quietly on the floor in front of the fire, enthralled, watching him skilfully transform a few pieces of driftwood into the best thing she had ever seen.

He had just finished it when the maroon was fired. Giving the little girl a kiss, he called to his wife that he would be back soon, grabbed his coat and ran off down the hill, never to see his family again. Mamie treasured the stool for the rest of her life.

Patrick 'Pat' Roche was the voluntary harbour master for Fethard and at fifty-five was the oldest of the crew. He had moved to Fethard from his native Bannow about twenty years earlier but, like so many men in the area, had to go away to sea in order to provide for his family.

During his time away he worked hard and saved hard before returning home with the intention of buying his own fishing boat, which would allow him to spend more time with his wife, Anastasia, and their two children. Initially he fished with his father-in-law, James Power, on the *Wayfarer* while he looked for a boat that would enable him to fulfil his dream of being his own master.

In the autumn of 1913 he found what he was looking for in Dunmore East, across the estuary in County Waterford. At twenty feet long, it was the ideal size; he could work it alone until his eleven year old son – also named Patrick but known as

Portrait by José Marques

PATRICK 'PAT' ROCHE
1858 – 1914

Paddy – was old enough to join him in a few years' time. (The Education Act of 1892 stated that children could be kept out of school if they were prevented by "*sickness, domestic necessity … or giving assistance in the fisheries, or other work requiring to be done at a particular time or season…*").

After being laid up for some time it looked neglected and was in need of a good deal of TLC before Pat would be happy for 'his boat' to take its place in the dock alongside *Wayfarer*.

On a fine day towards the end of September he went to Dunmore and sailed her back to Fethard. He tied her up just below the boathouse, where he could spend his spare time carrying out the necessary work. Throughout the winter months it had been a labour of love as he replaced planks, checked every screw and nail, fitted a new bilge pump and caulked every seam to make sure she was completely seaworthy.

After applying a couple of coats of paint at the beginning of the month she was now ready for the 1914 lobster season which would get under way in a few weeks' time, and had just completed the final job. He decided to name her Anastasia, in honour of his wife, and two days ago had carefully painted the name on the bow. Sadly he would never be able to show it to her, and he would never have the opportunity to fulfil his dream.

He had been working for a local farmer that day and when he came home for lunch in the afternoon he told his family he expected the lifeboat to be called out as there was a ship in trouble off the Keeraghs. He asked Paddy to listen out for the signal and had just finished his lunch when the young boy ran in excitedly, "*Daddy, Daddy, I've just seen the rocket; you'll have to go*". In later years Paddy often wondered how different his life might have been had he not told his father about the signal.

Pat's fourteen year old daughter, Mary, got his coat for him as he rushed off to join his crew mates. He would never see his family again.

John Kelly was a short, well-built man with a bald head and thick grey moustache who had sailed on merchant ships around the world for most of his life. He was described as being a 'low sized stocky man who was as strong as an ox' and had acquired a reputation as a 'hard man' and 'a great one for the language' – we can only assume that did not mean he was a linguist!

John married Elizabeth 'Lizzie' Ryan at the beginning of 1902 and a few years later, like his friend Pat Roche, gave up sailing the seven seas for a quiet life in Fethard, using the money he had earned at sea to buy a fishing boat and a piece of land. This was his third year on the lifeboat crew and he was one of the first to arrive.

Three of the crew lived on the Quay Road within a few hundred yards of the boathouse. Christy Bird's nephew, thirty-seven year old William 'Willie' Bird had the kind of weather worn face with lines carved by the wind, which was common to those who spent their lives fishing and farming. Willie caught up with Tom Handrick's brother, forty-three year old Mikey, a man with 'a voice like thunder', and together they walked up the road with Dolly who had not seen her father since the previous weekend and was making the most of this opportunity.

Christened Patrick Butler by his father, but known to everybody as Paddy Stafford, having chosen to use his unmarried mother's name, the final member of the crew was an expert boatman, slightly awkward looking at times but quick to respond in any situation. Like so many others in the area, he was a deep sea sailor, meaning he would spend anything up to a year at a

Portrait by José Marques

MICHAEL 'MIKEY' HANDRICK
1867 – 1914

time away at sea. Often described as 'Jolly', it was said he had a laugh 'like a spinning penny'. With a sense of humour that helped to keep everybody cheerful in any circumstance he was welcomed back into the lifeboat crew whenever he was at home.

Paddy was the last to arrive, even though he lived closest. When he was home from the sea he would stay with his aunt, Nanny, next door to the boathouse and when the maroon was fired she was cutting his hair. She insisted on finishing it before he left the house, not knowing it was the last time she would perform this service for him.

CHAPTER

7

True heroism is remarkably sober, very undramatic.
It is not the urge to surpass all others at whatever cost,
but the urge to serve others, at whatever cost.
— Arthur Ashe

Gathering the crew together, Christy Bird shared what information he had. Although these were experienced men who knew what to expect, he pointed out that the exceptionally severe weather conditions meant they would have to make their way into the wind facing waves of fifteen to twenty feet. He told them their lives would be at risk from the moment they set sail and the decision to launch was not one he could make alone.

There were no qualms from anyone, it was a unanimous decision, shipwrecks do not happen in good weather and this was what they had volunteered for. Each one of them had complete confidence in the boat, everything about her was workmanlike and she had been well built to withstand heavy weather.

Removing their flat caps, which were *de rigueur* at the time (except for Paddy Stafford who habitually wore a navy blue

Portrait by Jackie Edwards

WILLIAM 'BILL' BANVILLE
1880 – 1914

woollen hat he had brought back from America), they quickly donned the RNLI oilskins and sou'westers over their normal working clothes, already wet from the heavy rain. Some of them put on wellington boots whilst others retained their normal working boots. Last item to go on was the bulky Kapok filled lifejacket, which had replaced the cork jackets ten years earlier, and after checking each other's straps to ensure everything was secure, they were ready to go.

Strangely, one man was missing; Bill Banville who had first spotted the ship from the cliff top and raised the alarm in the village had not yet turned up, but with time being of the essence they could not afford to wait any longer.

With the tide close to its lowest ebb it was impossible to launch the boat from the slipway alongside the boathouse so the ground crew quickly hitched the carriage to two powerful horses, which were kept in the adjoining field, to pull it a quarter of a mile down the road. The unique smell of Fethard Dock, made up from a combination of dead fish, salt water and seaweed was borne on the wind and greeted them long before they reached it, unnoticed by most of them for whom it was a daily occurrence.

When the horses were unhitched, after pulling the boat across the small beach beside the dock and into the sea, the first problem cropped up – only nine oarsmen were present and they needed ten. Without hesitation, twenty-three year old Richard 'Richie' Bird stepped forward and volunteered to join them. He had never crewed the boat before but was well known to the rest of the crew as a strong and enthusiastic young man who worked as part of the shore crew, and had shared the washing duties with the cox on more than one occasion. The cox was well aware of his capabilities, he had known him all his life and knew he would not let them down; they were cousins.

The shore team knew exactly what was needed. Time is always of the essence in an emergency and they had trained many times to ensure the launch process was carried out like clockwork – but today was different. Perhaps it was an indication of what lay ahead but the launching did not go smoothly and everything that could go wrong did go wrong.

In a crisis, Christy Bird could always be relied on to be unflappable, and with a calm air of authority he took control of the situation. Under his direction the running gear was cleared, various ropes were untangled and, despite all the problems, she was launched in a little over half an hour, just as Bill Banville arrived on a dray cart.

Nobody knew what had delayed him and he had no time for an explanation but without a moment's thought he waded out to the boat and clambered over the side, minus his life jacket. As he climbed aboard he prophetically remarked, *"If I am to be drowned without it, I will be drowned with it"*. In a little over an hour, the truth of his words would unhappily be realised. Richie Bird was moved to take George Crumpton's place on the forward beam allowing George to assist Tom Handrick in the bow. Beside the very experienced Pat Roche, Richie would now have the added responsibility of raising the keel board if necessary, to reduce the draught when they were in shallow water. There were now fourteen men on board instead of the usual crew of thirteen. When it was all over, just five of them would return to their homes.

The instant *Mexico* struck the island the focus of the crew changed; there was nothing more that could be done for the ship, their sole concern now was survival.

CULLENSTOWN STRAND

The Keeragh Islands can be seen in the background

Photo by Steve Meyler

As water began rushing through the gaping holes in the hull Captain Eriksen issued orders to swing the mizzen boom over the rocks, which would enable the crew to crawl across to solid ground, whilst he attempted to rescue the ship's log from his cabin. Both attempts were unsuccessful, the boom had snagged and would not swing out, and Eriksen could not gain access to his flooded cabin.

He immediately ordered the lifeboat to be lowered and carefully selected two men to crew it; Hilmar Paulsen, an experienced twenty-two year old sailor from his hometown of Fredrikshald, and a tough Panamanian Indian deckhand with the unlikely name of John Smith. The first mate took charge of the davits at the stern as Smith climbed into the lifeboat but their run of bad luck was not over yet. The boat was swinging violently just a few feet above the foaming sea. Within seconds it became clear that continuing to lower it slowly would result in it being crushed against the hull of the ship by waves breaking across the stern.

Paulsen grabbed an axe and chopped through the ropes; the lifeboat dropped like a stone, landing undamaged but being pushed away by wind and waves. Throwing the axe to one side he jumped into the sea where Smith dragged him into the boat only to discover the rowlocks had been lost when it hit the water. They now had practically no control.

Fortunately the airtight tanks kept the little craft afloat and using the oars like paddles they did everything possible to get back to the wreck for the rest of the crew. *"As soon as we cut adrift we tried to rescue the other men. They were shouting to us and we tried to get alongside but the waves were beating us off. We tried to throw a rope but failed."*

Photo courtesy of Declan Hearne

HELEN BLAKE

On a training exercise outside Fethard dock
Christy Bird (standing) and John Mac are in the stern
Tom Handrick is standing in the bow

Showing what might have been if they could have got the rest of the crew on board, the wind and waves swept the little boat away and pushed them across open water towards Cullenstown strand, just a mile from the islands. *"We were hanging over the side of the lifeboat in all positions and expected every minute to be engulfed. Every wave swept us nearer to a ledge of rocks and when we struck the ledge, we took a leap from the boat."*

Struggling in their sodden clothing, the two men swam the last fifty yards through the breaking waves into the arms of George Galvin and his son (also George) who, with three other men, had waded into the boiling surf. The two men were dragged ashore in a semi-conscious state and carried up to Horgan's bar, a few hundred yards from the beach, where they were given hot food and drinks. After drying their clothes in front of a huge log fire they were taken to the Bar of Lough Coast Guard station.

A little earlier in the afternoon a telegram from Bannow had arrived at the home of Laurence Busher, captain of the steam paddle tug *Wexford,* informing him there was a vessel aground on the Keeraghs. Unable to get out of harbour, Busher contacted Frank Walsh at the harbour master's office and persuaded him to drive to Cullenstown. Arriving just before dark, they could see the ship on the rocks and immediately set out for Bannow where Andrew Cullen told them he believed the Fethard lifeboat had been lost. He also advised them about the two men from the schooner who were now at the Bar of Lough station.

On arrival Paulsen and Smith furnished Busher and Walsh with details of the *Mexico* and her crew, and what had happened on the island. Busher said he then *".... asked the men would they come to Wexford with us".* They got back to the town at about nine o'clock where they were handed over to ship's chandler

William McGuire, the honorary agent for the Shipwrecked Mariner's Society, who took them to the Globe Hotel on the Quay and left them in the care of owner Tom Ashe. (Four years later, McGuire was elected Mayor of Wexford, succeeding his father in the role.) It was not the last time this charity would feature in the aftermath of the tragedy.

By the time the two men got to bed it was well after midnight but when they arose at eight o'clock on Saturday morning the owner's wife had washed and dried their clothes and had a hearty breakfast waiting for them. Their command of English was limited but their gratitude was obvious without the need for words.

McGuire joined them during breakfast and, completely unaware of the drama unfolding on the Keeraghs, walked with them to the railway station two or three minutes away to board the train for Waterford where they were met by McGuire's counterpart, Edward Jones.

From Waterford they took another train to Kingstown (now Dún Laoghaire) where another of the charity's volunteers secured passage for them to Holyhead on the *TSS Scotia*, which later in the year was requisitioned by the British government for the war effort, serving with honour as an Armed Boarding Steamer. Within a couple of hours of disembarkation in Wales they were on a bus to Liverpool, sleeping for the whole journey.

At Innyard Point, about a hundred yards from the dock, there is a semi submerged row of rocks that juts out into the sea and on board *Helen Blake*, the first task for the crew was to make sure they were well clear of them. There was no time to settle in, they had to be co-ordinated as soon as the shore crew cast off and then row in unison straight out from the beach with the boat being rolled around by the incoming waves, before they could turn into the wind to face them head on.

Each man knew what was needed for this and they worked together like the well drilled team they were, with young Richie Bird fitting in and playing his part like a veteran.

After clearing both the beach and the dock a shudder went through the entire crew as they recognised the enormity of the task in front of them. With strong winds and huge waves thundering in on their port bow, there was no way they could row a boat weighing almost four tons against an incoming tide; to do so would have needed an exceptional effort and would have sapped every last ounce of energy before they even reached the wreck.

Aware of this, the cox made the decision to ship the oars and raise the sails, which would conserve energy as well as enabling them to cover the three miles between the mainland and the islands in a much faster time. It was no easy ride, however, tacking into the wind and being thrown around by the enormous seas. The two men in the bow took the brunt of it, having to turn away from the crashing water every time they hit a wave head on. It took every last bit of the cox's skill to keep her on course.

Constantly changing direction as they battled head on into the weather, it took them a long and worrisome hour to reach the stricken schooner. From the moment they left the dock, the wind started getting stronger and the sea became ever more violent. The conditions were the worst they had ever seen with peaks and troughs all around them and the white plumes of breaking waves as far as they could see. All they could do was

Portrait by José Marques

CHRISTOPHER 'CHRISTY' BIRD
1862 – 1914

Coxswain, Helen Blake lifeboat

hold on tight and hope for the best whilst in the stern, Christy Bird and John Mac gripped the tiller together using every last bit of their energy and skill to keep her on course.

At times, as the boat heeled over, they questioned if they would make it and for a fleeting moment Christy even contemplated turning back. It was a thought that left his mind almost as quickly as it had arrived; there were fellow sailors in danger and he was determined to do everything in his power to help them. None of the men had any idea of what they would find when they reached the casualty and they silently wondered if the crew would still be alive.

Like fishing and coastal communities around the world, the people of Fethard had learned to respect the sea, and had become accustomed to tragedy. Perhaps it was this knowledge, or some sixth sense, that caused the shore crew, unusually, to remain on the little beach, watching silently long after the lifeboat was no longer visible. Some of them would later say they had a strange foreboding about the planned rescue.

Captain Eriksen later described the scene in the same matter-of-fact manner as one of his log book entries, *"We saw the lifeboat coming out from Fethard. We were all on the ship at this time watching the lifeboat struggling through heavy seas. The waves were mountainous high and in addition rain and hail was falling heavily"*. On *Helen Blake*, the hail hitting their oilskins sounded like a machine gun, and the noise could be heard above the storm.

Approaching the Keeraghs, the cox could see the stricken schooner in the towering waves held fast by the rocks. He knew that as the waves rolling in from the Atlantic and across the Celtic Sea hit the shallow water around the Keeraghs, the energy normally used to drive them forward escaped vertically, increased the height and made them unpredictable.

The only way to effect a rescue would be to get between the ship and the shore so Christy Bird formulated a plan he hoped would allow them to get the crew safely off. His intention was to steer to windward and come around the wreck on their port side.

Every rescue has an element of danger, but this was beyond dangerous and their chances of success were fifty-fifty, at best. If they stood off there would be no chance of saving the crew, so that was not an option; it was a calculated risk and they had to take it.

About a cable length (two hundred yards) from the *Mexico* the cox headed into the wind and gave the order to drop the sail, allowing the boat to drift down towards the ship. Edging in precariously close, Bird gave the order to raise the drop-keels to avoid catching on the jagged rocks just a few feet below the surface.

The plan was working. The lifeboat was within a few yards of the ship and they were ready to take the crew on board. Suddenly, appearing to come out of nowhere, a massive wave swamped the boat, causing it to flounder in the rough seas. The men braced themselves as an attempt was made to get her away from the wreck, which towered over them, but without success.

"Let go the anchor!"

The cox's shout could be heard clearly over the crashing seas and though there was no panic in his voice, the urgency was obvious to everyone. Bowman Tom Handrick complied with the order but was instantly knocked off his feet, losing his grip on the cable which ran out to its full length making the anchor ineffective.

Incredibly, a second, even bigger, wave poured over them, closely followed by a third, tossing the boat around in the direction of the island. Only a couple of hours after low tide, a vicious array of sharp rocks were hiding below the surface waiting for their next victim – they had already ripped gaping holes in the steel hull of a ship that dwarfed the tiny lifeboat.

As soon as they felt the impact and heard the sickening sound of splintering timber, the crew knew the boat was doomed. Everything seemed protracted. It was like they were seeing things in slow motion, as they were thrown violently from their seats.

They had no way of knowing it and no time to think about it, but for many of them the shattered boat was the last thing they would ever see before their life was extinguished.

CHAPTER

8

I learned that courage was not the
absence of fear, but the triumph over it.
The brave man is not he who does not feel
afraid, but he who conquers that fear.
– Nelson Mandela

In *Helen Blake's* bow George Crumpton, whose place on the
oars had been taken by Bill Banville, just had time for a fleeting
glance toward Tom Handrick, who was trying to get back on
his feet. The two neighbours could each see the fear in the other's
eyes before both were hurled into the air. Tom, on the port side, hit
the water first and was immediately dragged beneath the surface
in one of the deepest sections of the channel. George, on the other
side, was closer to land and somehow made it ashore but it could
so easily have been the other way around; they had changed places
a number of times since leaving the dock an hour ago.

The same scenario was repeated in the stern where Christy
Bird, who had been clinging tightly to the tiller, was thrown into
the water, where he drowned, whilst his friend Mac ended up
safely on the island.

Struggling in the foaming sea, visibility was reduced to no more than a couple of feet, just enough for Richie Bird to see Pat Roche vanish beneath the waves as he struggled to stay afloat himself and reach out for the shore, before everything went black and he lost consciousness.

The pitiful shouts and screams of men who were taking their final breath were cut tragically short as the sea, which for so long had provided their living, now turned on them and took their lives. For some of them there had hardly been a chance to take a deep breath before hitting the water so within a few seconds they would have gulped in their first mouthful of water, and seconds after that they would have been unconscious. Even those who did manage to fill their lungs would have been fortunate to survive for much more than a minute.

Watching from the *Mexico*, Captain Eriksen later reported that it took just three minutes for the lifeboat to be *"broken to fragments"*. One of the schooner's crew said he had never felt so helpless looking down at the melee below him where he could see men being battered to death against the rocks, *"… and the sea became almost red with their blood"*.

Courage is usually defined as strength in the face of pain or grief, and the truth of that definition was demonstrated beyond question by the *Helen Blake* survivors during the next hour, and in the days to come.

Forty-three year old John Kelly, sitting amidships, lived up to his reputation as a hard man when the boat struck. Within seconds a hole appeared beneath him, the deck had vanished and he gulped in air as he just dropped into the sea. Straightaway, his leg got caught up in a rope and after fighting to clear it before it dragged him to his death he surfaced in a maelstrom of white water, gasping for breath.

Grabbing hold of a piece of rock in an attempt to pull himself on to land, he was instead pulled back into the sea by the back-wash. He was tiring badly now, but as a piece of the lifeboat's mast floated by, he reached out for it and stuck it under his belt to provide some added buoyancy before being almost knocked unconscious as he was flung against the hull of the schooner.

He grasped a rope hanging from the deck but with his energy sapped and fingers numb from immersion in the cold water, he was struggling just to hold on. Hearing a shout he looked up to see the captain who threw him a smaller line which he was able to wrap around his arm. With a strength born of desperation he managed to cling on to the rope as the sailors hauled him on board the crippled ship in a state they described as *"half-dead"*.

George Crumpton, a well-spoken man with a soft voice that generated confidence in those around him, spoke most eloquently as he recalled the terrifying moment they hit the rocks, *"The boat was, in a moment, in splinters, and we were in the sea struggling for our lives. How it was I climbed, I know not, but I found myself, after a good deal of struggling, well up on the ledge"*. Lying with his foot wedged between two rocks, and with the sea surging over him, he was close to drowning when a wave like those that had swamped the boat lifted him and propelled him farther up the shore.

Without knowing how he got there, Richie Bird, the young volunteer who had blacked out in the water after seeing Pat Roche disappear, regained consciousness to find he was lying on a rock beside Crumpton. Exhausted by their ordeal, and in pain from their injuries, the two men nevertheless managed to clamber up the incline to a small cliff overlooking the rocks where there was a clear view of the wreck. *"When the crew of the 'Mexico' saw us, they started shouting through the storm and appealing that something be done for them".*

The Fethard men shouted back with instructions and from the schooner a rope was dropped into the water where the current carried it towards the island, stopping a few feet short. Crumpton, whose mild manner belied his steely determination, was very agile for a big man and in order to grab the rope he leant over the cliff, putting himself in imminent danger of being dragged back into the raging sea. It was a display of what Captain Eriksen later described as *"intrepid courage"*.

Using this line the two men pulled ashore a hawser which was secured to an outcrop by Bird who, though not a regular member of the crew, was definitely proving his worth. The sailors on board *Mexico* referred to him as *"the boy hero"*. George Crumpton had nothing but praise for him saying, *"I cannot tell you how much I admired that youth's bravery all through"*.

Pulled taut by the crew, the other end of the hawser was attached to the ship's mast ready for evacuation. Drawing on every last ounce of strength, the pair were now able to bring the crew of eight safely off the ship, as they tentatively slid down the rope one by one. At times Crumpton had to step into the water to help some of them negotiate the last few feet. The two lifeboatmen were overjoyed when they realised the fourth man in line was their own crew mate John Kelly, who then remained on the cliff to help his colleagues until the last of the men, Captain Eriksen, had been brought to safety.

John Mac recalled how, after being thrown from the boat, he was knocked against the rocks and swirled about in the breakers, which had proved fatal to so many of his friends. At one point

Portrait by Raymond Foley

PATRICK 'PADDY' STAFFORD
1865 – 1914

he had to dodge underneath a portion of the wrecked lifeboat. After being borne backwards and forwards some half-dozen times he was ultimately caught by one tremendous wave and dashed towards the cliff above the shelf of rocks.

"I put my hands in front to save my head," he said, *"and by doing so managed to break the force of the impact somewhat, but it wasn't sufficient to prevent me getting a bad gash on the head. The next thing I remember was that I was at the mouth of a little alcove in the cliff, at the end of which a beam of wood had got caught. On my hands and knees with my head bleeding profusely, I managed to clamber on to the wood and get a hold of it. While there I saw several of my mates being swirled about, as I had been, and I am sure that more than one was, by this time, dead or dying. Garrett Handrick was one of those that were swept nearest to me; he was about four yards off when I crawled down and caught him by one of the hooks of his lifebelt. With the other hand I grasped a ledge of rock and in that way I held out against a couple of successive waves."*

Typical of the entire crew, their bravery and selflessness was demonstrated when Garry, who after swallowing a great deal of water was choking and rapidly losing consciousness, told Mac to let him go and save himself. In his down-to-earth, no nonsense style, Mac's response was, *"I suppose they are all gone now but the two of us, and we will go or come together"*. With every muscle in his body protesting at the effort, Mac hauled his friend onto the rocks where he rolled him over on his side and *"bruised the water out of him until he came to"*.

"From where we were, there were some twelve feet of smooth, straight cliff to negotiate in order to get to safety, but fortune was on our side – the air-boxes of the boat were driven into the

very cove where we were and with these and the aid of a piece of rope we clambered to the top". Once there, they joined their three colleagues who by now had brought everybody ashore from the *Mexico* to the comparative safety of the island. In an interview eight months before his death, Mac said, *"I took off every stitch of clothes and wrung them out – that's the time I was cold!"*

The adrenalin rush was now beginning to wear off and was rapidly being replaced by fatigue which began tightening its grip on the men as they longed for an opportunity to sleep. Richie Bird appeared worst affected with his pain obvious to everyone. All colour had drained from his face, he was walking with difficulty and his body cried out to lie down and rest.

Ignoring their exhaustion, the five men stood together in silence on the small cliff, lashed by the wind and rain, scanning the foaming water for any sign of life, still struggling to understand what had happened. It was a heart-rending scene as tears poured down the cheeks of these tough men attempting to come to terms with the dreadful realisation that the rest of the crew, nine of them, nine of their friends, had cruelly been taken by the raging sea.

9

*We will never be defined by tragedy
but, instead, by how we respond to it.
– Kevin Brady*

The whole episode around the Keeraghs, from the time the schooner rammed into the rocks through to the last man getting his feet on solid ground, appears to have lasted for somewhere between two and three hours, though for the men involved it must have seemed like a great deal longer.

Coast Guard records for that day indicate *Mexico* struck the rocks at around four o'clock in the afternoon, which was the same time *Helen Blake* was launched from Fethard. It took the lifeboat sixty minutes to reach the scene, it was around six o'clock in the evening by the time they managed to secure the line between the island and the wreck, and Captain Eriksen, the last man off the ship, was brought ashore almost an hour later, at seven o'clock, just as darkness was closing in.

Eriksen's report is contradictory on this point stating that *Mexico* went aground an hour earlier, at three o'clock, but the simple explanation for this is that it is likely the ship's clocks had never been changed since leaving the Azores, which are an hour behind GMT.

Earlier in the afternoon, the Coast Guards had also alerted the Kilmore lifeboat station, farther around the coast, of the impending disaster and at about the same time as the Fethard men reached the island, *The Sisters* was launched to assist in the rescue.

In the dark of night both weather and visibility deteriorated considerably and the lifeboat was unable to reach the wreck in the heavy seas. Disheartened, the crew made their way back to their station, which they reached at half past nine. Back in Kilmore they were given an update on the situation and coxswain John Kehoe made the decision for the crew to stand by throughout the night, waiting for another opportunity to venture out. He was a fisherman, he knew many of the Fethard men, he knew the Keeraghs and he was determined they would do everything possible to help.

It was thirty minutes after midnight when an RIC constable knocked on the door of Captain Busher's home in Henrietta Street, just a few hundred yards from Wexford harbour, to let him know a message had been received from the Coast Guards saying his tug was needed at the Keeraghs as soon as possible. By the time he could get his crew together the tide would be too low to sail so Busher advised the constable he would go to the Harbour in the morning at six o'clock to make the necessary arrangements.

In Kilmore, Kehoe could wait no longer, impatience was getting the better of him and at half past five on Saturday morning, with the full backing of his crew he decided on a further attempt to reach the wreck. There had been no improvement in the weather overnight and from the moment the boat cleared the harbour walls, it was clear they were fighting a losing battle. Heading straight into the southwest gale meant they were unable to use the sails so for almost an hour the ten oarsmen rowed with all their strength, directly into the oncoming waves with enormous seas constantly breaking over their bows and flooding the boat. It was a brave attempt, one that required a great deal of courage, and one that sapped every ounce of their energy.

Despite their best efforts, the violent winds and the strong current were relentlessly pushing them back, making it impossible for them even to round Crossfarnoge Point (known locally as Forlorn Point), no more than a few hundred yards from the harbour. There was no lack of resolve on anybody's part, and there was certainly no lack of audacity, but it soon became obvious that to continue would be nothing short of foolhardy and Kehoe was left with no choice but to turn the boat around and return to their station again, getting back at half past six.

Thirty minutes earlier Captain Busher had arrived in the Wexford Harbour Master's office where he telephoned the various Coast Guard stations and was told they needed his tug at the Keeraghs as soon as possible. Having seen the wreck for himself the previous day, he explained that he would be unable to render any assistance without a lifeboat, and asked to be connected to Rosslare Fort.

Disappointment and determination in equal measure was obvious to anyone in Kilmore who cared to look and three hours after their last attempt, despite their tiredness, the crew of *The Sisters* insisted on having a third shot. This time they were successful in rounding Forlorn Point after which they rowed themselves to near exhaustion, fighting against the tide and getting to within about half-a-mile of the islands where they could clearly see the wreck.

Fifty-one year old Kehoe had spent almost forty years in boats and knew the waters around Kilmore as well as anybody in the village. Most importantly, he knew when enough was enough and had to accept that in the current conditions there was no realistic prospect of them being able to help the stranded men. His responsibility now was to ensure the safety of his own crew so with great skill he brought the boat around and the exhausted men, dismayed they could take no part in the rescue, rowed back to the harbour for the last time.

On this point the Board of Trade report is contradictory, stating that on the third attempt *The Sisters* made it to within half a mile of the Keeraghs, something that is generally disputed throughout the area, including Kilmore.

The larger of the two Keeragh islands, the North Keeragh, contained, and still contains, the ruins of a stone house. This had been built specifically for the benefit of shipwrecked sailors over a hundred years earlier by Thomas Boyse, owner of the four thousand acre Bannow estate, which included the islands. According to the Reverend William Hickey, writing in 1868, Boyse kept the house stocked with *"stores of potatoes, whiskey, wood, candles and matches"*.

The stores were no longer there, but most of the walls were still intact and it would have provided a very valuable and much needed refuge for the men if fate had not determined otherwise.

KEERAGH ISLANDS

Ruins of the stone house can be seen in the centre of the large island

Photo by Steve Meyler

Because of the location of the wreck, the survivors had ended up a few hundred yards away on the smaller island where they were totally devoid of any shelter.

The term 'island' is almost a misnomer for the South Keeragh; it is barely more than a big rock with an area of grass covering around one and a half acres. At high tide this can often be less and during a storm like they were experiencing the grass can vanish completely. Where they were stranded gave the impression that if the twelve men stood around the edge of the 'dry land' they could hold hands.

With a maximum elevation no more than thirteen feet above sea level and the rocks surrounding it being pounded by waves that were way in excess of that, there were torrents of sea water continually rushing across the island adding to the men's already considerable discomfort and misery, and in some cases sweeping them off their feet.

The five *Helen Blake* survivors all had injuries of one type or another that were in need of attention. For the first couple of hours or so adrenalin had pumped through their bodies keeping the pain at bay but now the hurt was beginning to take effect and without the benefit of pain killers, dressings or any other first aid equipment, there was very little that could be done to alleviate it.

Everyone had grazes and contusions, some worse than others. Garry Handrick had twisted his ankle, George Crumpton had a hip injury and several abrasions on his arms and legs, Richie Bird's agony was clear for everyone to see as violent pain lanced through his back whenever he turned his body. It was later discovered he had bruised his spine, making his efforts earlier in the evening all the more remarkable. As the night progressed, he wondered what his parents, both in their sixties, would be thinking; when he left the house nobody knew he would be on the lifeboat.

Most of it had been washed off by the rain but John Mac's face still had large patches of blood from the gash on his forehead while John Kelly was in a much weakened state with numerous cuts and bruises from his struggles in the water. As bad as the situation was, it could have been much worse; they were fortunate that, other than Richie, none of them had suffered any debilitating injuries, and they could all still move around.

On shore watchers with telescopes and binoculars later said before it got too dark they had seen some of the men moving around with what appeared to be bandages on their heads. That was after *Mexico's* Swedish steward had stepped in to tend to the wounds using handkerchiefs and any other pieces of cloth he could find, first to wash the open cuts with salt water and then as makeshift bandages. His biggest problem was the clothing stuck to the men's arms and legs with blood. They winced as he dragged the dried blood away with the wet cloth but, if nothing else, this at least meant the bleeding had stopped. Working patiently and methodically he gradually separated clothing from skin and got everyone cleaned up.

There was nothing he could do to help with the bruises, strains, twisted ankles or any of the other unseen injuries so in those cases it was left to the cold to numb the pain – in some cases, the agony – the men were suffering.

Drained of their energy, cold, tired, and weighed down by their heavy, saturated, clothing, the rescuers and the rescued eventually began to settle down – although, in the circumstances 'settle down' is a relative term – for the start of what was to become an incredible feat of both endurance and survival.

Friday night was spent in the open, completely exposed to the elements, and as darkness enveloped the island the temperature quickly dropped. In the cold of the night, the thirteen men could do very little but sit down on the wet grass and pull their coats over their heads to fend off the worst of the rain. They huddled together in the desperate hope of providing each other with some warmth, and a modicum of shelter from the still raging storm and the spray from the angry waves sweeping in from the Atlantic.

Helen Blake's crew removed their lifejackets and spread them on the ground to see if they would afford some insulation from the ground, but they were so full of water they did little to improve the situation.

Those on the inside of the huddle received some shelter but their colleagues on the outside bore the full brunt of the storm as it snatched their breath away so every twenty or thirty minutes they attempted to relieve this by changing position. At times the wind was so fierce they were in danger of being blown off the island and had to lie flat on the ground, often in two or three inches of water – something akin to lying in a river bed.

The first couple of hours had crawled by and with it being impossible for them to get any sleep, the rest of the night seemed to go even slower. In the early hours of the morning Captain Eriksen's voice emerged from the darkness as he recited the Lord's Prayer in Norwegian, *"Fader vår, du som er i himmelen..."* He was gradually joined by others in the group, each praying in his own language. After that they sat in silence with only their fears for company.

Shortly before daybreak the gale appeared to subside but the wind was still force six or seven and, coupled with a rising tide, caused the waves to break closer and closer to the men, showering them with tons of salt water. Added to this was the cold air blowing in from Iceland with the result that two or three degrees Celsius was reduced to an effective temperature of minus five or six by the wind chill factor.

Throughout the night their body temperature had gradually decreased so they felt even colder, making mere survival an outstanding achievement, and something none of them were later able to explain. The whole of Western Europe was being swept by gales that week and it was so cold farther up the coast in Dublin that people were ice skating on the lake in Phoenix Park.

Conversation between the men was almost non-existent; there was nothing anybody could say that would help themselves or their companions; most of them were in shock, and there was neither desire nor energy for idle chit chat. Despite their overwhelming tiredness, sleep remained almost impossible and whenever anybody did manage to doze off they were wakened again within a few minutes as everybody in the group shifted position.

It was unquestionably the longest night of their lives as hour after endless hour they endured the relentless screaming of the wind and the thunder of the breaking seas, competing with rain and sleet to swamp the island. As the wind penetrated every inch of their sodden clothes it seemed to suck the last vestiges of warmth from the bodies of the thirteen men and only sheer willpower enabled them to make it through the night, clinging on to the hope they would be rescued when morning finally came. It was a forlorn hope, and one that would be raised and dashed time and again over the next three days.

During the night it became clear that António Luis da Cunha, the Portuguese deckhand who had joined the ship in the Azores, was in a particularly bad way. His breathing was shallow, he was shivering uncontrollably and he was rambling, with '*Mamãe*' (Mummy) being the only word anybody could understand.

When dawn broke on Saturday morning it was seen that Richie Bird was also shivering badly and both young men were so numb from the cold they found it impossible to move their arms and legs. It was obvious they were suffering from severe exposure and their companions did what they could for them, taking it in turns to massage their frozen limbs in an attempt to restore circulation. It was a thankless task. Though Richie slowly improved as the day wore on, António never had a chance to recover. He passed away shortly after nine o'clock that morning.

John Mac, was holding him in his arms when he passed away, *"trying to stop him from freezing"*, and described him as *"a fine young chap with the greatest head of black hair I ever saw"*. George Crumpton, who was sitting beside them when the end came, had nothing but praise for the young sailor, saying he never uttered a word of complaint and *"… to the last he bore his sufferings without repining or murmur"*. It was a very sad and lonely end for a courageous young man whose untimely death affected everybody on the island.

Garry Handrick found an axe lying around on the island which was identified by Sigurd Lie as the one used to free *Mexico's* lifeboat on Friday, and though their aching bodies cried out with the effort, between them they managed to use this to scrape out a shallow grave for António.

Photo by Steve Meyler

ANTÓNIO'S GRAVE
Cill Cemetery, Cullenstown

The unfortunate young Portuguese was wrapped in a few pieces of sailcloth that had washed ashore from the *Mexico* and laid in the hollow where his shipmates covered him with rocks and a few sods of grass. As the wind and the rain still found its way into every gap in their clothing and hit their oilskins with a noise that almost drowned out everything else, the remaining twelve men stood in silence as Captain Eriksen said prayers beside the makeshift grave.

António's body was exhumed a few days later by four local men, led by fifty-six year old George White, and taken ashore to be given a Christian burial in the tiny Cill graveyard beside the ruins of an equally tiny chapel near Cullenstown strand, within sight of the Keeraghs. There are only a few stones left now to show where the chapel once stood, and the graveyard is no more than a mound of earth in the middle of a field, overgrown with brambles.

It is there that he lies at rest in an unmarked, and uncared for, grave alongside sailors from other ships who suffered a similar fate, including seventeen from the *Demerary*, the ship which had grounded on the same rock as the *Mexico*.

There appears to have been no contact by the Portuguese authorities at the time. Even in later years, in marked contrast to their Norwegian counterparts, they showed no interest in the tragedy – or the death of one of their citizens. It is not known whether António's family, fifteen hundred miles away, were ever informed of his death or where he is buried. In October 2017 the Azores daily newspaper, *Açoriano Oriental*, published a full page article appealing for any relatives to come forward but, regrettably, this produced no results.

10

The friend who can be silent with us in a moment of despair
or confusion, who can stay with us in an hour of grief and
bereavement, who can tolerate not knowing... not healing,
not curing... that is a friend who cares.
— Henri Nouwen

The shore crew had remained on the beach for around half an hour before making their way back to the boathouse where they unhitched the carriage, leaving it at the top of the slipway, and returned the horses to the field across the road. There was no point in going home; if everything went well, *Helen Blake* would be back in another couple of hours.

John Mac's brother Tom, the man who had fired the maroon that signalled the alarm earlier in the afternoon took the big brass telescope from the side room in the boathouse and set it up on the hillside by the ruins of an old windmill overlooking the dock. From here there was an unhindered view of the Keeraghs and he would be able to follow the progress of the rescue. He was just in time to see the lifeboat making its way past the wreck before dropping the sail and turning into the wind before he lost sight of it as it went between the island and the ship. Thirty minutes later it had still not reappeared and alarm bells started to ring.

Many people from the outlying farms and houses around Fethard were still unaware the lifeboat had been launched as they excitedly made their way to the Young Farmers dance. The scene that greeted them on arrival was not at all what they had expected. There were no sounds of music or laughter, the boat-house was empty and a very sombre crowd was gathering on the hillside. Standing beside Tom, who remained on the telescope, were Sam Cook, nephew of *Helen Blake's* previous coxswain, and thirteen year old James Morrissey whose father was on the boat. Between them they gave a running commentary on what was happening on that desolate piece of rock three miles away.

Thirteen year old James had not been at home when his father left so he ran all the way down to the dock to see him, arriving just after the lifeboat had pulled away from the shore. Sadly he was denied the opportunity to say a last goodbye.

Joining the throng was Mary Bridget Handrick who, like everybody else, felt powerless as she stood watching, hoping and praying. The wind was almost blowing them off their feet and the rain was lashing down leaving their clothing completely soaked, yet nobody once complained about the weather. Their only concern was for the safe return of the fourteen men on that little boat.

By the time darkness descended, temperatures had dropped considerably and as the Keeraghs faded from view there were fresh concerns for the men's safety. Slowly people moved into the boathouse where the decorations put up for the dance now looked somewhat incongruous. Standing together in the gloom they felt in some way connected to the men, who by now they believed were on the island. It was late that night before most of them could bring themselves to leave the boathouse and return to their homes.

Tom Mac walked home through the storm with Mary Bridget, each of them lost in their own thoughts, their own hopes and their own fears. John was only a couple of years older than Tom, but he had always taken the role of older brother seriously and looked out for him when they were young lads. In much the same way there was a real bond between Mary Bridget and Garry, who had taken care of her since their father died. Additionally, of course, she was thinking of Mac and what might have been that evening if circumstances had not dictated otherwise.

After a slow, almost hesitant, walk back to the village the majority were still reluctant to go to their homes. Everybody wanted to help but there was almost nothing that could be done except to provide comfort by keeping each other company and praying with families for the safe return of their menfolk. An air of hopelessness permeated the entire area and, feeling helpless, many of the local men gathered in Foley's Hotel where they would usually have been served by Tom Handrick, unaware they would never see him again.

For most of the evening families of *Helen Blake's* crew had been joined by friends and neighbours sharing their grief as they stood on beaches and cliffs staring out across the angry sea. With no reports to the contrary, it was assumed everybody from the schooner and the lifeboat had made it safely on to the island and it was hoped that food, and perhaps even some form of shelter, had been salvaged from the wreck of the ship. There was no way of being sure, of course, and very little sleep was had in Fethard that night.

In between looking after the children, Mary Anne Morrissey had spent much of the afternoon in the children's bedroom where she had an unobstructed view over the top of John Ryan's farm-yard to Fethard Dock, about half a mile away. She returned to her viewpoint when the children were in bed even though in the dark of the night there was nothing to see. Earlier in the day she had a premonition that things would not end well and though it was irrational, she felt that if she moved away she would be abandon-ing her husband. Her love for James never faded and in the years ahead she would often return to that window to stare and to pray, broken hearted, alone with her thoughts and her memories.

Mary Bridget Handrick was restless when she got home. After changing out of her wet clothes and warming herself in front of the turf fire, she put away the shoes and clothes that had been laid out in readiness for the dance. Sitting in the dim light of the fire she shed a tear as she thought of Mac and Garry in the cold and rain, not knowing if they were safe, or if she would ever see them again. Her tiredness was almost unbearable but – like the men on the island – sleep was impossible.

She did what she could to comfort her mother, who had spent the night praying, but after pacing around the tiny room for what seemed like hours, she put on her coat again and set out into the night. Ignoring the cold, rain and dark she walked the mile or so to Windy Gap as though she was on autopilot. There she found Margaret Cullen in her cottage, looking intently through the window as if by some miracle she would be able to see the islands through the near total blackness of the night.

Praying and hoping for the best, Margaret secretly feared the worst and had been standing outside the doorway of their tiny cottage for the greater part of the evening, completely oblivious

Portrait by José Marques

WILLIAM 'WILLIE' BIRD
1877 – 1914

to the worsening weather. Earlier they had been drifting in and out of vision through the mist, but in the fast falling darkness the Keeraghs soon became a dull outline before completely vanishing from view.

Three year old Bridie and her fourteen month old sister Cathy had gone to sleep, but the other seven children, even Dolly who was just six, sensed something was wrong. In this instance, no news was definitely taken as bad news and the three eldest children stood with their mother doing whatever they could to console each other.

Margaret was six years older than Patrick but they had known each other since they were children, and had been sweethearts for as long as anybody could remember They eventually became husband and wife sixteen years ago when Margaret was thirty, since when Patrick had worked hard to provide for their growing family. He had a well-deserved reputation as an accomplished fisherman and three years earlier had acquired the first motor fishing boat in the area. He also ran a ferry service across the small channel to Bannow and would frequently be hired as pilot for the coal ships entering Bannow Bay, on their way to the unloading pier at St Kearns.

One by one the rest of the children eventually went to bed, with the exception of fifteen year old Ellen who stayed up with her mother and Mary Bridget. The three of them now sat around the fire spending the night in silence and sorrow, listening to the howling wind outside and waiting to see what the morning would bring. Young Ellen had the additional burden of worrying as much about her mother as her father and while each took some comfort from being together, there was nothing any of them could say to console the others.

Like the men on the island, they had suffered the longest and most fraught night of their lives, but at first light the families again started gathering on the cliff tops. As the morning progressed they were joined by dozens of other onlookers, all of whom were both anxious and apprehensive as they crowded along miles of coastline, enduring the ferocity of the worst storm in living memory to watch the drama unfold.

As the haze dissipated around mid-morning, bringing the Keeraghs back into view, the crowd stirred and there was a note of excitement in their conversation. They were back in contact, not physically but emotionally, and for those with binoculars, visually. Much as they tried, however, it was hopeless attempting to identify any of the shadowy figures that could occasionally be seen moving around on the island; all anyone could do was pray their loved ones were safe.

Unknown to the survivors or those on shore in Fethard, the Kilmore lifeboat had earlier put to sea in its vain attempt to reach the islands.

Three other boats were now making ready to join the rescue attempt.

chapter
11

Here's a health to every lifeboat
crew around green Erin's shore,
may God them steer from all rocks
clear, now and for evermore.
– John Codd

Between Wexford town and what is now Rosslare Europort there was a promontory known as 'The Fort', so called because of a structure which had been built there in the seventeenth century by the Confederates of Kilkenny as a defence against seaborne invasion (although, when Cromwell's forces besieged it, they surrendered without firing a shot). The fort itself was long gone but the tiny spit of land retained the name, and remained a guardian of the sea with the establishment of the Wexford lifeboat station and a small group of houses where the nucleus of the crew lived.

Officially the Wexford lifeboat, the *James Stevens* was known by everybody as the Rosslare boat, because of the station location. Forty-three year old coxswain Edward 'Ned' Wickham with his wife Margaret and their five children lived in the largest of

JAMES STEVENS
The Rosslare lifeboat

Photo by Steve Meyler

ROSSLARE FORT
The fort has gone; all that is left are a few rocks

the houses and it was there the telephone rang early on Saturday morning. On the other end of the line was Captain Busher who asked Ned if he was aware of the situation on the Keeraghs. This was the first the lifeboatman had heard of the disaster and after briefing him, Busher asked if he would go with him to assist in the rescue. The two men had worked together before and Wickham replied without a pause.

"Yes, will you bring me down?"

"To be sure; I'm casting off now and I'll be with you in half an hour".

This was by no means an unusual situation; as long ago as 1859, the steam tug *Erin* had towed the Rosslare Fort lifeboat to aid the twelve hundred ton emigrant ship *Pomona* with four hundred passengers on board. By the time they reached it, the ship sank and only the mast was visible; just twenty-four people survived. One of those drowned was Belfast publican Henry Lavery whose two year old son went on to earn fame as an artist, probably most famously known for one of his paintings of his wife, Lady Lavery, which adorned Irish banknotes from 1928 to 1975.

Only three crew members lived at the fort. Next door to Ned was his thirty-seven year old brother James, known to everybody as 'Jem', who together with his wife Mary and their son, shared the house with his brother John, his widowed sister and her son and an employee of the boat repair business run by the three brothers.

The third member of the crew was twenty-nine year old bowman William 'Bill' Duggan, who lived alone.

A call was put out for the rest of the crew and in the way of RNLI volunteers throughout the country, they all responded instantly ensuring the boat was ready to put to sea just sixty minutes after Ned had taken the call.

At exactly half past seven Ned Wickham launched *James Stevens* with the oarsmen, including sixty-nine year old Christopher Doyle and his son Andy, rowing a few hundred yards offshore where *Wexford* was waiting to take her in tow to the Keeraghs.

Half an hour later, at eight o'clock, a message was sent to the lifeboat station at Dunmore East informing them of the wreck and asking for their assistance. The maroon rocket was fired and the crew poured down to the harbour unaware of what task was in front of them but ready to do whatever was needed.

Ninety minutes after receiving the message, just as António was being interred in his temporary grave on the island, the *Fanny Harriet* was leaving harbour and raising the sail.

Lifeboat coxswains around the coast are experienced seamen with an intimate knowledge of the waters in which they operate, and Walter Power was one of the best. As the owner of the fifty-foot *Lydia Ann*, he had fished the area regularly and was only too aware of its fearsome reputation as 'the graveyard of a thousand ships'. Steering well clear of the coast, they battled their way around Hook Head before beating into a fearsome headwind through another nine miles of turbulent seas to reach the stranded men.

Having suffered through an indescribably harsh night on the island before undertaking the harrowing task of burying one of their group, the morale of the stranded men was understandably at rock bottom. Soaking wet, continually lashed by sleet and

WEXFORD

Built in South Shields in 1888
Leased by the Admiralty July 1915 – April 1918
Stationed in France during 1919
Registered in Sunderland 1922
Sold for scrap and broken up 1956

rain, blown around by gale force winds, shivering in effective temperatures hovering around freezing point and with no indication of what was happening back on shore, they truly were between the proverbial rock and a hard place.

Facing the full force of the howling wind there was no possibility to get comfortable. They spent their time shuffling aimlessly around the island, but even that was difficult. The combination of spray, rain and wind hit them from all angles with such force it felt as though they were being pebble dashed at times. During the night the numbing cold had eaten through their clothes leaving them with stiff joints and tight muscles making their legs feel like they were full of lead.

All they could do was hope against hope that help would come soon and they would be freed from what was beginning to feel like a prison. It is fortunate they were unaware of what lay in store for them over the course of the next few days; without that hope to cling on to, it is possible that some of them may have just given up, with dire consequences.

Back in Fethard the first indication of the gravity of the situation, and what had really happened, came at around two in the afternoon when the village was stunned by the news that six bodies had been washed up on the strand at Cullenstown. Bill Banville's youngest brother, twenty-eight year old Robert, and his friend Alex Cooper made their way from Fethard to carry out the unenviable task of identifying the bodies, which were later described as being, " ... *frightfully mangled, especially the heads of the unfortunate men* ...".

Robert was relieved to find his brother's body was not there and believed this meant he had survived. They were able to identify five of the dead as Christy Bird, James Morrissey, Pat Roche, Tom Handrick and his brother Mikey.

The sixth body, that of forty-nine year old Paddy Stafford, was unrecognisable and was mistakenly thought to be a member of *Mexico's* crew. He was so badly disfigured it was not possible to determine his identity until some days later, and even then it could only be identified by a St Joseph's Cord which he habitually wore around his neck. Pat Roche's mother arrived shortly afterwards offering to identify her son's remains but thankfully Cooper and Banville were able to persuade her otherwise.

The body of Willie Bird was recovered in the ensuing days but it was to be almost another seven weeks before Bill Banville, the man without a life jacket, was given up by the sea on Easter Sunday. He too was unrecognisable and could only be identified by the repairs carried out on the boots he had collected on the day of the disaster.

It was a further nine days before Patrick Cullen's remains were discovered by local man Edward Monahan who was walking his dog on Crosslake Strand, between Bannow and Cullenstown. One of his feet was missing and it is believed that after being thrown into the sea he was trapped by some of the wreckage, remaining there until his foot broke away at the ankle allowing the body to free itself and be carried ashore by the tide.

An inquest was carried out by John Roche, Deputy Coroner for South Wexford, who gave the cause of death as drowning. His body was then placed in a coffin and taken to Fethard in a cortege fit for a hero.

The state of the sea made it impossible for *The Sisters* to approach the island but rather than give up, they managed to lay off about half-a-mile offshore with the oarsmen fighting the wind and tide to keep he on station. They remained for an hour looking for an opportunity to get in close as, minute by minute the sea worsened. Eventually, fifty-one year old Kehoe had to admit defeat. He had spent almost forty years in boats and knew when enough was enough. Reluctantly, he had to accept that in the current conditions there was no realistic prospect of them being able to help the stranded men. His responsibility now was to ensure the safety of his own crew so with great skill he brought the boat around and raised the sail.

The wind was behind them for the return trip and the sea was running so fast they were in serious danger of broaching (turning broadside to the sea and sliding down one of the huge waves, to a watery grave). The drogue anchor was deployed to slow them down and this, coupled with skilful handling of the rudder, enabled them to make it safely back to harbour where the weather was so bad that 'for the safety of the lifeboat', she had to be housed overnight.

In the Hook Lighthouse, Patrick Higginbotham had been on duty through the night but even though his replacement, James Deveaney, had taken over, he remained transfixed at the top of the tower, one hundred and fifteen feet up, with his telescope focused on *Fanny Harriet* as she fought her way through shifting winds and unpredictable waves around Hook Head. Without realising it, his thoughts were exactly the same as the men on the lifeboat – would they make it.

The distance to be covered was just nine miles as the crow flies but tacking into the wind almost doubled that, as well as increasing the discomfort level. Their wet weather gear did little to stop the rain or the sea spray from soaking the well drilled crew who, with waves breaking over the bow one minute and hitting them broadside the next, gave a masterclass in sailing in adverse conditions.

By one o'clock, four hours after leaving port, she was at the Keeraghs, just a few hundred yards offshore. Ever mindful of what had befallen the *Helen Blake*, Walter Power was the picture of concentration, edging his craft slowly and carefully through the surf, all the time raising the hopes of the survivors who could see them clearly. The men on the island had first spotted the lifeboat ten minutes earlier as it appeared through the haze, and had rushed to the shoreline shouting and waving to attract attention.

As it approached, the Fethard men recognised many of the Dunmore crew, having previously carried out joint exercises with them. They had the utmost confidence in them so it was heart breaking for both the survivors and the crew when, despite making repeated attempts to manoeuvre her in close, *Fanny Harriet* was repelled every time by the massive waves rolling in from the Celtic Sea and gaining height as they bounced back from the rocks.

In the meantime, the *James Stevens* from Rosslare was on the way. Their station was over twenty five miles from the Keeraghs, more than twice the distance from Dunmore but they arrived just half an hour later, thanks to the power of the tug boat.

Few paddle steamers were built as sea going vessels, they were generally more suited to river and harbour work, and *Wexford* was no exception to this. She spent most of her time shunting ships around the harbour and was certainly out of her comfort zone in stormy seas, which speaks volumes for the skill and courage of Busher and his crew.

All through the six hour journey the tug battled into the heavy seas with its giant paddles crawling over the giant waves before descending into a trough waiting for the next one. At times the crew lost sight of the *James Stevens* at the other end of the tow rope one hundred and fifty yards behind them before it re-appeared, rarely cresting a wave but instead punching its way through in an explosion of spray. The Rosslare men were having a rough ride coming to a standstill as the tow rope slackened off and then lurching forward as they were dragged through an oncoming wave; it was like hitting a wall of water.

Wexford had to moderate her speed to avoid swamping the lifeboat, but even then Ned Wickham's crew needed to bail by hand in addition to operating the bilge pump for the entire journey. The sea was so bad as they approached Carnsore Point the tug had to reduce speed even further to prevent the lifeboat foundering.

Captain Busher towed them clear of the coast and around the notorious Barrels lightship where some years earlier the weather was so bad the lightship had dragged its anchor and was almost washed ashore. From there it was on to the Coningbeg lightship putting them in a position to approach the Keeraghs to windward.

The seven man crew on the lightship watched nervously as the tug towed the lifeboat past them to within about a mile of the islands where it cast off the tow and stood off as Jem Wickham raised the sail. Tentatively, they crept in closer to join the rescue attempt.

There was great excitement and their morale was quickly lifted as once again the men from Fethard recognised many of those on board the new arrival. One of the survivors later told Ned Wickham, *"When we saw you come 'round on Saturday, we knew we would be saved; we knew that if anyone could do it, you could"*.

Confidence was so high on the island that Captain Eriksen said a final prayer beside the grave of António and then got his crew lined up in preparation for evacuation from the desolate rock before shaking hands with Mac as a congratulatory gesture.

Against all the odds, they had survived, and believed they were about to be rescued.

CHAPTER

12

You make a living by what you get,
But you make a life by what you give.
– Winston Churchill

Both Busher on *Wexford* and Wickham on *James Stevens* had reputations that inspired confidence in everybody. During his twenty-four years in command, the fifty-seven year old tug captain had previously rendered assistance to various ships in distress and had personally saved a number of lives, which resulted in him being awarded medals by Lloyds and the Royal Humane Society. (Busher's son, Clem, emulated his father's bravery a few years earlier when, during a gale in the Bristol Channel, he tied a line around his waist and swam out to a sinking ship. His heroism resulted in the entire crew being saved.)

Ned Wickham held an enviable record that had gained him the respect of every lifeboat man in the country. Much like Richie Bird, he had first volunteered in an emergency when a boat was short of a crew member – the big difference being that Wickham was just eleven years old at the time! Since then he had saved an astonishing one-hundred-and-fifty-one lives, and had been awarded the King Edward Silver Medal by the RNLI. He took over from his father as coxswain of the Rosslare lifeboat in 1898.

Throughout the ages, seafarers have adhered to an unwritten law of the sea which requires them to go to the aid of fellow mariners in distress. It makes no difference whether the problem is in the middle of the ocean, or a few yards offshore, and the fishermen of Fethard had no intention of flouting that law. There were men in distress on the Keeraghs, and they were not just fellow mariners, they were friends and relatives.

As the wind appeared to have abated slightly, three local men – Marks Barden, Ned Brien and Charlie Cook (*Helen Blake's* previous coxswain, and next door neighbour of James Morrissey), together with 'the Peeler Kelly', one of three constables based in Fethard's Royal Irish Constabulary barracks, made an impulsive and courageous attempt to reach the islands, proving the old saying that referred to wooden boats and iron men was still apt.

Helped by others on the beach, they launched Paddy Molloy's twenty-four foot fishing boat, *Kate*, into the teeth of the storm. With only two sets of oars the four men faced a seemingly insurmountable task in tackling the huge waves but, against all the odds, they were making good progress until the gale once again gathered intensity, forcing them to turn back with less than half the distance covered. In the heavy seas it took all their skill, and all their strength, to get the boat safely back to the beach. (In later years the *Kate* was fitted with an engine from a Renault car and continued to be fished in Fethard by Paddy's son Patsy until the 1960s.)

Several attempts were made by both lifeboats to reach the stranded men and get a line to them as they circled the island looking for an opening in the waves they could exploit, unfortunately without success. With all the lifeboats being of similar construction, both crews were only too well aware that, throughout the rescue, they were never more than a few minutes away from sharing the fate of their RNLI colleagues from Fethard.

At around five o'clock, with the strength of the wind rapidly increasing and the waves becoming ever more threatening, the rescuers were left with no choice but to run for shelter.

They had left the island empty handed but their presence there was by no means an empty gesture; the pluck and resolve shown by both crews could only be described as exceptional. In a display of seamanship it would have been difficult to better anywhere in the country they took their little wooden boats into the turmoil of white water that most other vessels would do everything possible to avoid, and brought them out safely.

Ignoring waves that tossed them around and could have crushed them in a moment, they had constantly edged closer and closer to needle sharp rocks that had already punched holes in the steel hull of a ship that dwarfed them.

When it was all over, Jem Wickham, second cox on the Rosslare boat, reflected on what they had done, *"The sea that night would frighten anyone but our Irish blood was up and there were human lives at stake"*. He was a modest man who spoke from the heart and whose words reflected the attitude of all RNLI volunteers. *"Of course, we don't have the greatest opinion in the world of ourselves, but any Irishman worthy of the name would have done the same"*.

The Dunmore boat fought its way to Fethard, reversing the route taken by the *Helen Blake* twenty four hours earlier. On the cliff tops, the crowds saw the lifeboat heading in their direction and started to make their way to the dock. Local fishermen had to hastily reorganise the boats, moving them around and packing them in tightly to make room for the lifeboat. Very few of the boats had left the dock during the past week because of the weather, and three of them had now lost their owners on the Keeraghs.

When the *Fanny Harriet* docked, the quay was thronged with families and friends of the stranded men who bombarded the crew with questions. Everybody wanted to know if they had seen their husband, their father, their brother, their son. Walter Power and his crew had seen men on the island, and had recognised some of them, but they could not say for certain who was there or, perhaps more importantly, who was not there.

Tom Mac and Mary Bridget were overjoyed to hear John was safe, but disappointed when there was no news about Garry. Young James Morrissey, who had spent the whole day with Tom on the big brass telescope, was eager for news of his father but was left downhearted when there was none forthcoming.

Margaret Cullen, watching the lifeboat from her vantage point outside the cottage at Windy Gap, repeated a silent prayer over and over, *"Please, God, bring him home to me"*. Her sixth sense had come into play and she was certain something had happened to Patrick. Whilst she remained at home with the young ones, fifteen year old Ellen went to the dock with Mikie and Patsy but, like so many others, came away disheartened. There was no news of their father.

Rebecca Crumpton's younger sister, Annie Cruise, had stayed with her the previous evening and was now at the dock hoping

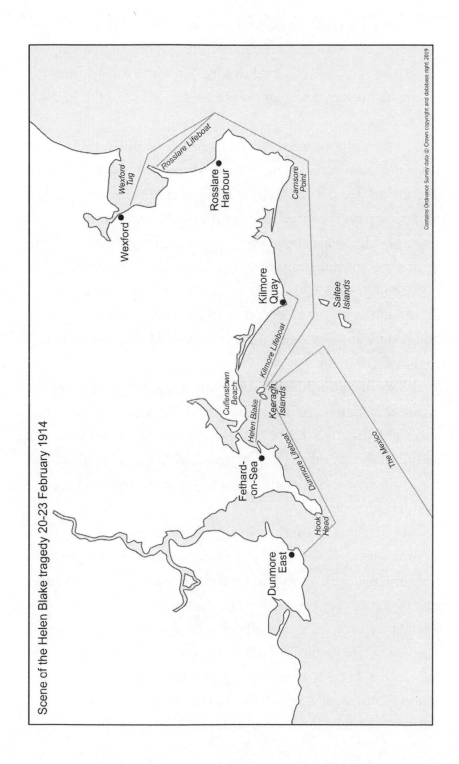

Scene of the Helen Blake tragedy 20-23 February 1914

Wexford Tug

Rosslare Lifeboat

Wexford

Rosslare Harbour

Carnsore Point

Kilmore Quay

Saltee Islands

Cullenstown Beach

Kilmore Lifeboat

Helen Blake

Keeragh Islands

Fethard-on-Sea

Dunmore Lifeboat

The Mexico

Hook Head

Dunmore East

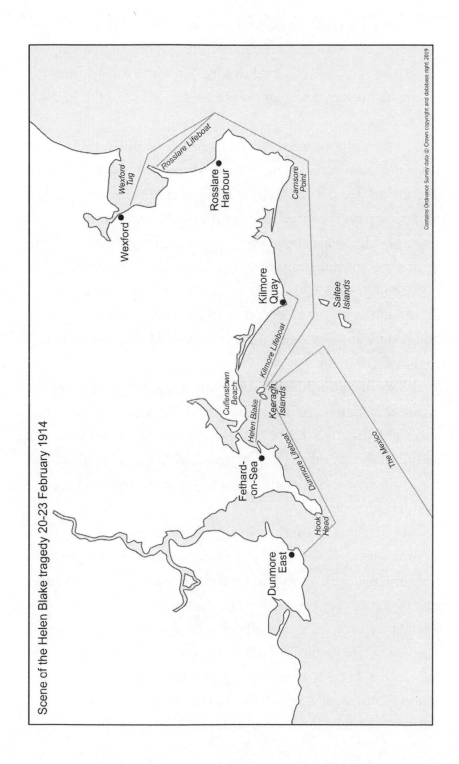

Contains Ordnance Survey data © Crown copyright and database right 2019

to return with good news. Unfortunately it was not to be; the Dunmore crew were unable to confirm George's presence on the island. Lizzie Kelly had to rely on others for information as she had been unwell and was not able to make the journey to the dock.

All the other families were there but, woefully, their questions did not always produce the answers they wanted to hear. The crowd was packed so tight that some of the local men had to clear a path for the exhausted lifeboat crew as they walked up to the big house above the quay where they were given hot drinks before being transported to the village.

Accommodation was provided for the entire crew in Foley's Hotel and at last they could strip off their sodden clothing and restore some warmth to their bodies while a hot stew was prepared for them.

Wexford had already raised the anchor by the time the Rosslare boat reappeared from the far side of the island and immediately steamed to meet them. A line was thrown to the lifeboat and used to haul aboard a four hundred and eighty foot hawser which would be used to tow them to Waterford harbour.

Approaching Hook Head everybody was on edge, they were entering the turbulent and unpredictable 'Race of the Hook', a phenomenon well known to local fishermen where the waters exiting the estuary are met by the incoming Celtic Sea and then joined by tides coming around the coast from Wexford, throwing everything into confusion with waves chopping and changing by the minute. In earlier times the Vikings had named the estuary Vadra Fiord (weather fiord) due to the exceptionally dangerous tides experienced in the area, especially in bad weather.

JAMES STEVENS CREW
Left to Right
Back: John Walsh, Christopher Doyle, Bill Duggan, William Shiel
Front: Andrew Doyle, Philip Duggan, John Mitten, Mogue Furlong,
Ned Wickham, Jem Wickham, William Walsh

The keepers in the lighthouse prepared themselves for the worst, watching in horror as the boats were caught up in the swirling currents and rough seas, pushing them towards rocks that had claimed so many boats and ships over the years. With a diameter of eight inches the hawser was big enough to tow a ship but with both boats being thrown around in different directions it was placed under immense strain. At half past six, about a mile and a half up the river it eventually split, leaving the lifeboat floundering.

The cox ordered the sail to be raised and within two minutes they had regained command of the boat. Visibility was still very poor as they followed in the wake of the tug so Busher blew the whistle every minute to help keep them on track. Approaching Duncannon lighthouse they passed over the site of Cromwell's flagship, *Great Lewis* – one of the earliest shipwrecks recorded in the area when it was sunk by gunfire from the nearby fort in January 1645, after being caught up in strong tides and currents.

According to Ned Wickham, *"We sailed up to Cheekpoint, where we reached about ten-thirty at night, fifteen hours after taking the boat out, and during all that time we had nothing to eat nor nothing to drink unless water. It was terribly cold all day, being sleeting nearly all the time. Every man of the crew had to remain in his place all day, there being no room to move about"*. *Wexford* dropped anchor and secured *James Stevens* alongside with two ropes.

Completely disheartened, the colour visibly drained from the survivors' faces as they stood together on the tiny island, silent, disconsolate, unmoving, watching as the boats, their only contact with the outside world, disappeared into the distance, and with them the realisation there would be no rescue today. They were all experienced seamen, they understood just how difficult and dangerous it had been, but that did not make it any easier to accept.

They had seen the efforts made by the crews from Rosslare and Dunmore and they knew Wickham and Power would never give up trying. The big question on everybody's mind, however, was whether the boats could get to them before it was too late. Throughout the day their hopes had been raised and as the adrenalin kicked in again they had forgotten about food and ignored their hunger, but now as daylight started to fade all the old feelings came back to them with the energy appearing to rush from their tired bodies.

During the last century it was believed the islands had been home to a colony of the Northern Hemisphere's only flightless bird, the now extinct Great Auk, and in years to come they would be transformed into a bird sanctuary, but throughout the weekend there was not even a seagull that might have provided some nourishment. Shortly after the disaster, rabbits were introduced to the islands for the benefit of anybody stranded in the future.

This was a precarious time for everyone; as survival experts know only too well, if you stop fighting them, the twin evils of starvation and dehydration will take advantage of you. To hold them at bay it was essential they remained positive. (In recent years it has been discovered that when you give up fighting, and stop believing you will survive, your body temperature drops and it becomes a self-fulfilling prophecy.)

This time it was captain Eriksen who came to the rescue and under his direction, helped by Mac, the twelve men scoured the island to gather up a few more pieces of sail-cloth together with some timbers that had washed ashore from the schooner. Using these they managed to fashion a makeshift shelter just as daylight faded, moving away to provide a dawn elsewhere, and leaving them to face another miserable night. They huddled underneath it in preparation for a second night on the island, hoping it would keep the worst of the weather at bay.

Their hopes were short lived and the benefit proved to be more psychological than physical. The island was solid rock with a few scant inches of soil on top which meant there was no drainage so, as the rain continued to come down in torrents, they spent the night with streams of water flowing all around them, adding to their misery. They were all outdoor men, tough men, who were accustomed to working in harsh conditions, but what they were going through now was beyond anything they had experienced before.

Whenever the cold became unbearable, they ran up and down the island in an almost futile attempt to generate some warmth. Mac with Garry, and Kelly with Crumpton, took it in turns every few hours to help Richie to his feet and half-carry him around the island. It helped, but at a cost, with the young man experiencing stabbing pains throughout his body as his blood circulation was restored. They probably did not know it, but walking around might well have saved their lives. In severe cases of hypothermia, if you remain lying down the blood gathers around the heart and vital organs. When you then stand up it rushes to the legs and can cause heart failure.

During the hours of darkness they craved sleep even more than food, but it was equally scarce. The Fethard crew had not slept for almost forty-eight hours and for many of *Mexico's* crew it was even longer. In their current environment, however, sleep could be dangerous. In the screaming gale and relentless rain, the wind chill factor was still producing minus temperatures and with them a serious risk that inactivity could lead to a quick death.

This was not a first for Eriksen. Like most Norwegians, he understood the dangers associated with the cold and he knew from experience the staggering pace at which death could follow when low temperatures, combined with strong winds, caused the body to lose heat rapidly. He also knew that removing wet clothing would do nothing to help.

Everybody was already displaying the first signs by shivering, which is a result of the body attempting to compensate by producing heat through muscle activity. As the body temperature drops the shivering stops, dizziness and disorientation kicks in, and the body only maintains heat around the vital organs – brain, heart and lungs. Blood circulation to the arms and legs shuts down while the heart rate becomes slow, irregular and weak before the individual finally slips into unconsciousness.

It was vital to prevent this happening so Captain Eriksen set up a rota where everybody took it in turns to sleep for an hour – not that many of them managed it – before being woken up and moving around to keep the blood circulating.

He was an imposing figure on the island, with a voice that resonated and inspired confidence. The Wexford Free Press described him as *"completely unnerved"* saying, *"... the bluff old captain of the Mexico, true to the best traditions of the hardy Norsemen, saw to it that everything that could be done was carried out to save his crew"*.

In the black sky, the moon and stars were hidden behind the heavy clouds for most of the night making the island so dark it was not even possible to make out the details of the person beside you. In the early hours of the morning the rain stopped for a short time and there was a break in the clouds giving everything a faint, and eerie, luminosity, but it quickly vanished when the rain resumed and the cloud returned.

With no energy, or appetite, for conversation, each man was more alone than ever, spending the long night harbouring his own private thoughts and fears. For *Helen Blake's* crew, in the forefront of their thoughts were the nine men who had been lost; they all knew their families, they knew how they would be affected and, worst of all, they knew they would be able to do nothing to ease the suffering.

For most of the men from Fethard, Saturday night in the village would have been an opportunity to relax for a couple of hours, meeting friends for a drink and catching up with the latest news and gossip. This Saturday was different; tonight in Nolan's, Foley's, Thompson's and many other public houses for miles around, they were the latest news, and the only topic of conversation.

George Crumpton was thinking about his wife and young Tom, just eighteen months old, questioning if he would ever see them again. Rebecca was the love of his life and, though he did not know it at the time, she was pregnant with their second child, who would be born towards the end of the year.

Captain Eriksen re-played the final hour of the *Mexico* in his mind time and again, analysing everything he did and speculating as to whether there was anything he could have done differently that might have saved his ship. He could not think of anything that would have caused a different outcome.

Mac's thoughts were of Mary Bridget and the dance that never happened; he wondered where she was now, what she was feeling, and if he would ever get another chance to take her out.

Richie Bird was suffering his agony with a degree of stoicism rarely seen, but alone in the cold of the night he questioned why he was even there. When Bill Banville turned up at the dock, he could have got off the boat but instead chose to stay. He could not say why he had made that choice, but he was pleased he did. When he helped bring the men ashore from the schooner the feeling he got was like nothing he had ever experienced before. He was unable to see them, wherever he looked all he could see was darkness, but he knew they were there. It was incredible to think that without him and his thirteen colleagues the men from the *Mexico* might now be dead. It was a feeling lifeboatmen around the country would understand.

He was now in more pain than he had known was possible and whatever he did, however he moved, he could do nothing to make it any less. Additionally, he could not stop thinking about António, who had succumbed to the cold just twelve hours earlier. As doubts started to creep in, he wondered if he would get off the island before the same thing happened to him.

CHAPTER

13

Eternal Father strong to save
Whose arm has bound the restless wave
Who bids the mighty ocean deep
Its own appointed limits keep
O hear us when we cry to Thee
For those in peril on the sea

News of the disaster spread rapidly around the world and in less than twenty-four hours it was being reported in newspapers from Manchester to Montana. In London a meeting was hastily convened at the RNLI offices in Charing Cross Road. Present at that was management committee member Lord Beresford, son of the Marquess of Waterford, who had some knowledge of the area and enquired as to what assistance could be rendered.

It was agreed that the Chief Inspector of Lifeboats, retired Royal Navy Commander Thomas Holmes, would travel to Fethard to lend his support. With just an overnight bag that he kept in his office he took a taxi for the short journey to Paddington where he would catch the eight-forty-five boat train.

Fog and heavy traffic made it a slow journey and by the time he got there the train had steam up and was preparing to depart. With the sleeper car already fully booked, he took a seat in the first class carriage where he could relax for a few hours.

It was a giant of a train with almost five-hundred tons of rolling stock pulled by Saint Class locomotive, *Clevedon Court*. Three of the fourteen carriages would be dropped off a few miles from Bristol before entering the Severn Tunnel and three more, including the dining car, were to be left in Swansea by which time the fireman would have shovelled some five tons of coal. A new locomotive was scheduled take over at that point for the final stage of the two-hundred-and-sixty mile journey to Fishguard where it would arrive at twenty-five past one – almost two hours faster than the same journey takes in 2018.

Arrival of the train coincided with the docking of the overnight ferry from Rosslare but it would be a further three hours before *SS St Patrick* left port for the return trip. Rather than sit around in the waiting room, Holmes made himself known to Captain O'Brien, also ex-Royal Navy, who invited him on board early and provided him with a cabin for the short voyage.

Winds of force six to seven were blowing in the Irish Sea making it a very rough crossing but, despite that, just over three hours after departure passengers were disembarking in Rosslare where the RNLI had arranged for Holmes to be met by a chauffeur driven car.

Kilmore Quay was only about fifteen miles away but the incessant rain had played havoc with the unpaved roads, making some areas more like a mud bath, creating huge potholes which tested the driver's skill to the limit, and more than doubling the time the journey would normally have taken.

At Nicholas White's hotel, a couple of hundred yards up the hill from the harbour, Holmes ordered breakfast while waiting for coxswain John Kehoe who arrived twenty minutes later after attending Mass in nearby St Peter's Catholic Church, where the congregation had prayed for those on the island. Kehoe brought him up to date with the situation based on his own experience and messages relayed from the various Coast Guard stations. With the storm still raging, it quickly became clear the problems in attempting a further rescue attempt from there were insurmountable.

Back in the fashionable two-seater 'De Dion' roadster for another uncomfortable and unpleasant journey, his driver, Jim Hearne, took him through Carrig-on-Bannow, less than two miles from Cullenstown. On a clear day it would have been possible to see the Keeraghs from there but on that day visibility was no more than a half a mile. Adding to the problem of potholes, broken branches and other debris scattered on the roads were being blown around with such violent intensity that on more than one occasion Hearne had to bring the car to a halt to prevent any damage. Crossing the Owenduff River at Wellingtonbridge he joined the New Line – a road built in the previous century by the British military to facilitate the movement of troops between Wexford Town and Duncannon Fort. Through Saltmills they crossed the bridge between Tintern Abbey and Bannow Bay before arriving in Fethard in the middle of the afternoon. Within ten minutes everyone in the village was aware of his arrival.

Having secured a room at Foley's he met George Bassett who was able to provide him with details of everything that had happened in the past forty-eight hours. There was just time for a quick wash and a cup of hot tea before he climbed back in the car, which by now had attracted a small crowd who followed him to the dock. Perhaps this was the miracle for which they had all been praying.

There had been a slight abatement in the weather, the sea was marginally calmer, waves were no longer breaking over the wall, and Holmes asked Walter Power on the waiting *James Stevens* if he would make another attempt to rescue the stranded men.

Fethard man Marks Barden, one of those who had attempted the rescue in the Kate the previous day, was taken on board. His local knowledge would be used to pilot the boat. It was an exceptionally hazardous trip with gale force winds blowing them in every direction and colossal seas crashing over the fo'c'sle threatening to swamp them at any moment. They also encountered the extra problem of the wind being against the tide, which has the effect of making the waves steeper. Their wet weather gear did little to protect them from the elements and within minutes they were soaked through, baling out and spitting out salt water.

The wind was whipping the water into a frenzy and Commander Holmes watched in amazement and admiration as Walter Power's men, piloted by Barden, manoeuvred the boat through the maelstrom to within a few hundred yards of the island. Barden was sixty-eight years old but very powerfully built with the strength and agility of many men half his age. The sight of the lifeboat once again raised the hopes of the stranded men who could hardly believe it had launched in such appalling weather.

The euphoria was short lived, however, as, despite their persistence and another remarkable display of courage, the would-be rescuers were forced back time and again by the mountainous waves, dashing the hopes of the survivors, who by now were very

Portrait by José Marques

WALTER POWER
1856 – 1937

Coxswain, Fanny Harriett

DUNMORE CREW

William Power (2nd Coxswain), Patrick Power (Bowman), Thomas Power, Michael Power, Patrick Power, Phillip Myler, Patrick Myler, Pat Brown, William Bond, George Cunningham, William Burke, James Donovan weak and beginning to lose hope. It was a despondent and weary crew that returned to Fethard.

One of the new motor lifeboats might have weathered the storm better but it is doubtful that it could have got close enough to effect a rescue. Such musings were hypothetical anyway; although one would replace *Fanny Harriett* in Dunmore in a few months, the nearest on that day was in Wicklow, over ninety miles along the coast.

Visibility from the island had been poor all day with even the Saltee Islands, only a few miles southeast of them, invisible since daybreak and now, as evening approached, it deteriorated further. Forcing their eyes to penetrate the obscurity of the rain and mist, the men on the island could occasionally see outlines of people gathered on the cliffs above Cullenstown strand but there was no possibility of making out any detail. Looking towards Fethard the view was even worse; they knew where the dock should be, where the cliffs overlooking Grange beach should be, where Windy Gap should be, where every point along the coast should be, but through the driving rain there was nothing to be seen. That did not stop them looking, however, and like those on shore, they stared into the distance hoping for a miracle.

Mac looked towards Grange and wondered if Mary Bridget was there; what was she thinking, did she even know he was alive? It seemed like a hundred questions were running through his mind, over and over again. He wondered what he would say to her when he saw her again, if he saw her again, and he started to formulate sentences and phrases in his mind.

Captain Eriksen thought of his wife; she had pleaded with him to retire at the end of the summer but he allowed himself to be persuaded to do one more voyage, a decision he was now beginning to regret as he too wondered would he ever see her and his family again. At home in Fredrikshald, Marie Louise had attended the nine o'clock service in Immanuels Church with their daughter, Tora Louise, so far unaware of the drama unfolding almost eight hundred miles away.

When the Norwegian government became aware of the tragedy instructions were sent to Edward Betson, their consul in Dublin, to ensure they had representation in Wexford. Betson dispatched a Mr Stordahl who arrived early on Saturday evening, in the company of Harrison Cox, representing the underwriters of *Mexico*. The two men went straight to a meeting with the local Lloyds agent, Tom Walsh, hoping to be brought up to date with events, but what he told them is anybody's guess. His statement to the newspapers indicated that his grasp of the situation was very different to the reality.

Perhaps he had seen the wisp of smoke from the meagre fire the survivors had lit but that seems unlikely as it certainly would not have been visible from Wexford. It is more likely that information regarding the fire had been relayed to him, and based solely on that he appears to have allowed his imagination to run riot.

According to Walsh the men on the island had built a shelter, had a fire going and were *"in possession of plenty of provisions obtained from the ship before it broke up"*. He also declared that *"when the ship struck the rocks, the bow was forced up on the rock, and the crew would not have had difficulty in climbing on to the island"*.

The press, in a hurry to get something out to their readers, and never shy about getting their facts wrong, were only too happy to print his story. Proving the old adage that you should never let the truth get in the way of a good story, the *Northern*

Whig, a Belfast newspaper, went even further, quoting an unnamed member of the *James Stevens* crew as saying he saw eleven men on the island, none of whom could speak English and motioned by holding their fingers to their mouth to demonstrate they were hungry and thirsty.

In Fethard this should have been a special day at home; the day when 'Daddy' did not go to work, the day when the children could spend some rare and valuable time in his company, the one day of the week when the whole family could be together. Tragically, on this Sunday it was not to be.

Despite the atrocious weather that hung around all morning, hundreds of people walked miles to attend Mass where the tearful congregation prayed together for the safe return of the men. Denis Foley took Margaret Cullen and the children in his pony and trap. Michael Rossiter, on whose farm Pat Roche had been working on Friday, collected a distraught Anastasia and the two children; fourteen year old Mary had been standing outside the gate all day on Saturday, crying and refusing to come in *"... until Daddy comes home"*.

Bill Banville's brother, Robert, who had borrowed an ass and cart to take his mother and father, collected near neighbour Lizzie Kelly; it was the only time she left the house during the whole of the weekend. Godfrey Taylor, the lifeboat committee president, collected Garry Handrick's mother and Mary Bridget and then drove his car to Fethard for Tom Mac. After dropping them off at Poulfur he attended the service in Fethard before returning to Poulfur to collect them when Mass was over.

The Marchioness of Ely sent her car to pick up Mary Anne Morrissey and the children. Since receiving the news that her beloved James had been found at Cullenstown, Mary Anne had been inconsolable and later said she thought she would never be able to stop crying.

Young James, who had spent the previous day standing by the big brass telescope and relaying information to others, showed a maturity beyond his age doing everything he could to comfort little Mamie. She refused to let go of the stool *"Daddy made for me"* just two days ago, and it had to go with her in the car. No member of the crew's families walked to Poulfur that day.

George Crumpton, who was instrumental in getting the men off the *Mexico* and on to solid ground, was the only member of the Church of Ireland on the crew and his wife, Rebecca, chose to walk the hundred yards or so to the church at the top of the village, carrying young Tom in her arms. She did not walk alone however, she was joined by more than a dozen neighbours who had stood in the rain, waiting on the street to accompany her and provide what little comfort they could.

Packed to the rafters, with people standing in the aisles, the front rows in both churches were left empty for the distressed families. It was heartrending as the services came to an end and the final hymn, *Eternal Father, Strong to Save,* was sung with additional vigour and passion by both congregations.

Nobody went home when they left the churches; there was a feeling of emptiness in all of them, they wanted to do something but, of course, there was nothing they could do. Like a procession many of them made their way through the driving rain to the cliff tops and looked out to sea, still hoping for a miracle.

The fishermen and the sailors in the assembled crowd could see the hopelessness of the situation; they knew there could be no possibility of a rescue attempt today, but they kept their thoughts to themselves.

Mary Bridget's eyes were hurting from the effort as she stared out to sea, willing them to see something and desperate to know if Garry was alive, and whether Mac was still okay. Eventually the crowds slowly started to disperse, leaving close friends and family alone until they too were forced to leave as the cold and the rain penetrated through to their aching bones.

In the afternoon the smoke being generated by the wet wood on the island could be seen and this brought some relief as people rushed back to their vantage points. Everybody had an opinion; the fire would be used for cooking, to boil water, to dry their clothes and generally bring some comfort to them in the shelter everyone assumed they had.

Spirits were further lifted when they saw the *Fanny Harriet* leave the dock, with Commander Holmes on board, and face the onslaught of the sea. When the lifeboat returned later in the day, the quay was again crowded but this time the questions were silent; the faces of the crew told them everything they needed to know. There was no good news, and with night taking over from day they solemnly made their way back to their homes.

Throughout the weekend the community lived up to its reputation for taking care of each other and neighbours made sure none of the grieving families were left alone. As tears flowed freely and frequently in houses throughout the village, fires were made, meals were cooked, children were looked after, prayers were said and, perhaps most importantly, there was always someone to talk to, someone to listen, and a shoulder to cry on.

CHAPTER

14

Never give up, for that is just the
place and time that the tide will turn.
– Harriet Beecher Stone

On Saturday evening, the Dunmore lifeboat crew joined the Fethard Coast Guards for a meeting with Commander Holmes in Foley's Hotel, their intention being to put a plan together for the following day. Forty-two year old Ned Brien from the Coast Guard's lifesaving apparatus team had been on board the *Fanny Harriett* for the rescue attempt in the afternoon and believed it would be possible to fire a rocket from the boat. The others were not sure. It had never been done before. Brien drove his point home with vigour – everything else had failed, what was there to lose? Fortunately, his reasoning won the day and it was agreed they would go ahead in the morning, provided the weather allowed.

True to form, another problem presented itself when they found there were no rockets available in the village. Sixty-five year old David Palmer, the number one man on the rocket team volunteered to go to the Coast Guard station in Arthurstown, eight miles away, to see if they had any. It was not an easy journey in the atrocious weather conditions but he was in luck and the others were waiting for him in Fethard when he returned well after midnight with four precious rockets.

In a few short hours, their plan would be put to the test.

Sunrise over Fethard would not happen for another two or three hours, but at four o'clock on Sunday morning John Mac's youngest brother, Patrick, and the rest of the Coast Guard apparatus team lined up on the quay to see their colleague depart. Marks Barden, who would act as pilot for the Dunmore crew, helped Ned Brien in securing the rockets on board *Fanny Harriet*. Then they waited.

The hoped for abatement in the weather had not materialised and neither did it seem likely to; even the sun appeared to have admitted defeat with no sign of it breaking through the heavy clouds that continued to blanket the area. Waves were still breaking over the wall of the dock. Rain was coming down in sheets. Winds had once again reached gale force. The weather was described anecdotally as 'the worst for fifty years'. They continued to wait.

The hours dragged by, until late afternoon when, after much discussion, Walter Power made the reluctant decision not to venture outside the shelter of the dock. There was no lack of nerve, no lack of resolution, no lack of courage, but to take the boat into the open sea would be reckless and irresponsible. The risk to his crew would be too great. Everybody was crestfallen when he gave the order to 'Stand down'.

After an uncomfortable night on the tug the wind was still blowing at gale force and at seven o'clock a decision was taken by Captain Busher and Ned Wickham to leave Cheekpoint and make for Waterford. In port they were able to use a telephone to let people know where they were. Michael O'Connor, the lifeboat secretary in Wexford, arranged for funds to be made available to them, and told them to go to the Imperial Hotel on the quay and order lunch for all hands. After this, the tug took on seven tons of coal and booked a pilot to take them down river in the morning.

According to press reports, one crew member on the *James Stevens* was particularly anxious as they waited in Waterford harbour with *Wexford*, hoping for a break in the weather. Twenty year old Phillip Duggan was due to be married on Monday morning and in the current situation that did not look like even a remote possibility. The anxiety of his bride-to-be, the paper said, *"was compensated by the knowledge that he was engaged in a noble cause"*. Whether this is true or not is a moot point. His fiancée, Mary Sheill – if indeed they were even engaged at the time – was only sixteen years old and it was to be a further two and a half years before they walked down the aisle.

There was no respite on the Keeraghs as the storm continued to rage through the night and when dawn arrived on Sunday morning it found the survivors suffering with freezing temperatures gnawing at their faces and chilling them to the bone.

High tide at around eight o'clock brought even more problems. The intensity of the storm had increased, the waves were higher than ever and as the sea careened across it, the island was submerged in over a foot of fast moving water. All they could do for the next hour or so was stand or kneel, holding on to each other and the remains of their shelter. It was a frightening time and in their weakened state there was a very real possibility they would be washed into the sea.

As the wind dropped and the tide receded, the rain and sleet were temporarily replaced with snow. After what they had just been through, this was seen as a godsend and the men immediately gathered what they could in an attempt to slake their thirst, without realising it might well do more harm than good. When you eat snow two things happen; firstly body heat is used up melting it in your mouth and secondly, when you swallow it, it cools the body from the inside, accelerating dehydration.

Monstrous seas were still crashing over the rocks on every side of the island and although nobody spoke of it, each one of them was only too well aware that any further rescue attempt that day would be unachievable unless there was a dramatic improvement in conditions. They had all reached the depths of despair with a real danger that in their lethargic condition they would give up and just wait for nature to take its course.

What do you do when there is nothing to do? What do you say when there is nothing to be said? They were not the first 'castaways' to suffer this dilemma, and like those before them, they had no answer. Stand up, walk around, sit down, lie down, stand up, walk around, sit down; it was a never ending cycle. Survival was their number one priority, their only priority, but now monotony and boredom had become their enemy. Additionally, for many of them loneliness was also becoming a problem.

There were twelve people on the island but loneliness is not caused exclusively by being alone, it is mainly a state of mind and it is entirely possible to feel lonely surrounded by thousands of people; it can also be exacerbated by fear.

Photo by Steve Meyler

CULLENSTOWN

*From this vantage point on the cliffs above the beach,
crowds watched the drama unfold on the Keeragh Islands,
which can be seen in the background*

Even answering the call of nature added to their difficulties. At low tide the little cliff at one end of the island offered some small measure of privacy but this was offset by its proximity to the rocks and the spray from the breaking waves. For most of the time privacy had to take a back seat.

Much time had been spent discussing possible ways of getting on to the *Mexico* where there was known to be food, but it was hopeless. The masts that had been clearly visible the previous day were now gone, consumed by the sea and taking with them the rope used to bring the crew ashore, and the hull, which had appeared to tower over the island, was now barely discernible amongst the rocks, having keeled over and sunk deeper into the channel.

On a summer's day with calm seas it is quite possible to wade between the islands but any attempt to reach the wreck in the current conditions would have meant certain death. By a strange quirk of fate, both vessels, which ended their days together on the Keeraghs, had also started life in the same year, 1905.

As the crew looked with sadness at the remnants of their ship, Sigurd Lie was amazed to find lying between the rocks, the watch he had lost as he came ashore. It was obvious at first glance it would never tell the time again but he later said it would serve as a reminder of the horrific experience he had gone through.

Visibility was poor throughout the day and at time the blinding rain and the thick black clouds overhead gave the impression that night had arrived early. They were wet, they were cold, they were hungry, they were thirsty, they were in pain, the wind was tugging at their clothes and they had no idea how long that situation would last.

Suddenly, in mid-afternoon all that was forgotten for a while when a loud shout from the *Mexico's* crew caused the Fethard men, who were about a hundred yards away, to hurry towards them wondering what had happened. Andersen, the steward, had discovered half a dozen dry matches tucked inside a pocket in his jacket and the elation was almost tangible as everyone forced themselves into action, gathering pieces of wood to light a fire. Without thinking about it, most of them headed in the direction of the *Mexico*.

There was no shortage of driftwood and wreckage around the shoreline and it did not take long before they had collected a pile large enough for a beacon. The exception was Mikhail who went in the opposite direction, but he did not shirk his responsibilities making a number of trips to bring back three or four times as much as any of the others.

Again it was a case of solving one problem and replacing it with another. Excited at the thought of a fire, they had forgotten the wood was all so wet it would be impossible to light.

It looked as though their plan might fall at the first hurdle, until John Kelly provided a solution. Most of the men carried a knife – a standard piece of equipment for those who worked on boats and ships – and Kelly's plan was to first of all cut away an inch or so from the outside of the wood, the wettest part, and then cut what remained into shavings and small pieces of kindling, which would be easier to burn. It was slow work and as soon as it was done the men put the pieces in their pockets or underneath their little shelter in an attempt to keep them dry.

In the meantime, those without knives laid a bed of stones that would keep the fire clear of the wet grass, and then built a makeshift wall about a foot high to shelter it from the wind.

Everybody searched their pockets and between them managed to find a few scraps of paper which, coupled with the wood shavings, they hoped would be enough to start a fire.

Under the shelter Richie Bird played his part drying a piece of quartzite, which made up the bulk of the island's rock and would be used to strike the matches. Two men held a piece of canvas over the top to keep the rain off as Andersen set about lighting the little pile.

The first match blew out straight away and the second went the same way. The third attempt almost succeeded with the paper igniting, before being blown out seconds later. There were only three matches left and as delight was quickly turning to despair, they made a shelter of sailcloth around the little wall.

It worked. The fourth match lit the paper and wood shavings and after what seemed like an eternity the flames reached up, raising a cheer from the men. They took it in turn to hold the canvas over the fire as it was carefully fed first with kindling and then with larger pieces which had been stacked around the fire to dry out sufficiently for them to burn.

The wet wood was producing more smoke than heat, but the important thing was that it was providing *some* heat. Not all the men had gloves and for those who did have them they were just one more item of wet clothing from which they got little or no benefit. The result of this was that everybody's fingers had turned white and almost all feeling was gone from them. As they warmed them in front of the flames, the pain in their hands was agonising but by rubbing them vigorously they were eventually able to get some feeling of normality back into them.

Permanently wet clothes meant cold had been their constant companion since Friday evening and, even with a little shelter now built over it, the fire was fighting an endless battle with the weather to provide any meaningful heat. In their weakened state doubts began to creep in with silent questions being asked: *"How long can we last?" "Will we be rescued in time?" "Will we ever see our families again?"*

For the crew of *Mexico* it was even worse. They were hundreds, and in some cases thousands, of miles from home, and even if they were saved they would still have to make their own way back, probably by signing on to another ship after they had been paid off by *Mexico's* owners.

For many of them this was the time when private deals were made with God as to what they would do if their life was spared.

As second coxswain, John Mac was seen as the de facto leader of the *Helen Blake* survivors. He was a quiet man, well liked and well respected by the crew, who, despite his own weakened state, did whatever he could to keep spirits high.

Under his leadership the men from Fethard continued to see themselves in the role of rescuers throughout the ordeal and working as a team did whatever they could to ensure the survival of everyone. Christy Bird would have been proud of them.

With seven different nationalities on the island, communication could have been a real problem but fortunately Sebastian Riley was English, Captain Eriksen, First Mate Lie and Steward Robert Andersen spoke very good English and the rest of *Mexico's* crew had a smattering of the language.

The remaining twelve men had now gone without food or water for two days, with the added misery of unremitting salt spray. Additionally, the cold weather was causing stress hormones to be released which in turn caused their bladders to fill leading to urination, which further accentuated their thirst. Their condition was rapidly spiralling downwards and every one of them was now starting to display advanced symptoms of dehydration.

They looked up to the sky in the hope of catching a few drops of water to ease their craving but the driving rain felt like needles as it hit their face doing little more than wetting their lips, and even that had a taste of salt. A small bottle of wine and a small bottle of brandy, which first mate Lie had managed to bring ashore with him, provided a psychological boost but in reality, as diuretics, probably did more harm than good.

John Kelly had fished for lobsters in the vicinity of the islands and knew there would be an abundance of them in the rocks a few feet below the surface. There were plenty of small ropes amongst the flotsam on the island and tying a few of those together and around his waist he stepped into the water with his crewmates holding the other end.

The current was too strong for him to go where the lobsters were likely to be so he had to make do with gathering a few barnacles from the rocks above the tide line, although in the breaking waves it was nearly impossible to tell where that was. The raw crustaceans were salty and rubbery but were eagerly devoured and there were no complaints.

At great risk to his own life, Garry Handrick volunteered to scour the rocks in the shallows for more, the same rocks that had almost ended his life a couple of days earlier. Taking the life line from Kelly, he edged his way along the edge of the rocks, struggling to stay upright in the swirling foam. Filling his pockets with the little creatures he made his way back to his fellow survivors who wrenched them from the shells and wolfed them down in an instant. He could only make two forays into the water before his fingers became too cold to hold the stone he was using to release their grip on the rocks.

Dutch deckhand Cornelius Wagenaar was a giant of a man and had been watching from the back of the group, leaving the little arthropods for those he felt were in more need, and as Garry stepped out of the sea he moved forward, taking his place knee deep in the freezing water. He only managed to get a few more before he too had to call it a day when he started shivering almost uncontrollably. In front of the little fire his crewmates massaged his body through his sodden clothing and gradually restored some circulation.

For two days the men had scoured every inch of the island in their search for food, frustrated that on board *Mexico*, just a few yards away but impossible to reach, there were enough provisions to keep them going for weeks. Spirits were temporarily raised when they found four tins of preserved beef, a tin of salmon and two tins of pineapple that had been washed ashore from the wreck. Added to the few barnacles gathered earlier from the rocks, this helped to alleviate the hunger of the twelve men, but did little for their biggest problem, which was still the lack of fresh water.

It was a constant temptation to drink the rain water that had gathered in indentations in the rocks or had been collected by the canvas awning but this was so badly tainted by sea spray it would have made them sick and intensified the dehydration. Already, the majority of them had developed swollen tongues during their time on the island.

Speaking about their time on the Keeraghs, after being rescued, George Crumpton probably spoke for all of them when he described the thirst as becoming unbearable, adding, *"I could not open my mouth yesterday morning it was so parched, and I think I would not have got through if we had to endure the strain much longer"*.

Heroes are made by the paths they choose,
not the powers they are graced with.
– Brodi Ashton

Perhaps tiredness was making them irritable – and sometimes illogical – or perhaps they were just sticking to what they knew, but for most of the day the crews of *Helen Blake* and *Mexico* had drifted around on the island in two distinct groups, even by the fire they sat on opposite sides. Nothing had been said, no decision was taken, there was no tension; it was almost tribal in the way it just happened.

The Fethard men had a common bond. They had known each other for years, in most cases since they were children, their crew mates had been swept away less than forty-eight hours ago, and they felt more at ease together sharing their hardship, and their loss. As they wandered around the island together they often found themselves drawn to the shoreline where they would stare at the sea, subconsciously searching for the friends they had lost.

The crew of the schooner had also been through a lot, facing death together more than once in the past few months and their shared experiences had helped mould them into a single unit, with one exception. Mikhail, the Russian deckhand, was never really part of the group, always a few feet away from the others and, according to John Mac, even the Captain appeared to be wary of him.

Spirits dropped rapidly after seeing the *Fanny Harriet* make her way back to Fethard. They were now back in one group with one mutual goal; to stay alive. Of the three longest and coldest nights the men had ever encountered, this one, the third on the desolate island, was the worst yet and the sustained cold drained their bodies of every last ounce of energy reserves. By now most of them could no longer even remember what it felt like to be dry and warm.

When sunset arrived the light of day did not stay around for long. The night was moonless and the only visible light was the intermittent flash from the Hook lighthouse as it fought to punch a hole in the mist from the top of the black and white tower almost nine miles away where it stands guard over Waterford Harbour, warning ships to stay away from the dangerous coast line. For *Helen Blake's* crew it was a tenuous link with home; they knew the tower and they knew the lightkeepers, and that knowledge brought some small comfort to them.

Despite all their best efforts, a combination of wind, rain and wet wood meant the men were unable to keep the fire going and as the flames were slowly extinguished, so once again were their hopes. Garry Handrick recalled that during the ordeal, *"We only had a little bit of tobacco and it got saturated with salt water, but we chewed and ate it"*.

Having re-built their rudimentary shelter, they maintained their rota for sleep beneath it and there was nothing more they could do except remain huddled together. Their attempts to run around to generate warmth were pitiful and in the darkness they faced the constant risk of being blown, or falling, into the sea.

The combination of rough clothing and salt water was doing nothing to aid their comfort and many of them were suffering excruciating pain. Over the past forty-eight hours, chafing had become an ever increasing problem to the point where one survivor described the inside of his thighs as being 'red raw'. With nothing useful to say, and no energy to say it, they kept their feelings and ever increasing anxieties to themselves.

Young Richie Bird had more to worry about than most. His youthful looks were exaggerated by the fact that he was the only member of the crew without a moustache and now, suffering with almost unbearable pain, the pallor of his skin added to his pathetic demeanour. He had stayed under what remained of the shelter for most of the day, wrapped in a few pieces of sailcloth to keep the worst of the weather at bay. Despite his pain he never once complained, with his resilience providing inspiration for everyone.

Alone with their thoughts, the stranded men were in the midst of the worst storm to hit the coast in a generation. They were hemmed in by seas so ferocious that even in the shelter of Wexford town the newly laid railway line on the quay was torn up and the heavy sleepers were washed along the street in water up to four feet deep.

In the dark of night, they thought the rain would never stop. Like a demented drummer, it beat out a constant rhythm on the canvas over their heads, adding to the relentless roar of the wind as it raged across the island threatening to take their meagre little refuge with it. Local tradition amongst fishermen was that no one had ever escaped alive from a shipwreck on the Keeraghs and this did nothing to stimulate their resolve.

Everybody knew their time was limited; if they did not get off tomorrow, they would never get off, and infuriatingly there was nothing they could do to help themselves. *Mexico's* crew hoped for the best while the Fethard men placed their faith in Ned Wickham and Walter Power; they knew them, they knew their reputation, and they knew they would never give up so long as there was even the slightest chance of success. Silently, they prayed they would make it in time.

As the light of a new day started to push the night away the bedraggled survivors were in a very bad way. Without exception, they were displaying advanced signs of hypothermia. Parched throats meant speech was painful, some of them could barely walk and they had to help each other to keep moving and maintain blood circulation.

John Mac was looking for barnacles close to the seashore when he thought he saw the shape of a boat coming towards them. Afraid his eyes were playing tricks on him, he kept watching for five or ten minutes before the realisation of what it was dawned on him.

At six o'clock on Monday morning the sea was a little less boisterous and even the sun looked as though it might attempt to break through the clouds as dawn crept slowly across the horizon. On the quayside in Fethard, the Coast Guard apparatus team were again joined by family members and friends to see the *Fanny Harriet*, with Commander Holmes on board, leave Fethard for its third rescue attempt.

This time the rockets and the firing apparatus were safely loaded into the bow compartment under the supervision of Coast Guard Ned Brien, another of the men who had made the valiant effort in the *Kate* on Saturday.

Ned was comparatively prosperous for the time having built an enviable reputation as an excellent stone mason involved in the construction of many of the finest buildings in the area, and responsible for the magnificent natural stone wall surrounding Templetown church. Though the language was no longer in general use, Ned and his family were all fluent in Irish. A native of Bergerin, about twenty miles from Fethard, he married local girl Ellen Foley in 1893 and soon became a popular figure, immersing himself in numerous community activities – in later years he founded the Fethard Cycling Club.

Less boisterous the sea may have been, but it was by no means a smooth ride or an easy trip and by the time they reached the Keeraghs the weather had changed again. The wind had resumed its ferocity and the combination of low tide and a heavy ground swell made it almost impossible to get close in.

Unwavering in his determination to help the stranded men, who were now waving furiously, Walter Power circled the island, allowing Marks Barden to study the shoreline, carefully searching for the right anchorage. Barden knew the Keeraghs as well as any man but still had to go around twice before finding a suitable spot.

Eventually they dropped anchor two hundred yards off the north shore, opposite Cullenstown strand and level with Ballymadder Point, where they got some shelter from the island itself. From this point the cox took the risky decision to allow the boat to drift in on the anchor cable until it was about a hundred yards from the rocks.

Nobody had ever tried firing rockets from a lifeboat before so it was to some extent a matter of trial and error. With the boat pitching and tossing in the heavy swell, timing had to be perfect if they were to have any chance of succeeding. At half past seven everyone held their breath as Brien fired the first of his rockets, with a line attached. It fell short.

Without hesitation, and with an exceptionally skilful display of seamanship, the crew put themselves in harm's way, moving the lifeboat ever closer to the rocks as Ned readied the apparatus to fire a second rocket. This time it succeeded and as it landed on the island the wearied men found renewed energy from somewhere letting out a muted cheer as they grabbed the line and secured it to a rock.

The feeling of relief was almost palpable. Tears unashamedly rolled down the cheeks of many of the survivors as they looked at the small rope. It was not over yet, but this really was a lifeline. After being marooned on the island and exposed to the elements for over sixty-two hours they had now established their first physical contact with the outside world and some of them dared to smile for the first time in days.

Coxswain Power had the foresight to tow a small rowing boat behind *Fanny Harriett* and this was now attached to the line, ready to be pulled towards the shore by the stranded men. It seemed luck was against them again; the boat was smashed to pieces by the sea before even reaching the island.

The look of anguish on the faces of the twelve men was painful to see and the lifeboat crew quickly improvised by attaching to the rope a spare life jacket and a life buoy they had

DUNMORE EAST

From the harbour entrance the Hook Lighthouse can be seen on the horizon

Photo by Steve Meyler

brought from Fethard dock. These were then pulled ashore by the men on the island accompanied by shouts from the crew urging them to get into the life jacket.

Much as they wanted to get off the island, nobody dared to venture into the churning sea. Not only was it difficult for them to make any kind of physical effort, but they feared they would be drowned before they reached the lifeboat. After what seemed like an eternity but in reality was probably just a few minutes, and ignoring his debilitating injuries, including his still untreated head wound, Mac led by example.

He squeezed into the life buoy so the lifeboat crew could haul him, half submerged, his mouth filling with water, through the lethal surf and safely on board. It had worked but it was an extremely dangerous manoeuvre and drowning had been a very real possibility. As others around him continued to hesitate, John Kelly, with a commitment born of desperation, grabbed the lifebuoy and followed Mac to safety.

At around the same time, the Rosslare lifeboat, *James Stevens*, reached the scene with Ned Wickham at the helm. Having spent the night in Waterford they left there in tow of the *Wexford* at around three forty-five that morning for an uncomfortable five hour trip in a sea described by Busher in a casual understatement as *"very, very bad"*. As they pulled alongside the Dunmore boat, and with nobody else prepared to chance their luck in the lifebuoy, second cox William Power passed the rope across to Jem Wickham.

At forty-five feet *James Stevens* was bigger than the other lifeboats making it virtually impossible for them to get any closer to the island so they dropped anchor just a few yards away. They were towing a thirteen foot boat (punt) taken from the tug which they planned to use to continue with the rescue. Wickham's idea was to put two of his crew in this and send them ashore to bring off two survivors at a time.

Ever mindful of what had happened to the *Helen Blake*, he came up with an ingenious, but exceptionally risky, plan. *"We knew that the small punt would be swamped with the two men on board just as she would reach the island. We knew the only chance of saving these two men and the two men they would take on board from the rock, was by all hands pulling as quickly as possible back to the lifeboat. The speed and force of bringing her back with the weight of the men on board would automatically drive the water out over her stern sufficient to keep her afloat whilst coming back to the lifeboat"*.

Ned Wickham made it sound simple but it was a plan fraught with danger for everyone involved. He went on to say that *"… two of my crew, my brother Jem Wickham, and bowman Bill Duggan volunteered to man the small punt"*.

What he failed to say was that all ten members of his crew had bravely volunteered.

CHAPTER

16

Home, home, home from the sea
Angels of mercy, answer our plea
And carry us home, home from the sea
Carry us safely home from the sea
— Phil Coulter

It was an awe-inspiring combination. Bill Duggan was still only twenty-nine years old but had already been serving on the lifeboat for ten years during which time he had established himself as a first class lifeboatman, and had been involved in a number of rescues. On one occasion, away from the lifeboat, he was helping the Coast Guard who were using a breeches buoy to bring the crew of a grounded schooner ashore when the captain fell into the sea. Almost instinctively Duggan rushed into the churning foam and carried the semi-conscious man to safety.

Jem Wickham who had served as second cox for sixteen years had no less a pedigree. He once single-handedly saved two men who were floating out to sea on a plank after their boat had foundered in heavy fog. In Wexford harbour he saved the life of his own father when his boat capsized. Together, on their fishing boat, the two men had saved the life of a ship's pilot when they went to his aid after he fell overboard from a steamer entering the harbour.

Although appearing to take it in their stride as if it were an everyday occurrence, what they were about to do was a real act of derring-do. Their actions took incredible courage and nerves of steel – they knew there was no guarantee the plan would work, and they knew their chances of survival were probably less than fifty-fifty. With no let-up in the wind and with massive waves still pounding both the rocks and the lifeboat, the punt was bobbing around like a cork, in constant danger of capsizing at any moment.

The little boat was brought alongside and the line from the island was attached to the bow together with another running back to the lifeboat – the punt would have to be spun around when they reached the island. After removing their boots and oilskins, the two men carefully climbed in with their weight reducing the freeboard – the distance between the sea and the top of the gunwales – to just a few inches.

During the tow from Waterford, the crew had borrowed some tools from the tug and used them to shorten two of the lifeboat's oars. These were now put to the test as they fitted them in the punt and rowed to the island.

The first trip went without a hitch, exactly as planned. Clinging to the line to avoid being washed away, Hernández and Riley waded into the water carrying Cornelius Wagenaar between them and lifted him aboard. Hernández climbed in after him, while Riley returned to the island, and the lifeboat crew started pulling as fast as they could with the water gushing out over the stern of the punt. The plan was working.

The next trip was almost their last, and improvisation was once again the order of the day. *"The second trip to the island our little boat got a plank from the bottom stove in and we stopped the crack by packing in bread and canvas"*. In his casual, easy going, style Ned could make even the most incredible event sound like an everyday experience, and once again the real story is in what he failed to say.

The violent action of the sea had driven the punt on to the rocks where it was trapped and without a thought for their own safety, Duggan and Wickham jumped overboard into the swirling waters to lift it free. It took just a few minutes but all the time they were being smothered by huge waves and had to fight them to get the boat away from the rocks. When they climbed back in it was half full of water so one of them sat on the bottom to cover the hole and slow down the flow while the lifeboat crew hauled it back. Bread had been put in the punt in case they too got stranded, and they used this, wrapped in canvas, to plug the hole before calling on the lifeboat's pump to help bail it out.

Richie Bird was one of the last to leave the island and was in almost unbearable pain as he was helped to the boat by John Kelly and Garry Handrick. In total, the little boat made five trips over the next hour and successfully brought the ten remaining men back to the lifeboat. Watching events from close quarters, one of the Dunmore crew described the rescue to perfection when he said it was, *"The bravest act I ever saw"*. Commander Holmes later echoed those sentiments in his more formal manner, stating, *"… the service was one of great personal risk to those who undertook it"*.

When everybody was safely on board *James Stevens* the punt was cut free and within minutes was lost beneath the waves. The two lifeboats pulled away, rowing hard through the surf surrounding the islands before raising their sails as they made their way into open water where the tug was waiting. George Crumpton, Garry Handrick and Richie Bird were transferred to the Dunmore boat, joining up again with John Mac and John Kelly. Commander Holmes boarded the tug and made his way to the bridge to offer his thanks to Captain Busher and his crew.

The crew of the *Mexico* were transferred to the *Wexford* where the tug's crew felt that at last they had an opportunity to play a real part in the rescue. On board, the survivors were wrapped in blankets and could feel the heat from the constantly stoked boilers. They could not remember the last time they were warm and some of them were almost in tears with the realisation of how close to death they had been. *Wexford's* mate, John Harpur, gave Jorge Hernández a pair of his boots and Big Bartle (Bartholomew) Carty, a giant of a man with a heart to match, *"cooked them a good hash which was most welcome"*.

A welcoming roar indicated engines being brought up to full power, a line from the tug was attached to both lifeboats and the paddles started to turn with Busher pointing the bow towards Fethard. Pure adrenalin had provided the energy for them to wade through the water to the punt and now, as that drained away from their bodies, the traumatised survivors were too weak to do anything except thank their saviours. Thirst remained their overriding concern and, although it was a painful experience, they eagerly drank what little water was on board.

Above Cullenstown strand an array of 'spyglasses' – an eighteenth century name for a small telescope but used locally for all telescopes and binoculars – had been pointed at the Keeraghs since first light on Monday morning, watching every move as the two lifeboats edged in perilously close to liberate the stranded men from their anguish, and a spontaneous cheer erupted when they saw the last of the survivors taken from the island.

For the people in Fethard it had been a tense time, particularly for those who were on the quayside at daybreak when the Dunmore lifeboat set out. They had followed its progress across the open water but when it moved to the north of the island, lost sight of it. A short time later the tug with the *James Stevens* in tow hove into view, making its way towards the island, but again the lifeboat moved out of their line of vision when it went to join the rescue.

The only thing they were able to see for the next couple of hours was a sporadic wisp of smoke from the *Wexford* as it stood off from the islands, waiting.

Those two hours seemed like an eternity but suddenly it was over. Not long after nine o'clock the sails of the lifeboats appeared from behind the island and those with telescopes or binoculars resumed their running commentary to the others gathered around them. Within half an hour or so they could see the column of smoke from the tug increase as the engines were brought up to full power. Then they saw it turn into the waves, heading in their direction. Like Cullenstown, a cheer went up and families of the crew started to hug each other in the belief that the ordeal was over. Their loved ones were coming home.

Those who had been watching events from Grange beach or nearby cliff tops quickly made their way to the dock; some riding their bicycles through the village, others walking across the Little Burrow and then on to the stepping stones to cross the narrow waterway below the boathouse.

The tide was too low to attempt getting into the dock so the tug untied the *Fanny Harriett* and stood off in the bay allowing Walter Power's oarsmen to take it the last few yards to the little beach alongside.

It was a little over sixty-six hours since fourteen men had boarded the *Helen Blake* and launched from the same spot.

Five of them were now coming home.

chapter

17

Memories, even bittersweet ones,
are better than nothing.
– Jennifer Armentrout

It was strangely quiet as the boat approached the beach; the rain had stopped and with the wind now little more than a breeze there was not even a slight swell on the sea; the mist had been dissipated by the weak sun which had managed to find a gap in the clouds. For the first time in days the Keeraghs were clearly visible as the crowd stood in silence, waiting. Over twenty people were on board making it nearly impossible to see who was there and who was not, and amongst those waiting there was a mixture of excitement, relief and anxiety.

Communication with the island had been non-existent since the disaster so nobody still knew for certain who was safe and who was missing. The bodies of Bill Banville, Patrick Cullen and Willie Bird had not yet been recovered and although Paddy Stafford had been found at Cullenstown, his body was yet to be identified.

Four families who had spent the last three days hoping and praying were devastated when the lifeboat got close enough for them to see the five survivors and realise their loved ones were not amongst them. The empty ache of desolation in their hearts left them unable to speak as tears of sorrow streamed down their cheeks. All they had now were memories; hopes and dreams and plans for the future had all gone in an instant, memories had now become their most precious possessions.

For others there were tears of joy as their men came ashore to be welcomed by friends, relatives and onlookers alike, including Fethard lifeboat committee president, Godfrey Taylor, and his wife Dorothea Marie.

Their appearance came as a shock to those waiting; they had been away for three days but looked as though they had aged ten years. Keeping up appearances as he alighted from the boat, and confirming his reputation as a hard man, John Kelly was the only survivor capable of walking unaided to the beach. The other four, still struggling with untreated injuries inflicted by the rocks when they were thrown into the sea, and suffering the effects of hypothermia and dehydration from their time on the island, had to be carried ashore by waiting family and friends.

Tom Mac carried his brother on his back and left him in the care of Mary Bridget who was waiting with blankets, before going to assist Garry Handrick who had already been carried from the lifeboat.

After a cursory examination by a doctor they were each taken to their homes where, for the first time since Friday, they enjoyed the luxury of dry clothes with some hot food and drink, followed by a well-deserved and much needed sleep in a warm bed. After nearly three days of having their ears assaulted by

JOHN 'MAC' McNAMARA
Being carried ashore by his brother, Tom.

FANNY HARRIETT
Returning to the 'Wexford' after bringing the survivors home

the thunderous roar from the combined sounds of the wind, rain and sea, there was now a glorious silence which they initially found strangely disconcerting.

Bill Banville's brother Tommy had returned from the dock as soon as he saw the *Wexford* heading for Fethard, to let his parents and Lizzie Kelly know they were on their way home. A little over an hour later James and Mary Banville were distraught when they discovered their son was not amongst the survivors. Lizzie had spent the past few hours heating water for a bath which was waiting when John came home, but he was too drained to take advantage of it. Lizzie burst into tears and hugged him as soon as he walked through the door but it was a measure of his tiredness that, having discarded his wet clothes in favour of dry woollen long johns, he was asleep almost as soon as his head hit the pillow.

Leaving young Tom at home with her sister, Rebecca had been waiting for George Crumpton and was overcome with emotion when she saw he was safe. Richie Bird's two brothers carried him home where his mother stripped off his wet clothing, wrapped him in blankets and put hot potatoes under his arms to warm him up before putting a mattress in front of the fire for him.

Local doctor William Shorten was joined by Dr Garrett Hickey from New Ross and together they visited all the survivors during the afternoon tending their wounds and providing whatever medicine was necessary. All five were weak and suffering the effects of exposure, most of the wounds had healed but the gash on Mac's forehead had re-opened and needed stitches. Richie Bird was given an injection to ease the pain he had endured since Friday evening. Fortunately, there appeared to be no crippling injuries.

Confined to bed, sleep was fitful for all of them as they relived their terrible ordeal over and over. Asked in his 1954 interview how he felt after the rescue, John Mac said, *"I don't remember beyond that they kept me in bed for a week and I couldn't quench my thirst, but if a fella's anyway tough at all, he's able to put up with a lot when he's put to it, and, though there was never much of me in it, I was tough"*. This was not bravado or ego; it was a simple, matter of fact statement, and one that applied equally to every one of his crew mates.

Largely unnoticed in the excitement, Ned Brien and Marks Barden also came ashore, leaving *Fanny Harriet's* crew to row back to the tug. The two lifeboats were then taken in tow again with the Dunmore boat being released about a mile from her home port. Captain Busher later told reporters that as they continued the journey up the river to Waterford the crew of the *Mexico* had been most emphatic that had it not been for the sacrifice of the Fethard lifeboatmen they would also have perished.

By the time they reached Waterford it was dark but that in no way diminished the enthusiasm of well-wishers who crowded the quay and applauded as the distressed sailors disembarked to be met, and taken care of, by Edward Jones and his team of volunteers from the Shipwrecked Mariners' Society – a charity that some years earlier had benefited from the will of Helen Blake. They all appeared to be in a dreadfully weakened state and arrangements were initially made for them to be admitted to hospital.

Remarkably, after a few hours rest their condition improved such that hospitalisation was no longer deemed necessary, with one exception; Cornelius Wagenaar was suffering badly from the effects of exposure and had not fully recovered after his time in the water collecting barnacles, with his feet and legs so swollen he was unable to walk.

During their two day stay, Captain Eriksen, First Mate Lie and Steward Robert Andersen were given rooms in the Munster Hotel at the eastern end of the quay, close to the fourteenth century Reginald's Tower, which was home to Waterford's Chief Constable, Patrick Cahill. The rest of the crew – Sebastian Riley, Hernández and Mikhail – were provided with accommodation in the Kilkenny Hotel, a few streets away. The entire crew were fitted out with new clothes and every one of them underwent thorough medical checks. After three days of misery, they were all only too happy to sit out their short stay in Ireland's oldest city – founded by the Vikings one thousand years earlier – by remaining in the comfort of the hotels. The exception to this was Mikhail who wandered up and down the quay on Tuesday searching, unsuccessfully, for a ship to join.

A reporter from the *Freeman's Journal* who interviewed Andersen as soon as he set foot on the quay, wrote, *"… the sailor spoke with the greatest indifference of sufferings which he and his marooned fellow sailors underwent on the rocks. 'It was just a little cold', he said"*. The Swede finished the interview politely by saying, *"I must go and warm myself"*.

At four o'clock the following morning *Wexford* took the *James Stevens* in tow again, getting back to Rosslare Fort at three in the afternoon. As the crew went home for the first time in three days, quickly returning to their normal routine while they waited for the next emergency, the shore crew took over, washing the boat and seeing to it that it was made ready to go to sea again at a moment's notice.

CREW OF THE MEXICO

On board SS Arklow preparing to leave Waterford.

Captain Eriksen is in the centre, First Mate Sigurd Lie is on the left, holding the ship's log.

Two of the crew were already in England, one was in hospital and one had died.

Commander Holmes remained in the area for a few days gathering information which would be used in the official inquiry at a later date.

The day after the rescue was Shrove Tuesday and Margaret Cullen's younger sister, Statia Keating, who had gone home with her after the survivors had been brought ashore, made pancakes for the young children in an effort to retain some semblance of normality for them. Lent would start tomorrow but they would not be giving up anything this year, instead Margaret wondered if she could find enough to feed them each day.

Fearful that *Mexico* would break up and damage other shipping, and aware of the problems this could have for the owners, Eriksen is reported to have sold the wreck to coal merchant Michael Murphy for just five pounds before leaving Waterford. Bearing in mind that a representative of the underwriters had arrived in Wexford a couple of days earlier however, it seems unlikely that this story is true.

On Wednesday evening the crew, with the exception of Wagenaar who was still in hospital, were ready to leave and as they boarded the *SS Arklow* bound for Liverpool, their original destination, Captain Eriksen was elated to be presented with *Mexico's* log book which had been found by a Coast Guard on a beach some miles from the Keeraghs. A reporter from the *Waterford Standard* interviewed them before leaving and reported they looked in perfect health, showing no signs of the harrowing ordeal they had been through.

SS Arklow was owned by the Clyde Shipping Company, which coincidentally also owned ships with the names *Dunmore, Saltees* and *Coningbeg*. Another coincidence that came to light, and amused Captain Eriksen when he was told about it, is that the original names for Bannow and Keeraghs (Bannoe and Keeroe) were a combination of Norse and Gaelic.

It was just six days since *Mexico* had gone aground when they arrived in Liverpool and were reunited with their ship-mates Smith and Paulsen, who had again been cared for by the Shipwrecked Mariner's Society.

An employee of Vogt and Maguire, the ship's agent, was on the quayside to meet them and from him Eriksen discovered the reason for the telegram he had been handed before leaving the Azores (*Proceed on the fastest possible sailing directly to Liverpool*). During the voyage from Laguna, ship owner Alf Rød had sold *Mexico* to a French company in Le Havre and their representatives were waiting in Liverpool to take it over.

Sebastian Riley was met by his parents who had initially read about the disaster in the *Manchester Guardian*, and then been relieved to receive a telegram sent by him from Waterford. A couple of weeks after returning home he began studies for his First Mate's ticket and a few months later enlisted in the Royal Navy where, by an amazing coincidence, his first posting was to the *Cymric*, which had been pressed into service as a Q-ship at the outbreak of war.

They were now in one of the busiest ports in the world packed with ships of all sizes and nationalities, with no short-age of berths for experienced seamen. The captain still felt a responsibility for his former crew and his first job on Thursday morning was to arrange for them to be paid by the ship's agent and for Cornelius Wagenaar's pay to be sent to him in Waterford. He then spent a day and a half assisting the men in finding new ships, which would take them to the four corners of the earth where many of them would soon be caught up in 'the war to end all wars'.

Mikhail, the Russian, declined the captain's help and went his own way, securing a berth as a stoker on the four thousand ton British steamer *SS Branksome Hall,* bound for Port Said in Egypt. She was sunk by a U-boat four years later, during the final months of the war but before that Mikhail had returned home to serve in the Imperial Russian Navy. It is not known if he survived the war.

Norwegian Consul Jens Bull, assisted by ships' captains, Anton Haug and Ingvar Thom, who were in port, held an inquest on Friday into the sinking of the *Mexico*. The following day in front of local solicitor Theo Eskrigge, Captain Eriksen swore an affidavit to be used by the official inquiry before taking a cross country train in the company of Robert Andersen. In Hull the Shipwrecked Mariners' Society continued to assist them, this time by helping them secure passage to Norway and Sweden where they would join their families.

Within forty-eight hours of their arrival in Liverpool, everybody had gone their separate ways and though it was unlikely they would ever meet again, their ordeal on the Keeraghs remained with them, binding them together for many years to come.

CHAPTER

18

But darkest of all is the cloud of
grief o'er Fethard hangs today,
For her brave heroic lifeboat men
whose lives were cast away.
– Matty Barden

The week following the disaster was a time of confusion and despondency with Fethard a sea of mixed emotions; joy and relief for relatives of the survivors, sorrow and grief for those of the deceased. Last week everybody had been going about their normal life, this week their whole world had been turned upside down. Nothing was as it had been, and nothing would ever be quite the same again; it was as though the heart and soul had been ripped from the village.

The bereaved were in a state of disbelief and needed a scapegoat, someone to blame, somewhere to vent their anger, and much of this was directed at Christy Bird, unfairly, but perhaps understandably – he was the cox, he was in charge, he took the decisions, it must have been his fault. There was no logic in their reasoning, it was based purely on emotion and at that time they were unaware of exactly what had happened. The lifeboat had been hit by three successive waves that towered over it and appeared to come out of nowhere. One hundred and eighty seconds later it was all over. Unhappily, there was nothing anybody could have done to change the outcome.

Monday, the day of the rescue, was a wretched day in the village, with joy and mourning strangely and pathetically mixed. For many, the ecstasy of welcoming home the survivors was quickly replaced by the depression of the first funerals, which took place a few hours later.

Just two hours apart, Christy Bird was buried in Fethard village and the Handrick brothers were laid to rest side by side in the Old Templetown cemetery, beside the crumbling church of the Knights Templar.

The following afternoon James Morrissey's coffin was carried shoulder high from his home on Sunny Row, followed by his family, through an avenue of mourners who lined the street from one end to the other. Contemporary press reports describing the scene said, *"It was a silent and mournful assemblage, so silent indeed that one felt the overwhelming bereavement which the village had suffered has made even sorrow inarticulate"*.

The numbers attending the funerals exceeded the population of the village as people from miles around came to honour the brave men who had paid the ultimate price in their quest to help others.

During the same week, Paddy Stafford was interred in Poulfur and Pat Roche in his native Bannow where, regrettably his grave was left unattended for years; eventually the original headstone was broken and discarded by vandals. Two of his

Photo by Steve Meyler

JAMES MORRISSEY'S GRAVE

St Mogue's churchyard, Fethard on Sea
Christy Bird is buried beside the bush obscuring part of
the church, John Mac and George Crumpton are just a
few feet away and Bill Banville is at the front of the church.

grandchildren returned it to its rightful place and placed a new plaque alongside it in later years.

In 1923, just one day after her twenty-fourth birthday, Pat's daughter, Mary Roche, married Peter Fitzpatrick and over the course of the next twenty-four years they became the proud parents of thirteen children, including a set of twin boys. Peter died in 1948 at the age of fifty and was buried on his youngest child's second birthday. Before her death in 1961 Mary said her only regret in life was that she never saw her father's grave. After Paddy and Mary left home their mother, Anastasia, remained in the family house, living alone with her memories of Pat until her death in 1953, having spent just ten years short of a century on earth.

Willie Bird's body was found two days after the rescue, on 25th February, and was buried in the family plot in Old Templetown, close to the Handrick brothers.

Following the discovery of Bill Banville's remains in April, his brothers, Tommy and Robert were two of the pallbearers who carried the coffin to his final resting place close to the entrance to St Mogue's church in Fethard. His parents were heartbroken as they stood by the graveside and his sixty-nine year old mother later said *"Poor William was the best of a boy; he gave me every penny he ever earned"*.

Ten days later, when Patrick Cullen's cortege reached Fethard he was met by an inconsolable Margaret with lines of sorrow etched into her face, and taken to Poulfur church to lie in repose. Mary Bridget Handrick and the five survivors were amongst those who remained with her throughout the night beside the sealed

CREW OF THE WEXFORD

Left to Right

*Engineer John McDonald, John Harpur,
Bartholomew 'Big Bartle' Carty, John Furlong,
Peter Hamilton, Captain Laurence Busher*

coffin; she cried the whole time and said it felt like her heart was breaking apart. Since the tragedy, Mary Bridget had felt a sense of guilt that her two men had survived whilst so many others had been bereaved.

The next day, Friday 23rd April, exactly nine weeks since Patrick had rushed from home to answer the call, the sun was shining but an aura of gloom and despair covered the cemetery where what seemed like the entire village had gathered to pay their last respects to a hero who was buried just a few feet from his old friend Paddy Stafford.

Standing at the graveside with tears running down their cheeks as they said a silent farewell to a loving husband and father, the sorrowful sight of Margaret and their nine children was heart rending and could not have failed to touch anybody.

The younger children, who used to love the way their Daddy would throw them in the air and catch them, were too young to understand what had happened and for them the upset was gradually forgotten, but for the older ones the sadness and the sorrow were always there.

For Margaret the pain never went away; she tried to put on a brave face for the children but for years she cried herself to sleep. When she opened her front door it was to a view most people would find idyllic, but for her, and the children, the uninterrupted view across the bay to where the Keeraghs, although low lying, appeared to dominate the skyline, served as a constant, and painful, reminder of their great loss. As a result of bronchitis and heart failure, she was eventually reunited with her beloved Patrick on 20th February 1941, the twenty seventh anniversary of the tragedy.

Shortly after Patrick's burial, money was allocated from the relief fund to provide identical and easily recognisable headstones for each grave so even in death they retained a link with their former crew mates.

For some time after the rescue, it was as though a cloud had descended on Fethard as it wallowed in the gloom of calamity and families struggled to come to terms with the loss of their loved ones. Normality did slowly return to the village but the survivors could never forget those three days and nights of hell on the Keeraghs, or what the sea had done to their friends and colleagues.

They had endured the worst Mother Nature could throw at them and for sixty-two hours on the island had lived with the constant fear of death, during which time all their efforts were focused on survival.

Now they were being thrust into the limelight time and again by the media, the RNLI and various other organisations wanting to honour their bravery – and raise funds. It was not something with which they were entirely comfortable, for various reasons. Most importantly, they did not see themselves as heroes; their view was they had just done what they were trained to do and, as Jem Wickham later put it, *"... any Irishman worthy of the name would have done the same"*.

The brain works hard to supress traumatic events but the loss of their friends and particularly the sight of them being thrown around in the water and hurled against the rocks remained vivid in their minds for the rest of their lives. As the realisation of what they had been through, and what might have been, started to sink in, some of them were showing signs of what is today recognised as Post Traumatic Stress Disorder, and nightmares became commonplace for them.

In terms of the initial goal it had been a successful rescue, but Fethard and its people had paid a very high price. For every member of *Mexico's* crew who was saved, a member of the *Helen Blake* crew lost his life. These were nine fellow villagers, nine individuals, nine breadwinners, snatched away in the prime of their lives leaving behind grieving family members, including three widows and a total of sixteen children who would grow up without a father.

It was a loss that could never be replaced, and a loss woefully made all the worse by the RNLI who, in their service book detailing the cost of the rescue, appeared to show a total misunderstanding of what transpired that weekend, and a complete lack of respect for the men who had put their lives on the line. Rather surprisingly, and very disappointingly, the records say no lives were saved by the crew of the *Helen Blake*; an assertion that is very much at odds with what happened on the island on the Friday evening and what Captain Eriksen told Captain Busher on board the *Wexford* tug.

It is also contradictory to a statement made at their own annual meeting by the Earl of Selborne, a former First Lord of the Admiralty: *"… only the other day there was a terrible disaster on the Wexford coast. The Norwegian schooner Mexico went ashore on one of those rocky islets off the coast. The Fethard Life-boat with a crew of fourteen men went out to the rescue in what, as far as I can gather from the accounts in the papers, must have been about as bad a gale as ever raged, even on that coast. The boat was smashed to pieces on the rocks, nine of the crew were drowned, and five, most happily, were thrown actually on the rocks or were just able to scramble on to them. And these five on the rock were able to help to rescue the whole of the crew of the Mexico, because they were able to make fast a line which was passed from the mast of the Mexico to some portion of the*

rock, and the whole of the crew of the Mexico passed down that rope from the schooner to the rock. So that even at the moment of disaster to the boat and the sacrifice of the lives of nine of their mates, the five survivors were able to accomplish the purpose for which the Life-boat had set forth".

The up-market *Pall Mall Gazette* paid tribute to the men who had lost their lives, saying, *"The country can ill spare men who are thus ready to take their lives in their hands at the call of duty".*

CHAPTER

19

Can I see another's woe,
and not be in sorrow too?
Can I see another's grief,
and not seek for kind relief?
– William Blake

*H*elen Blake was not replaced. A decision had been made in July 1913 to close the Fethard station and provide a new motor lifeboat at Dunmore East, which would provide cover for Ballyteigue Bay. The new motor boat, *Michael Henry*, arrived there from Newhaven on 12th March 1914 just seventeen days after the rescue. In his book, *The Last Fethard Lifeboat*, John Doyle, who had known some of the survivors, said, *"The people of Fethard would have been better off had it arrived two months earlier"*. In fact, just three weeks earlier would have changed everything.

In June 1995 the RNLI decided to re-establish a lifeboat station in Fethard and the following year, eighty-two years after the disaster a new D-Class inshore lifeboat, specifically designed as a light and highly manoeuvrable rapid response craft, arrived in the village.

Initially housed in the refurbished boathouse it was later moved to a new purpose built station, opposite the site of Bill Banville's old house. When the search started for a new crew, many of the volunteers included descendants of the 1914 crew including one of the current helms of the boat, Eoin Bird, grand-nephew of Richie and cousin of both Christy and Willie. His ancestors would have been proud of him.

On the practical side, with so many families left without a breadwinner, it would have been a major struggle just to feed themselves were it not for the kindness of others. The people of Fethard, of course, did what they could and shared what they had, but the generosity spread way beyond the village and donations to the various disaster funds which had been set up for them came pouring in.

The *Wexford People* newspaper started the ball rolling with a 'shilling fund', and even closer to home, the Kilmore fund had raised the equivalent (in 2018 terms) of almost five thousand pounds before the end of the first week. Donations arrived from all around the world, from people who had never before heard of Fethard.

Luis Bolnes, in Laguna, sent a very generous one hundred pounds, Guinness employees sent sixty pounds, the cadets on a training ship in Liverpool sent eight pounds five shillings and there were literally hundreds of donations exceeding one pound – the equivalent of one hundred pounds in 2018.

Twenty-five pounds was received from David Midgley & Sons, to whom the cargo was consigned, and who faced a tragedy of their own less than eighteen months later when one of their employees, Jack Law, was killed in the first days of the Battle of the Somme.

A number of newspapers, including *The Freeman's Journal, Dublin Daily Express* and *Irish Times* deserve an enormous vote of thanks for starting funds and publicising them to encourage people to contribute, which they did in their hundreds with the first donations arriving the day after the rescue, including a donation of two thousand pounds from the RNLI.

As a seafaring nation, Norway understood very well the sacrifices that had been made and was quick to show its appreciation with a generous donation of five hundred and fifty pounds voted by Norwegian Storting (Parliament), fifty-five from King Haakon and Queen Maud, and a further eight hundred and fifty from the shipping community of that country.

This was acknowledged at the RNLI annual meeting when they referred to, *"... the interest which Their Majesties the King and Queen of Norway have taken in our own Life-boat Service, the unprecedented honour they have done us in sending a subscription to our funds, and the unprecedented honour the Norwegian Parliament has done us in voting a subscription to our Institution".*

Charity concerts and football matches were organised throughout Wexford and the neighbouring counties where people were able to show their appreciation for the crew's selflessness. Wexford South MP, Peter Ffrench, who was born in Bannow, took an active part in ensuring the public were aware of the tragedy and the need for donations; he wrote numerous letters to newspapers and even raised the matter in Parliament.

In total over nine thousand pounds was collected – a staggering one point one million in 2018 values – but sadly it was not without controversy. Lancashire businessman Sir Charles Macara, president of the International Cotton Federation, had organised the first recorded charity street collection in 1891 to raise funds for families of twenty seven lifeboatmen who drowned going to the rescue of a German barque, also called *Mexico*. When he heard of the Fethard disaster he immediately launched an appeal in the British press, which attracted substantial donations. Just ten days after the rescue however, he was unjustifiably slated by Johnstone Wallace, Lord Mayor of Newcastle upon Tyne.

Between 1900 and 1910 Wallace had been Chairman of the Lifeboat Saturday Fund (founded by Sir Charles) which collected funds to help widows and orphans of lifeboat crews losing their lives through disaster. *"Consequently"*, he stated, *"there can be no need for any local effort or special fund to raise money for bereaved relatives. That the RNLI is able to do so is perfectly obvious ..."*

As mentioned earlier, the RNLI did indeed make a substantial donation, amounting to just over twenty percent of the total fund, but it fell far short of the amount needed. Sir Charles was very diplomatic in his response saying Wallace's comments were extremely unhelpful and would do nothing but harm to the collection.

All the various funds were amalgamated and a committee, including both the parish priest and the rector of Fethard, was set up under the auspices of the RNLI to distribute the funds. It was agreed the bulk of the money should be used to provide annuities for ten adults and sixteen children. Despite protest from some quarters, a total of three hundred and seventy pounds was justifiably shared between the survivors and those who had assisted in the rescue.

The *Irish Times* published an article which suggested, *"it may be found that too much money has been collected, that certain sums will remain that cannot wisely be devoted to the purpose for which they were originally intended"* and the surplus should be used in future disasters. *"In this way, we believe that the wishes of the contributors would be carried out".* A pompous and unpleasantly condescending comment as donations had been made specifically to the Fethard disaster/relief fund. Perhaps the good people at the *Times* felt that simple country folk would be unable to handle it if they received more than was needed just to feed themselves.

In the event, the balance of the fund was paid over to the local trustees who used it to good effect in helping dependents of the deceased as and when it was needed. The final distribution of funds was made in 1936 when the remaining nineteen beneficiaries each received the equivalent of almost three thousand pounds in 2018 values.

The Cullen family, Margaret and her nine children were, perhaps, the worst affected by the tragedy and a great deal of reliance was placed on eldest sons Mikie and Jack, barely into their teens, to provide for the family. A poignant photo of Margaret and the children published in numerous newspapers throughout England and Ireland is thought to have been largely responsible for the generosity shown by so many people.

Tragedy hit the family again four years later on 15th August 1918. It was a hot day and after the family had been to Mass to celebrate the Assumption of the Blessed Virgin Mary, three of the boys decided to go swimming in the sea just below their house. In the ebb tide, eighteen year old Mikie got caught in a current which dragged him under; Jimmy and Jack tried to help but got into trouble themselves and were fortunate to be saved by a man named Wade who was walking on the beach. Mikie's body was found on Grange Beach later in the day and like his father, the cause of death was declared to be drowning.

In January 1939, their daughter, thirty year old Dolly, married fifty-four year old seaman Paddy Barden and in the absence of her father, was given away by Martin Foley who, a quarter of a century earlier, had encountered Patrick riding his bike on that never to be forgotten day. History almost repeated itself at the end of the following year when Paddy's ship, the *Glenmoor*, was torpedoed and sunk en route from Cardiff to Alexandria. After being stranded alone on a raft for seven days without food or water he was eventually rescued by the British destroyer, *Havelock*.

On 23rd May, just one month after Patrick Cullen's burial, four of the survivors were joined by George Bassett, secretary of the lifeboat committee, on board a lifeboat towed by a horse for a massive Lifeboat Day parade through the centre of Cork. Richie Bird was unwell and unable to accompany his crew mates.

During the parade the people of that city showed great kindness and sympathy as they contributed to the disaster fund, with those in the poorest part of the city being the most generous. Later in the evening the five men were guests of honour at a banquet hosted by Lord Mayor Henry O'Shea who told them that by being there, he felt it was they who were conferring an honour on the city of Cork.

Anecdotally it is said that many of the donations sent from overseas were misdirected to Fethard, Tipperary so to avoid any further problems a decision was made to re-name the village Fethard-on-Sea, the name that is still used today even though the change has never been made official.

Ole Edvin Eriksen retired from the sea after the *Mexico* disaster and became a salmon warden on Iddefjord, a stretch

THE CULLEN FAMILY
A few days after the tragedy

Left to Right

Mary Margaret (Cissie), Ellen Mary (Nellie), Michael (Mikie)
Margaret holding Mary Kate (Cathy),
Bridget (Bridie), Mary Bridget (Dolly)
Back: John Patrick (Jack), James (Jimmy), Patrick (Patsy)

of water between Norway and Sweden, close to his home in Fredrikshald (now Halden). He remained active in his country's Sailors Association until his death at the age of seventy-two in 1921, the same year that his youngest son Tor, captain of a steamship, was hospitalised along with ten of his crew after contracting malaria during a trip to Africa. His eldest son Billie, who was also a sea captain, died in Bangkok seven years later.

A little over a year after the rescue, John Mac and Mary Bridget finally went to the dance together, which had been moved from its usual February date. During the evening Mac plucked up the courage to propose. She said, *"Yes"*.

chapter

20

The legacy of heroes is the memory of a great
name and the inheritance of a great example.
– Benjamin Disraeli

Thc wreck of the Mexico did not break up as expected
and the salvage operation was contracted to Thomas
Round & Co of Sunderland. They sent their ship *Salvor*
to the area and employed a number of local men, headed by
Bertie Downes, to carry out the work, paying them thirty shillings, plus food, per week. The valuable cargo of mahogany
and cedar was offloaded and towed into Bannow Bay by rowing
boats before being sold on.

When checked, it was found there were fewer logs than
recorded on the original inventory and this was put down to
some of them being washed away from the wreck before they
could be saved. It certainly had nothing to do with the fact that
there are a few houses in the area with mahogany furniture and
staircases – and even one with mahogany framework for a shed!

A crane was erected to bring the ship's machinery including
the donkey engine, winches and cranes ashore to find new homes

on ships around the country. The concrete base made for the crane can still be seen on the island. There was a gale during the salvage operation leaving the workmen stranded on the island but fortunately on this occasion they had the shelter of a hut and an adequate supply of food and water enabling them to weather the storm in relative comfort, and on full pay, until it blew over.

In November George Crumpton, the man who had risked his life on the island to catch the line thrown from *Mexico,* and had combined with Richie Bird to bring the crew to safety, became a proud father for the second time when Rebecca gave birth to William Robert, although very few people knew that was his name. He grew up to be a very popular man who for most of his adult life was rural postman for the area and was known to everybody as George – even his nephew did not know his real name until he collected his papers after his death.

Following the tragedy George continued to help his fellow man as an auxiliary Coast Guard, until the middle of January 1917 when he collapsed due to heart problems from which he never recovered. He died six weeks later on 27th February with Rebecca at his bedside and was laid to rest a few days later, six feet from James Morrissey, in the village he had served so well.

Richie Bird never fully recovered from his experience on the island; he suffered with recurrent pain for the rest of his life as a result of the damage to his spine caused when he was tumbled around in the sea. He was diagnosed with emphysema shortly after his time on the Keeraghs and this resulted in his death a little less than two years after the disaster.

The 'boy hero' was just twenty-five years old when he died on 14th February 1916 by which time the media had moved on

SURVIVORS OF THE HELEN BLAKE

Back: John Kelly, George Crumpton, Richard Bird
Front: Garrett Handrick, John McNamara

to new stories and his death went largely unnoticed by the press, but not by the villagers. Leading the large crowd of mourners at his funeral in Templetown were his family and the four remaining survivors.

Just three weeks later, on Monday 6th March, the four were together again but this time for an altogether more pleasant ceremony as John Mac married Mary Bridget in Poulfur church; best man was John's brother Tom who had fired the maroon to summon the crew on the day of the disaster, and there to give the bride away was Garry Handrick, whose life had been saved by the groom two years earlier.

They went on to have two sons, Nicholas and John, and lived a quiet, contented life in their small house at the top of Sunny Row, often calling on Mary Anne Morrissey to help out with odd jobs around the house and to ensure she was coping. She had been affected very badly by the disaster and never fully recovered. In 1950 she was admitted to the mental hospital in Enniscorthy where she died the following year at the age of eighty-two.

Mac later went to sea as an able seaman aboard the Waterford to Fishguard mail boat the *Great Western,* from which he retired on 15th June 1939, two days before his sixty-fifth birthday. On his retirement, or in his words, *"when I got past my labour",* the RNLI paid him a pension of one pound a week. The last of the survivors, Mac was five years past the three score and ten denied to his erstwhile crew mates when he died on 22nd October 1954 in Wexford County Hospital. Cause of death was given as Coronary Thrombosis, Cardiovascular Degeneration and Chronic Asthma. He was laid to rest in Fethard.

Ned Brien and his wife Ellen emigrated to America in 1920 to join their two sons, Thomas and Patrick, one of whom had

joined the priesthood. Perplexingly, Ned's birth name was Bryan but he described himself on his wedding certificate, and was known by everybody, as Brien, whilst at least one of his sons appears to have called himself O'Brien.

George Basset sold his various businesses in 1922 and with his wife Matilda and son Walter, moved to New Zealand, but not before buying a property for his sister, Mary, and transferring his post office business to her.

Marks Barden had been ill for a year when, in June 1923, he died of a brain haemorrhage at his home in Grange, just three days before the marriage of his twenty-three year old niece Mary Ellen Ryan who had lived like a daughter in the family house for most of her life.

Laurence Busher continued to work into his sixty ninth year, and died at home in 1927 due to dilation of the heart, after suffering with coronary artery disease for eighteen months. He was survived by his wife, Mary, and eight children.

John Kelly continued to work on his fishing boat becoming a familiar, and very popular, sight in the village for many years, selling freshly caught fish from the back of his ass and cart. He also farmed his small piece of land to provide potatoes and vegetables for the home, plus a little additional income. Following the death of his wife, Lizzie, he went to live with his sister in Waterford where, with his heroism all but forgotten, his death in February 1937 warranted just half a dozen lines in the *Waterford Standard*.

Two months later the same newspaper provided similar coverage to announce the death of Walter Power, coxswain of the Dunmore lifeboat. After leaving the lifeboat service Power spent a few years fishing in the *Lydia Ann* but eventually sold it and retired. Around half a century after his death, the boat was beached at Saltmills in Bannow Bay where it was left to rot.

Garry Handrick never married and never completely recovered from his ordeal. He acquired a few acres of land close to his home and spent the remainder of his life farming. After his mother died in 1919, he never spent a night alone in his house, instead making his way to Fethard every evening and sleeping in John Mac's house. Twenty years later parish priest Lawrence Kinsella contacted the RNLI on Garry's behalf and obtained an allowance of ten shillings per week – to be reviewed after twelve months. At the age of sixty eight he was taken to Wexford County Hospital where he was found to have a liver disease. He passed away on 7th November 1950 and was buried a few days later in Old Templetown, not far from Willie Bird and his namesakes, the Handrick brothers.

The next few years saw lifeboat president Godfrey Taylor endure a great deal of sadness. On New Year's Day 1915 his eldest son, forty-two year old Godfrey, serving as a Fleet Surgeon in the Royal Navy, was one of almost five hundred who lost their lives when the battleship *HMS Formidable* was torpedoed in the English Channel. His youngest son, thirty-six year old Charles, a Major in the Royal Irish Regiment, was killed on the 5th August 1917, during the first week of the battle of Passchendaele. Twelve months later the former land agent passed away peacefully in Dublin's Fitzwilliam nursing home.

That frightful weekend in 1914 also saw the emergence of a number of largely unsung helpers, all of whom played an important part in the rescue. At the top of this list must surely be the five members of Captain Busher's crew on *Wexford* who were crucial to the rescue and who, like the lifeboat crews, were prepared to put themselves in harm's way to help others.

Content to be in the background were the many women who provided hot food and drinks for the Dunmore crew in Fethard, and who spent endless hours comforting the families whose loved ones were lost.

At the annual meeting of the RNLI mentioned earlier, which took place just a month after the tragedy, the Earl of Selborne heaped praise on the *Helen Blake* crew: *"...It was indeed a noble example of what the men who man these boats, no matter whether they be Irishmen, Englishmen, Scotchmen, or Welshmen, can do, and what they will do, when the hour of trial comes. Finally – and if I speak briefly I am sure you will know that it is not because I do not feel deeply – it unifies men of all religions. It unifies Catholic and Protestant"*.

"I suppose in all the long annals of the RNLI there has been no more striking event than the rescue of the wrecked crew of the Mexico. The decision which had to be taken by the Fethard Life-boat was one of life and death to them. It was clear that unless they could get between the wrecked ship and the reef, their chance of saving the lives of the men on board was hopeless. To do so was well-nigh certain death. But there was a chance. They took that chance, and nine men perished".

"But, as the Chairman pictured it, it was the five survivors who rendered possible the ultimate rescue of the crew of the wrecked ship. I inquired from the Secretary as to what this gallant crew was composed of, and I found that there were both Catholics and Protestants there. So we see that even in the presence of death, in face of the great appeal of humanity,

Catholics and Protestants in Ireland, no less than in England, know how to answer that appeal, and know how to die together in its service".

At a meeting of the Wexford Harbour Commissioners on 3rd March a comprehensive fifteen hundred word report from Captain Busher detailing the involvement of the tug was entered into the minutes. A letter was also read from Commander Holmes asking for the commissioners' account *"for services rendered by the tug"*. The minutes record that, *"After a long discussion it was decided to make a charge of £200"*. This was made up as eighty hours hire at thirty shillings an hour, plus forty pounds for insurance and a similar amount for ancillaries such as repairs, extra coal, etc.

The following day a special meeting was convened when it was minuted that, *"After consideration it was decided to increase claim for use of tug from £200 to £300 as the risk being so very great"*. To the layman it may appear that this was not at all considerate, and it is difficult to understand what could have happened in the intervening twenty-four hours since the original figure had been determined *"after a long discussion"*. The risk was indeed very great, but it had not increased overnight and in hindsight, in the absence of any real explanation, this looks like a somewhat avaricious decision with an arbitrary figure – equivalent to an additional ten thousand pounds in 2018 terms – plucked from the air. It was not the first time the commissioners had inflated the value of their services; four years previously they had claimed two hundred pounds salvage in connection with the Dutch schooner *Nellie*, only to have it reduced by Lloyds of London to seventy-five pounds.

Interestingly, there is no mention in the minutes of any commissioner asking 'Why?' and nowhere are any of the decisions or proposals in connection with the Keeraghs rescue attributed to an individual. It is almost as though they were aware of how shameful their decision was and were hiding behind collective responsibility. The figure looks particularly high bearing in mind the accounts for 1908 showed the total income for the tug was just over nine hundred pounds for the year (there was virtually no difference in the value of money during that period).

Regrettably, this was not the last time petty officialdom would be seen to act controversially in connection with the disaster, and to show what many people considered to be their true colours.

CHAPTER

21

Man gives you the award,
But God gives you the reward.
– Denzel Washington

The scale of the events which had taken place during that terrible weekend in February, and the selfless bravery of all those involved, was recognised and applauded way beyond the confines of Wexford. The disaster and subsequent rescue were reported around the world in hundreds of newspapers, and generous donations were made to the disaster fund by individuals, companies and organisations at home and abroad.

A letter from the RNLI head office to Wexford solicitor Michael O'Connor, honorary local secretary of the institution, less than three weeks after the rescue, echoed the thoughts of many thousands. *"The Committee of management feel that the conduct of all concerned, both of the men who lost their lives and those who so strenuously and persistently strove to save the survivors, shows that the traditions of heroic conduct, which are inbred in our seafaring race, are a living and active force, inspiring the men of today as it did their fathers before them"*.

It was very well warranted praise for a group of ordinary men who had carried out an extraordinary rescue. With some rather puzzling anomalies in the list, the letter went on to detail the many awards that had been agreed and would be presented at a later date. The final paragraph of the letter said, *"The commit-tee has heard with some surprise of the very heavy charge of £300 which has been put forward by the Wexford Harbour Commissioners for the tug's services, and I have been instructed to ask that they may see their way to reconsider this charge ..."*

At a meeting of the commissioners on 16th March the secre-tary read a letter from Mr O'Connor in which he pointed out the charge was far in excess of what the Institution had expected. The rather curt response was, *"the amount charged is not in any way excessive"*. Before moving on to the next item they stated that, *"... according to Capt. Busher's statement, had he not been able to make Waterford Harbour, his boat would have been undoubtedly lost that night"*. An assertion of this nature does not appear in the statement read into the minutes two weeks earlier and neither is there any record elsewhere in the minutes of Busher having indicated such a concern, so it is unclear what statement was being referred to. Still no explanation as to why the fee originally agreed was increased by fifty per cent the next day.

Topping the list of awards detailed in the RNLI letter was the King Edward Silver Medal for Gallantry which was to be presented to Jem Wickham and Bill Duggan of the *James Stevens*, whose actions and bravery cannot be praised highly enough. Ned Wickham, who had been awarded the Silver Medal eight years earlier for his part in another rescue in

Photos by Steve Meyler

SILVER MEDAL

Awarded by King Haakon of Norway to
Richard Bird for ædel daad (nobel act)
His name was misspelled as Burd

Similar medals were awarded to nine others involved
in the rescue, including all the Helen Blake survivors

which six lives were saved, received the Silver Second-Service Clasp. All three men would also receive the thanks of the RNLI inscribed on vellum, and every member of the crew was awarded a gratuity of two pounds – to put this into context, the salary of the assistant county surveyor equated to less than two pounds per week.

Captain Busher of the *Wexford* was awarded the thanks of the institution on vellum plus a gratuity of ten pounds, while his six crew members each received three pounds. (Vellum is made from calfskin and will last indefinitely – the Magna Carta was written on vellum over eight hundred years ago and is still in existence today.)

Lifeboat volunteers do not do what they do for fame or glory, and when it finds them they are often uncomfortable in its presence. Even so, it is difficult to understand why no mention was made in the letter of any awards for the crews of *Helen Blake* or *Fanny Harriet*.

There were two rescues that weekend; on Friday the Fethard crew had brought eight men safely off the *Mexico* sacrificing nine of their own in the process, and on Monday the volunteers on the other two boats had brought twelve men off the Keeraghs. The first of those incidents appeared to have been forgotten.

Controversy raised its ugly head again at a meeting of the Wexford County Council on 6th May when a recommendation was read from the Finance & Roads Committee, *"With reference to removal of Fethard Life Buoy in connection with Fethard Disaster"*. The recommendation was to claim the cost of replacing the lifebuoy *"from Life Boat Institution"*. Not one councillor in the room was prepared to stand up and be counted by questioning the recommendation, and all those present unanimously agreed to support this unbelievably cold-hearted resolution.

It is difficult to understand the rationale behind this most disconcerting, and heartless, decision as it has always been accepted that lifebuoys are put in place so they can be used to save lives at no cost to the user. The decision was especially galling as this was the lifebuoy used by the Dunmore lifeboat crew to rescue John Mac and John Kelly. Perhaps reporters did not attend council meetings at that time but, for what-ever reason, no mention of this callous decision was made in the press.

On Sunday 26th July, just two days before the assassina-tion of Archduke Franz Ferdinand which led to the start of the First World War, the lifeboatmen and the crew of the tug travelled to Dublin where the awards were presented by the Lord Lieutenant of Ireland, Lord Aberdeen, at a glittering ceremony on the bandstand in Temple Gardens, as part of the city's Civic Exhibition.

Before the presentations a message was read from the King of Norway, *"Hearing that Your Excellency shall be presenting medals to the brave rescuers of the Norwegian vessel Mexico, I beg you to express my warmest thanks for their brave deeds"*.

The Monarch – the first King of recently independent Norway – further expressed the gratitude of his country when he awarded silver medals and citations on vellum to ten people involved in the rescue, including the five *Helen Blake* survivors.

In addition to the awards mentioned in the original letter, Walter Power, cox of the Dunmore lifeboat, was a late addition to the RNLI list and was awarded a very well-deserved Silver

Medal whilst his crew received a gratuity of two pounds each. The five *Helen Blake* survivors each received a gratuity of three pounds together with a vote of thanks from the RNLI inscribed on vellum. The inscription on John McNamara's certificate (opposite) is indicative of those awarded to the five survivors:

It had originally been planned for the crew of torpedo destroyer *HMS Forward,* which the previous month had been patrolling the coast of Wexford, to provide a guard of honour for the lifeboatmen, but it had sailed suddenly and unexpectedly from Dublin at seven o'clock the previous evening. According to the press, *"The abrupt departure was not considered especially significant"*. Unless, perhaps, it was you for whom the guard of honour was planned.

Captain Busher offered his thanks and said nothing pleased them more in Wexford than to go to the rescue of anyone in trouble, and as long as he was master of the *Wexford* tug he would always be ready to do his best. He was unquestionably an honourable and honest man sadly let down by his employers who regrettably did not share his public spirited attitude.

Ned Wickham spoke most eloquently on behalf of his crew when he thanked the Lord Lieutenant for the honour paid to them. He said the wreck of the *Mexico* was the worst they had ever dealt with, but should a similar disaster occur again on their shores they would not be found wanting; their lifeboat had so far been the means of saving one hundred and fifty one lives.

He also thanked the King, the government and the people of Norway, and Lord and Lady Aberdeen for the kindness shown to the crew of his boat, *"kindness that was only in keeping with that which Their Excellencies had shown to everyone since they first set foot on the green shores of Erin"*.

Representing the RNLI, Sir Godfrey Baring MP said, *"The records of the institution hold many a bright and glorious page but none more noble or poignant than that relating to the Fethard disaster"*. At the conclusion of the ceremony, the lifeboatmen 'were entertained to tea at the Exhibition by Lord Aberdeen'.

Reflecting on the awards many years later it is challenging to understand the thinking behind some of the decisions made by the RNLI awards committee. Glaring omissions and inconsistencies left an understandably sour taste in some quarters where it was felt, perhaps correctly, that some of the participants had been ignored and dishonoured.

A Silver Medal went to Commander Holmes who was described as directing the rescue operation, though in practical terms it is difficult to see how he could have been anything more than an observer on the Dunmore boat. Walter Power was the coxswain, and therefore in command, Marks Barden piloted the lifeboat to a safe anchorage where the rescue could be carried out, and Ned Brien both formulated and executed the plan to fire a rocket from the boat, without which the rescue could not have gone ahead.

On the Rosslare boat, Ned Wickham, who was in command, devised the plan which was carried out with unbelievable courage by his brother Jem, and Bill Duggan. Each one of the eighteen oarsmen on the two lifeboats did more than Holmes on that Monday morning to ensure the success of the rescue, so it is problematical to see the justification for the Commander's medal. It is perhaps telling that there was no mention of him playing any part in the rescue by any of the other participants when they were interviewed after the event.

Back in London a couple of weeks after the disaster, Holmes would have been required to provide a detailed report and it is possible that his recollection of the part he played in the rescue was greater than others remembered. Additionally, he was not at the scene when the *Helen Blake* came to grief to see the bravery of the crew, or the rescue of the men from the *Mexico*.

It is even more difficult to understand the reasoning, or lack of it, for missing Barden and Brien out completely, but if the two Fethard men felt any disappointment they never spoke of it and there were no complaints from them for this blatant injustice. These were a very special breed of men and on that horrendous weekend they were not looking for glory or recognition, the only thing on their mind was to get the survivors off the island. They had received all the reward they ever craved on Monday 23rd February when the *Fanny Harriett* brought five of their friends home safely and landed them on the beach beside Fethard dock.

It was a very different attitude to that of the Wexford councillors in attendance at the Dublin ceremony who were only too eager to be seen in the company of, and to ingratiate themselves with, the so-called elite of society.

Vice-chairman Charles Peacock and Councillor Michael Cloney seconded and supported a vote of thanks that had been proposed to the Lord Lieutenant for presenting the awards. They appear to have conveniently forgotten that twelve weeks earlier they had plunged the depths of despicability in voting to seek payment from the RNLI for the lifebuoy used to rescue two of the lifeboatmen in whose reflected glory they were now basking.

Perhaps they were merely following the lead set by the Chairman of the Council, John Bolger, who found his way on to the committee headed by Lady Adelaide FitzGerald of

Johnstown Castle which was set up to administer the funds raised for the dependents of the nine men who lost their lives. In this position the press could report his determination to carry out his civic responsibilities, again without mentioning the lifebuoy.

At the 1914 Annual General Meeting of the GAA (Gaelic Athletic Association) a very special, and very well deserved, honour was conferred on Jem Wickham and Bill Duggan when it was agreed to award them with Gold All-Ireland medals; the first, and still the only, time such medals have been awarded to anybody outside the field of play.

The medals were presented at a civic ceremony in New Ross by James Sinnott, Mayor of Wexford, with council leader Bolger once again getting in on the act. This time he said he was speaking on behalf of all his colleagues at the council (all of whom had agreed to charge for the lifebuoy) and stated that *"it was an honour to be associated with the presentation ... which had the sole object of paying a just debt of praise and gratitude to men who so nobly risked their lives for their fellow men"*.

The eloquence of the real heroes was made all the greater by the self-effacing style typical of all the lifeboatmen, when Jem Wickham in his response said he thought *"it was an act of Heaven that saved the survivors more than anything else"*.

22

In three words I can sum up everything
I've learned about life: it goes on.
— Robert Frost

On 21st February, less than twenty four hours after *Mexico* had run aground, the first known report of the tragedy was written by hand, though details of the writer are undetermined, and submitted to Augustine Birrell, the Chief Secretary for Ireland (effectively the British government minister responsible for governing Ireland) who received it two days later, by which time the rescue had taken place.

Probably due to its rushed nature, this was little more than a simple notification of the tragedy covering the basics of where and when it happened, the weather conditions at the time, information on the two crew members who made it to Cullenstown, the bodies that were washed ashore and the inquest planned for the Monday.

A little over six weeks later, on 9th April, a report was sent to the Chief Inspector of the RNLI providing details of tests carried out on the lifejackets (which they referred to as life belts) used by the crew, and determined what would seem glaringly obvious to most laymen, that, *"… the ideal belt would be one with waterproof qualities …"*.

It went on to state that Kapok, the material used in the life-jackets, had *"some small buoyancy, but nothing like sufficient to provide for the support of a body in the water"*, the buoyancy was provided by the millions of small air bubbles contained in its fibres.

One of the jackets recovered from the drowned men was described as, *"a solid saturated mass"* and weighed a stagger-ing twenty eight pounds. To put this in context, it would be like attempting to swim in rough seas, fully clothed, with a tyre from an average family car around your shoulders. Commenting on this, the report continues, *"… the wearer of this belt must have been brought into continual violent contact with rocky ledges until every particle of air had been forced out of the Kapok"*.

Ostensibly designed to save lives, the report seems to indicate that in this instance the jackets may have had the opposite effect and were of very little, or no, use to the men in the situation in which they found themselves. With such a weight attached to his body, a man would quickly be dragged under the water and drowned.

Kapok had been introduced in 1904 but any outsider looking at the contents of this report would surely be excused for believ-ing that any testing before they were put into service must have been rudimentary in the extreme, and the fact that the jackets remained in service for almost another sixty years seems to indicate that no lessons were learned from the tragedy.

Louth County Council in whose jurisdiction *Helen Blake's* sister boat, *General R Dudley Blake*, was stationed, sent a resolution to their counterparts in Wexford which was entered into the minutes of a meeting on 15th April. It tendered the sympathy of the Louth CC, *"to the relatives of the gallant men of Fethard who lost their lives in an heroic attempt to rescue the shipwrecked sailors of the Mexico, recently wrecked off the Wexford Coast"*.

At a meeting a month earlier, Wexford councillors had expressed their *"deep sorrow"* and formally passed a *"vote of condolence"* to the relatives. This contrasts rather sharply with their attitude just one month later when they passed the infamous resolution in connection with the lifebuoy.

A week later the RNLI settled their bill from the council to pay for a replacement lifebuoy, and the invoice from the Wexford Harbour Board, *"for services rendered by the 'Wexford' tug and Captain Busher"*.

Ireland was still under British rule at the time so the official inquiry into the tragedy was carried out by the Board of Trade, the government department responsible for all non-military shipping. This took place eight weeks after the rescue, on 21st April, in the Wexford County Council chamber and was conducted by Commander Warren Caborne, a very experienced investigator who had retired from the Royal Navy twenty years earlier after a distinguished career which resulted in him being invested as a Companion of the Order of the Bath (one of the most senior British Orders of Chivalry).

His report, dated 2nd May, ran to almost six and a half thousand words and covered every aspect of the incident from construction of the lifeboat to the training of the crew and from weather conditions to the role of the other lifeboats, giving special mention to the skills and efficiency of Coxswain Christy Bird.

Witnesses giving evidence included the Board of Trade's solicitor who confirmed *Helen Blake* had been built in 1904 before being placed in Fethard the following year, and George Rube who had supervised construction of the boat at the Thames Ironworks in London.

Incorporated in the report was the affidavit Captain Eriksen had sworn in Liverpool detailing the voyage and the loss of his ship, which he finished by saying, *"On my own account, and on behalf of the whole crew, I wish to record our most grateful thanks, and our very deep sorrow for the terrible disaster to the lifeboatmen who were trying to come to our rescue".*

John Kelly told the inquiry he believed the forward centre board was not lifted and, *"that is what lost the boat".* Other reports suggested the board had been lifted, but not secured in place. Kelly also pointedly addressed Commander Holmes stating forcefully, *"There is no truth in the tale that the lifeboat was capsized".*

Concerned as it was with the loss of the lifeboat and the circumstances leading up to it, very little mention was made during the proceedings of the time the men spent on the island, and most conspicuous by its absence was any reference to the separate investigation which had detailed the inadequacy of the lifejackets.

The omission of this from the inquiry is especially surprising as it would almost certainly have been fresh in the mind of Commander Holmes to whom it had been sent less than two weeks earlier, who was at the inquiry, and who had been on the Dunmore lifeboat during the rescue.

Holmes passed away in September 1933 after a *"distinguished career in both the Royal Navy and the lifeboat service".* In its obituary, the *Manchester Guardian* recalled the events of

1914, stretching the truth somewhat when it described rather spuriously how the survivors were marooned on the island *"until rescued by Commander Holmes and the lifeboats from Dunmore East and Wexford"*.

On 11th February 1915, just nine days short of the first anniversary of the tragedy, Wexford Council granted permission for a monument to be erected. Paid for with an allocation from the disaster fund, it was built by George Bassett in the heart of the village where it serves as a permanent reminder of the crew's heroism. It is a classically simple edifice featuring a Celtic cross on a stone plinth with details of the tragedy and the names of the heroes inscribed on slate.

Unlike most memorials, it was not fenced off or separated from the rest of the village in any way and, as a result, soon became an integral part of the village. Perhaps unaware of its significance, children played around it, people stood around it to talk with friends, and, today, cars are parked alongside it. In this way the *Helen Blake* and its crew once again became part of the fabric of village life.

Ned Wickham retired from the RNLI in 1925 after a remarkable forty years' service. His brother, Jem, took over as cox and Bill Duggan became his number two, both again bringing great credit to their lifeboat. Jem emulated his brother's achievement when he was awarded a Silver Second-Service Clasp in 1929 for his part in the rescue of five people from the British schooner *Mountblairy*. During his illustrious career his bravery was recognised with awards from five countries, Great Britain, Ireland, Norway, Denmark and the Netherlands.

There were two Duggans on the Rosslare boat, Philip was related to Bill by marriage and one of his descendants, known as Billy, maintained the family tradition as second cox of the Rosslare motor lifeboat *Douglas Hyde* where the cox was Richard Walsh whose two brothers had been on the *James Stevens* in 1914.

In November 1954 they both received RNLI medals for the rescue of seven men after hurricane force winds split the Liberian registered tanker *World Concord* in half. At eleven thousand seven hundred tonnes and two hundred metres long, this was the largest tanker in the world at the time. Fortunately it was in ballast when the accident happened and no environmental damage was caused. The lifeboat was at sea for twenty-six hours during the rescue, a feat that saw the crew awarded a case of rum by the Sugar Manufacturing Association of Jamaica for the longest winter service. Other crew members included Jack Wickham and Jack & Dicky Duggan.

Ned was in the news again over a hundred years later when the Duchess of Cambridge and naturalist Sir Richard Attenborough were amongst guests at the unveiling of a major new exhibit in London's Natural History Museum, in 2017. The exhibit was the skeleton of a twenty-five metre whale which Ned had killed with a home-made harpoon when it was stranded in Wexford harbour in 1891.

On 11th March 1915, the RNLI transferred the lease on the Fethard boathouse, which runs until September 2885 at a rent of six pence a year, to a group of trustees for the use of local fishermen. Unfortunately no longer in the pristine condition Christy Bird maintained, it still stands proud today as a lonely and silent reminder with history and sorrow etched into each one of its fifteen hundred granite blocks.

Photo by Steve Meyler

THE MONUMENT
Fethard on Sea

When he made his plea to the nation in 1823 for the formation of a National Institution for the Preservation of Lives and Property from Shipwreck, Sir William Hillary envisaged at the heart of the institution, *"a large body of men … in constant readiness to risk their own lives for the preservation of those whom they have never known or seen, perhaps of another nation, merely because they are fellow creatures in extreme peril"*.

Ninety one years later he would have been proud of fourteen unassuming men from Fethard on Sea who lived up to his vision, with nine of them saying a last goodbye to their loved ones before making the ultimate sacrifice in the service of their fellow man.

Over a century later it remains one of the greatest losses ever suffered by the Irish RNLI and, while the official report of the tragedy says nine crewmen lost their lives when the *Helen Blake* sank, it is seen as far more than that in Fethard on Sea where nine villagers, nine friends, nine relatives are today remembered with pride, along with the survivors and the crew of the *Mexico* whose lives they had saved, and who together endured those appalling three days and nights on the Keeragh Islands.

Standing in the shadow of the boathouse at three o'clock on the afternoon of 20th February 2018, looking across Ballyteigue Bay through a haze of rain, it is difficult not to be moved by the thought of what happened on that fateful day one hundred and four years earlier when joyful anticipation turned to horrific tragedy in the space of just a few short hours.

Ar dheis Dé go raibh a n-anamacha.

Helen Blake

The Mysterious Benefactor

An enigma, wrapped in a mystery

*Each person is an enigma. You're a puzzle not only
to yourself but also to everyone else, and the great
mystery of our time is how we penetrate this puzzle.*
– Theodore Zeldin

During the years 1886 to 1914 there were three different lifeboats stationed in Fethard, each one of them
bearing the same name, *Helen Blake*. Throughout the
twenty eight years those boats were in service very little attention was paid to the name they were given, or where they came
from. To everybody involved, the important thing was what the
boats did, not what they were called.

In later years, however, curiosity raised its head and questions
started being asked. Local school principal John Doyle answered
the first question, "Why *Helen Blake*?" In his 1970 book, 'The
Last Fethard Lifeboat', he states that the boat, "… *was provided
from a legacy of Mrs Helen Blake of Handcross House, Sussex"*.

A simple question, and a relatively straightforward answer
that was essentially correct, the money did indeed come from
Helen Blake, but through a somewhat circuitous route. In the

1905 RNLI Service Book it states *"… the lifeboat at Fethard (was) Presented to the Royal National Lifeboat Institution in 1884 by the late Mrs Helen Blake – per The Lords of the Treasury".*

With no explanation, the last six words in that statement raise a further question. "Why was the treasury involved?" And it does not end there; having discovered who the money came from, the obvious next questions are, "Who was Helen Blake?" and, "Why did she provide funds for a boat in Fethard?"

Whilst once again the questions appear to be reasonably simple and straightforward, the answers have proved to be somewhat more complicated – perhaps even mysterious.

We know Helen was a noted socialite in nineteenth century London, that she was responsible for the fabled Blake Millions, that her name was known around the world and that she had supposed relatives on virtually every continent. Yet even today, almost a century and a half after her death, nobody knows who she really was, and to misquote Winston Churchill, she remains, *an enigma wrapped in a mystery.*

We know she was Irish but according to newspaper reports of the time, and there were many hundreds of them, Helen Blake (née Sheridan) was born in Cavan / Mayo / Longford / Tipperary / on a boat in the Irish Sea. She lived in England / America / Australia, and she met her future husband in Dublin / Longford / Mayo / Mid-Atlantic, when he was a Lieutenant / Captain / General in the British army.

There are only a few things we know with absolute certainty from official records. Her husband to be was a Lieutenant-General when they met, they married in Scotland in 1819 when she gave her age as nineteen, she lived in London and the home counties, she was very wealthy, and she died in 1876 aged seventy-six, without leaving a will.

Of all the stories that have 'done the rounds' the one initially given most credence, and the most believable, is that Helen was born in a small village close to Claremorris in County Mayo in 1800, the daughter of schoolteacher Michael Sheridan and his wife Mary (née Jordan).

She had become the youngest of the family with the sudden death of her nine year old sister, Niamh, and three years after that, with little or no work to be found close to home, Helen's parents sent her to the nearby town of Castlebar when she was just fourteen.

Still grieving from the loss of her sister, and friend, it was a very unsettling and upsetting time for the young girl who felt betrayed by her parents. Although they were only fifteen or twenty miles away, they might as well have been on the other side of the world. The only time she saw her family during the next four years was on their occasional, and infrequent, visits to Castlebar, and on Christmas Day when she was given time off from her work to spend the day at home.

The fact that her employer was her uncle, the proprietor of Tyrawley Hotel on Bridge Street, did not make life any easier and she was required to work almost seven days a week – there was time off on Sunday to attend Mass but if there were guests in the hotel she had to work for the rest of the day, serving in the dining room.

Wednesday 17th March 1819 was St Patrick's Day, which was then celebrated as a holy day rather than the international party day into which it later evolved. There were only two guests in the hotel, and in the dining room, that day; two British army officers to whom St Patrick meant very little.

Forty-three year old Robert Dudley Blake who, according to British military records, was a Lieutenant-General at the time, was the sort of person who stood out in a crowd – not that the dining room could have been described as crowded – and not just because of his uniform; he radiated authority, had an impos-ing stature and at around five feet ten inches was considerably above average height for the time.

Helen was immediately smitten by the good looks of the dashing officer with his thick black hair and the fashionable 'mutton chops' sideburns. He was staying at the hotel for a few days with a Captain from his regiment, and she went out of her way to be in his presence whenever possible. In addition to serving in the dining room, she was responsible for cleaning the hotel, including the guest's rooms, so there were plenty of opportunities for them to meet.

On the second day of his stay Robert spoke to her and was impressed by how worldly wise she appeared to be for a young country girl. He made a point of talking to her again at breakfast on his last day at the hotel, asking about her family and her hopes for the future.

Helen wanted to travel, to see Dublin, to visit England, to discover new things. Blake was again impressed and was starting to see more than a mere servant girl. When he left the hotel he told her he would see her again when he came back in a couple of months, and left her a tip of half a crown – almost as much as she earned in a week.

Now it seems it was Blake's turn to be smitten. Captivated by her simple and vulnerable beauty he could not get the fresh

faced young girl out of his mind, engineering a reason to return
to Castlebar just one month later and again on a number of
occasions over the following six months.

For these subsequent visits he travelled alone, enabling him
to spend more and more time in her company, in the dining
room, the resident's lounge or anywhere else he could engage
her in conversation. Helen could not fail but to be overawed,
listening intently as he told her stories about England, his career,
and his family.

Like most officers of that era, who had to buy their commission in the army, Robert was from the wealthy landed gentry;
the Blake family seat was Twizel Castle, about ten miles from
Berwick-upon-Tweed and just a mile south of the Scottish
border. It was immortalised in Sir Walter Scott's epic twelve
hundred line poem, Marmion – a tale of Flodden Field.

Even though their lives were as different as chalk and cheese,
the unlikely couple of British officer and Irish colleen gradually
fell in love.

Twenty years since the Battle of Castlebar memories were
still raw for many of those in the area whose family and friends
had been killed in the battle, or hanged by the British. As a
result, such a liaison would have been very much frowned
upon in the locality making it necessary for their relationship
to remain clandestine. In a small rural community in nineteenth
century Ireland, however, that was easier said than done, and
many people became curious as the Lieutenant-General made
more and more frequent trips to the town.

After much discussion, the couple decided their only option
was to elope. This was an easy decision for Helen; there had
been almost no contact with her family whom she believed had

all but abandoned her after she left home, so she had no ties and relished the opportunity to escape from her mundane life. The fact that she was about to head off into the proverbial sunset with a dashing army officer with whom she had fallen head over heels in love made the decision even easier.

For Robert it was very different. He would be introducing into British society an Irish girl who would be viewed by the majority of them with disdain; the British upper classes of the day did not hold the working class Irish in very high regard.

He had no way of knowing how his family would react and he would be putting both his reputation and his career on the line. There were, however, three things that outweighed all his concerns; she was the most beautiful girl he had ever met, she was fun to be with, and he loved her.

This was an era when officers were entitled to between six and eight months leave each year so taking advantage of this he moved out of his quarters at the beginning of September. When he booked into the hotel in Castlebar a few days later, he had already planned the following month like a military operation.

Two tickets had been acquired for the mail coach, for which the Tyrawley was a regular stop on the journey from Westport to Dublin. Before leaving the city, he had also purchased new clothes for Helen so she would not stand out from the other passengers, or guests in hotels where they would overnight.

There were a number of people milling around as the coach prepared to leave on Monday morning and, even though they boarded at the last minute, the couple were once again caught out by the small community. News of their elopement was circulating around the town almost before the coach had left its boundaries.

CLAREMORRIS IN THE 1800s

Helen's father was summoned and, with her uncle, pursued them from Castlebar to Ballyglass and then on to Tuam, in neighbouring County Galway (coincidentally, the same route taken by the retreating British soldiers in the aforementioned battle) but they were too late and were unable to make up the lost time.

Love had won the day and the couple eventually made it completely across country arriving in Dublin two days later, fulfilling one of Helen's wishes that she had spoken of during their first meeting.

Three days were spent in accommodation Robert had arranged in Thomas Gresham's hotel at the top of Sackville Street. Most of their time was spent in the hotel, away from prying eyes but they did embark on something of a shopping spree to carefully selected shops, buying more clothes for Helen, and a trunk to transport them. It was the first step on the long road to a transformation that would allow her to blend in with Robert's circle of friends.

The young girl was completely overwhelmed by everything that had happened in the last few days; instead of working in a hotel she was now staying in one, in place of her two home-made dresses she now had a complete wardrobe and, above all, she now had a gallant and handsome man whom she loved taking care of her every need as she journeyed into the unknown.

On Saturday morning, five days into their journey, they boarded a ship to Liverpool and late that afternoon another of Helen's wishes was fulfilled when she stepped on to English soil for the first time.

Liverpool was a bustling town about half the size of Dublin in the early part of the nineteenth century but, thanks mainly to the port, was growing rapidly. It was already very different to the town described by noted traveller Celia Fiennes in the previous century:

"Leverpoole which is in Lancashire is built just on the river Mersy mostly new built houses of brick and stone after the London fashion; ye first original was a few fish-ermens houses and now is grown to a large fine town and but a parish and one Church, tho' there be 24 streetes in it. There is indeed a little Chappell and there are a great many dessenters in the town. Its a very Rich trading town, ye houses of Brick and stone built high and Even that a streete quite through Lookes very handsome – the streetes well pitched. There are abundance of persons you see very well dress'd and of good fashion, ye streetes are faire and Long, its London in miniature as much as ever I saw anything".

Taking two rooms at the Crown Inn they enjoyed dinner together and with a great sense of relief Robert felt that away from Ireland they could at last relax. Since leaving Castlebar he had travelled in civilian clothes to avoid drawing attention to himself but on Sunday morning he donned his uniform again to attend the service in St Peter's Church just a short walk from the hotel. In England he felt more comfortable but was surprised by the negative attitude of some people towards the uniform. He later discovered this was due to the news spreading of an incident just a month earlier in neighbouring Manchester when fifteen hundred troops and constables had attacked a peaceful demonstration. Fifteen people were killed and many were seriously injured in what became known as the Peterloo

Massacre, an event that led to the founding of the *Manchester Guardian* newspaper.

His plan was to travel to Glasgow as soon as possible so at six-thirty on Tuesday morning they boarded *The Royal Telegraph* outside their hotel. Heavy rain plagued them throughout the day turning the dirt roads to thick mud and even with four stout horses doing the work, their progress was at times reduced to walking pace.

By the time they reached the Crown & Mitre in Carlisle the clock had already struck midnight and there was just enough time for a bowl of hot broth before retiring to their rooms, exhausted. The majority of Wednesday was spent in front of a roaring fire after Robert decided to break the journey and take the first coach on the following day instead.

After an early breakfast, they were on the road again at seven o'clock on Thursday morning. The weather had improved and most of the roads had at least partially dried out so with a few rest stops along the way to change horses they arrived in Glasgow some fourteen hours later.

No time was wasted as Robert met with the Minister of the Gorbals Parish Church on the South Bank of the River Clyde on Friday, and then summoned a jeweller to their hotel on George Square to select a wedding ring.

24

Nothing is less important than which fork you use.
Etiquette is the science of living. It embraces
everything. It is ethics. It is honour.
— Emily Post

Exactly three weeks since leaving Castlebar, and accompanied by two employees of the Waverley Hotel where they were staying, they took separate Hansom Cabs to the Church to be married in a short ceremony on Monday 27th September 1819 – just one month after the birth, in Germany, of Prince Albert, the future prince Consort who they were destined to meet on a number of occasions.

When they returned to the hotel, their booking was changed from two rooms to one. Befitting his role as an officer and a gentleman, prior to their wedding Robert had insisted on separate rooms wherever they stayed.

Details of the marriage are unquestionably true, but the rest of the story appeared to be turned on its head when genealogist Leo O'Toole unearthed British census records where Helen gave her birthplace as 'Lancashire, River Mersey' (1851) and 'At Sea' (1871).

It looked as though at least part of the mystery had been solved but, conversely, all this information really does is add to the uncertainty.

O'Toole in his 2009 book, *The Cailíns Road To The Rich Man's Wealth*, points to a baptismal certificate from the Church of St Andrew in Dublin as proof of who she was, and who her parents were – John and Dorothy Sheridan.

There are inconsistencies on this certificate however; the Christian name is shown as Eleanor and the date is 19th December 1802. Whilst Helen is sometimes used as a diminutive of Eleanor, the date does not tally with Helen's stated age when she married. No date of birth appears on the certificate so although it is possible that she was not baptised until she was two years old, such a delay would have been almost unheard of in Ireland at that time.

Equally, there is no guarantee that the information she gave on their wedding day was correct, even though there was no reason to provide false information as the legal age to be married was not raised to sixteen until ten years later. Subsequent census records show how flexible Helen could be when it came to admitting her age; in 1851 she was described as being forty-seven, and twenty years later she had lost another six years when she gave her age as sixty-one.

If the baptismal certificate and the census records showed ambiguities relating to her name and her age, it is quite reasonable to assume there could also be a discrepancy in her place of birth, so we are back to square one, albeit with an extra spanner thrown into the works.

One thing of which we can be reasonably certain is that wherever she was born, her parents, whoever they were, could

Gorbals Parish Church, Carlton Place.

Pub.d by Wardlaw & Cunninghame,Glasgow, 9.th June 1821.

R.Scott Sc. Edin.r

GORBALS PARISH CHURCH

Where Helen and Robert married on 27ᵗʰ September 1819

have had no idea of the impact she would have on the rest of the world. From apparently humble beginnings she went on to become a lady of note in Georgian and Victorian Britain whose name would become known around the globe and who would be remembered with fondness and gratitude hundreds of years later in the village of Fethard on Sea in County Wexford.

Leaving Glasgow, the newlywed Mr & Mrs Blake took a coach to Edinburgh where they stayed on Princes Street for two days, which were spent enjoying the ambience of the city. On the second morning they visited Robert Stevenson's magnificent Regent Bridge which had been opened the previous month, and was situated a pleasant fifteen minute walk from their hotel.

Before their departure, Robert sent a letter by mail coach to book rooms in London. The journey south to the capital was a leisurely trip, so very different to their journey north a week earlier that Helen was moved to describe it as their honeymoon. She was still coming to terms with the events of the past month and Robert had decided to make the trip part of her education. Not surprisingly, she was feeling slightly uncomfortable by being served rather than doing the serving, although it was a role to which she had adapted very well by the time they reached London.

Their first night on the road was spent at the Blue Bell Inn in the picturesque village of Belford, no more than twenty miles from Twizel Castle, although Robert made no mention of this to Helen as he felt it was too early to meet the family. There were a number of unsubstantiated press reports alleging Robert kept their marriage secret from his family and friends for many years, fearful that Helen, being from a lower class, would not be accepted by them. Life after their marriage is reasonably well

Illustration courtesy of Sir Michael Blake

Photo courtesy of Norman MacKillop (www.NorthOfTheTyne.co.uk)

TWIZEL CASTLE

In its glory during the 19th century (top)
and as a ruin in the 21st century

documented and there is no evidence to support these contentions, in fact the reality was just the opposite.

Day two saw them in Bishop Auckland where Joseph Lonsdale of the King's Arms Inn appeared to sense Helen's disquiet and went out of his way to make her feel at ease. The half way point in their journey was York, which they reached on the afternoon of the third day, making their way to the White Horse Inn on Coppergate, a hotel that was popular with visiting army officers.

It was the first time in almost a month that Robert truly felt at ease, mixing with his own type. The city was recognised as being the most elegant in the north of England, and regarded by the moneyed classes as an attractive and stylish alternative to London, with shops and craftsmen to match anything available in the capital. Spending a full week there, it was the longest the newlyweds had ever been in the same place together.

On the recommendation of the innkeeper's wife, Marie Mayes, they browsed the shops in Stonegate before ordering two new hats for Helen which milliner Sarah Hodson in St Helen's Square delivered to their hotel three days later. In the flight from Ireland and the rushed journey to Glasgow, there had been no opportunity to acquire an engagement ring. To rectify this situation, and to complement the wedding ring they had purchased in Glasgow, Robert instructed Edward Jackson on Coney Street to design a ring with an emerald centrepiece and this too was delivered within a few days.

Accompanying a British army officer, Helen's Irish accent raised a few eyebrows and caused a few sideways glances from time to time in the establishments they visited but, then as now, money talks and nothing out of place was ever said. It was a foretaste of what life might be like in London without the proper education and preparation.

Sunday morning saw the couple attend the service in York Minster, presided over by the Archbishop, Edward Venables-Vernon, who in a private meeting the previous day had blessed their union.

The route from York to London could be completed in a gruelling twenty hours but Robert again decided to break the journey, this time in Peterborough where they overnighted at the Bull Inn. Arriving in London the following day they booked into the rooms Robert had reserved at James Mivart's hotel on Brook Street in Mayfair (later to become the world renowned Claridge's), while they looked for a suitable house.

Family friend, and Robert's former banker, Sir Thomas Baring introduced him to a gentleman who was experiencing business problems and within a few days he had purchased the man's house at 19 Adam Street, just off the Strand in the Adelphi district of London. Their neighbours here included portrait painter Thomas Stewardson and the former Lord Mayor of London, Christopher Smith.

Situated between John Street and Adelphi Terrace, the house was way beyond anything Helen could ever have imagined. A screen of Doric columns dominated the entrance hall beyond which was the main winding oak staircase with a skylight on the top floor flooding the stairs with daylight. Double mahogany doors led to the main rooms which boasted magnificent carved wood mantelpieces and decorative ceilings with exquisitely painted panels.

It was the biggest house she had ever seen and it looked to her as though the family cottage in Mayo would easily fit into just one of the rooms.

They were not destined to be there for long however; in the centre of London they would be part of a vibrant social scene and if Helen was to blend in with the highborn and titled ladies, she would first have to transform herself. Robert had already decided the best way to achieve this would be for her to attend boarding school in the country.

Adam Street was an ideal town house but it was not appropriate as their permanent residence. For that they would need a house in the country, ideally located somewhere in the Home Counties. The difficulty was that the majority of suitable houses tended to stay in one family, passed down from generation to generation, so there were very few on the market.

Once again Sir Thomas Baring came to the rescue. A former colleague of his had recently died and his son had made the momentous decision to sell everything and move with his family in order to take advantage of the opportunities that were opening up in the burgeoning United States of America.

Handcross House close to Crawley in Sussex was ideal and if Helen thought their London house was big, she was in for a shock. This was huge; in addition to the fifteen-room main house, it offered stables, a coach house, gardener's cottage and gate house, plus substantial grounds. It was beyond her wildest dreams.

Importantly it was also on the London to Brighton road, only around three hours from the coastal town. It was there, at the start of 1820, a place in the seminary run by the aptly named Matilda Manners was secured for Helen at a fee of thirty guineas per annum, plus two guineas for washing, ostensibly to complete her education.

Robert had other ideas, however, and at his request academic pursuits tended to play second fiddle, with Miss Manners concentrating on such topics as elocution, deportment, etiquette and other social skills which were a prerequisite if one was to be accepted by the upper echelons of society. It was very much a forerunner to the finishing schools which sprung up in the second half of the century.

Whenever they were in residence, the Blakes attended St Mary's Church in nearby Slaugham each Sunday, becoming very friendly with Rev. Robert Ellison whom they often entertained at their home. The deeds of Handcross required a tithe to be paid to the church and, as was usual at that time, this levy was paid in kind. A great tithe-barn for storing the Rector's dues stood close to the rectory.

Rev. Ellison died in July 1839, after which the couple's relationship with his successor William Sergison became distinctly cooler, as could be seen by the formality of a notice sent by Robert's agent twelve months later.

July 21ˢᵗ 1840. I am instructed by R. D. Blake, Esq., to inform you that the tithes of hay on his land in the Parish of Slaugham will be set out for you in the usual way the mowers being now at work cutting down the grass. I am, your obedient servant, John Pierce.

What caused the breakdown is unknown but it was further evidenced fourteen years later, in 1854, when Sergison's plans to make alterations to the church were thwarted by a faculty that had been granted to Robert (probably in exchange for a substantial donation) in March 1829 by Robert Carr, Bishop of Chichester. The faculty conferred to Handcross House one pew in the north-east corner of the nave and one on the south side of the main body of the church.

Three years later, in August 1857, a Court of Inquiry was convened in the St Michael in Lewes Church to determine if

HANDCROSS HOUSE
From a contemporary sketch

the then Bishop, Ashurst Gilbert, could revoke the faculty. This failed due to opposition from various quarters including Helen, on behalf of herself and 'future occupiers of Handcross House'.

Helen was very keen to please Robert and realising the importance of her schooling, threw herself into learning the ways of the gentry with relish. During the first term, their coachman would be waiting at the seminary entrance on Friday afternoons to take her back to Handcross, around twenty-five miles away, for the weekend. Helen then decided to remain at the school for the whole of the term, taking extra tuition during the weekends and immersing herself totally in her social studies.

During this period the couple rarely went to the town house in London. Robert knew just how imperative it was that she should be confident in the ways of the upper classes before being introduced into the pretentious social circles of the capital. Without the proper training she would soon be found out and with no second chance to make a good first impression, this would see her shunned by the other ladies. He was determined that would not happen.

We are the only real aristocracy in the world:
the aristocracy of money.
– George Bernard Shaw

During their first meeting in Castlebar, Robert had been surprised by how bright and worldly wise Helen was for a country girl. He now discovered she was also a fast learner. After less than eighteen months at the school, they were both confident she was ready to make her grand entrance. To him she had always been a beautiful young girl, but now she had become a beautiful and sophisticated lady, and the perfect excuse for a *soirée* was just six weeks away.

Having sent Mrs May, the housekeeper, on ahead with their trunks, the couple left Handcross at the beginning of July and moved in to Adam Street where Robert contacted his old friend Sir Thomas Baring once again. This time he sought his help in preparing a guest list comprising the cream of London society, before having invitations individually inscribed by a calligraphist and hand delivered by his coachman.

Gossip circulated around London every bit as fast as rural Ireland and curiosity was rife on Sunday 19th August 1821, one month after the coronation of George IV (from which his estranged wife Caroline of Brunswick was infamously turned away, three weeks before her death), when they welcomed their guests to celebrate Helen's twenty-first birthday.

Whether this was in fact her birthday, or she had simply plucked a date from the ether, is a matter of conjecture, but whatever the truth it made no difference to the enjoyment or success of the evening, which served its purpose in launching her into the social circles of the capital.

Robert had concentrated on quality rather than quantity so it was a comparatively small affair in terms of numbers, but huge in terms of influence with the fifty or so guests being la crème de la crème of British society. These were indisputably the movers and shakers of their time.

Miss Manners' Seminary had certainly done its job; Helen's posture was impeccable, her confidence unquestionable, and whilst elocution lessons may have softened her accent, she had lost none of her personality or her charm. She was different, she was fun, her smile lit up the room, she was the centre of attention and the guests could not get enough of her.

Nothing had been left to chance, from the carefully selected guest list to the best French wines and the finest tea from the Far East. Housekeeper Rosie May had brought in extra help to ensure everything ran smoothly, and had excelled herself with a sumptuous array of food.

Helen's dress was a masterpiece, exclusively designed by Geraldine Bailey, a young dressmaker who had trained in Paris and whose talents were in high demand amongst the ladies of the aristocracy. Tonight she looked exquisite in a stunning pale green satin evening dress with the figure hugging high-waisted regency style of the day, a 'festoon flounce' caught up with rosettes, and sleeves made of fine net clasped all the way to the wrist.

Tall, elegant, beautiful, with still just enough of a hint of the Irish brogue to make her both alluring and mysterious in equal measures, everybody wanted to speak to the General's young wife. Helen knew how to hold their attention and to keep them guessing, not revealing any information about her background. It was not long before the couple were the toast of London becoming what, in the twenty-first century, we would call 'A' list celebrities.

Whenever they came 'up to town', the pair found themselves in great demand and added a touch of glamour and levity to the lavish parties and balls held throughout the city, including the palatial homes of Piccadilly and Mayfair such as Burlington House, Devonshire House and Bath House, home of the Barons Ashburton where the ballroom comfortably accommodated in excess of five hundred guests.

That the Blake family were wealthy is unquestionable. The source of Robert's personal wealth, however, has never been fully explained and raises many questions.

Robert's grandfather, Sir Francis Blake, possessed estates in Northumberland covering thousands of acres, including the Twizel Castle estate which he inherited in 1717. Together with Robert's father, also Francis, he moved out of the crumbling castle seventeen years later and into nearby Tilmouth House, embarking on a costly and ambitious project to build a new five-storey Gothic revival mansion on the Twizel site, designed by architect James Nesbit from across the border in Kelso.

Some forty years later the project was abandoned, still unfinished. Described as an experimental philosopher, Sir Francis was a Fellow of the Royal Society, High Sheriff of Northumberland and took an active part in the defeat of Bonnie Prince Charlie's Jacobite rising for which, in 1774, he was rewarded with a Baronetcy.

Six years later Robert's father inherited the Baronetcy and the various estates, which he added to with the purchase of sixteen hundred acres around the village of Duddo, four miles from Twizel. Following in his father's footsteps, he went on to be knighted and to be appointed High Sheriff of Northumberland.

When he died in 1808 he left a complex ten page will, plus four codicils totalling a further eight pages, the net result of which was that Robert received a total of sixteen thousand pounds (the equivalent of approximately one point three million in 2018). It was a significant inheritance and one which could have seen the couple live out their lives in comfort and style. It does not, however, account for the huge fortune left behind when Robert and Helen died.

On the completion of the six months leave he had taken to marry Helen, Robert chose to be put on 'Irish Half Pay' by the army. This meant he was no longer attached to a regiment, but was allowed to maintain his rank, effectively making him a reserve officer with plenty of time on his hands. How he used that time and exactly how he amassed such wealth remains a mystery.

One report suggests he owned a shipping line where the ships included the *Blake* and the *Sheridan*, but this has never been substantiated. There are no records of any other business ventures. There were spurious reports in American newspapers that he made his fortune variously in California and Ohio, which

HELEN BLAKE
1800 – 1876

Portrait by Clive O'Sullivan

ROBERT DUDLEY BLAKE
1774 – 1850

Portrait by Clive O'Sullivan

can be dismissed due to the fact that he never even set foot on that continent.

Records do show the couple built a substantial property portfolio, not all of which produced income. For their personal use, in addition to Handcross House, the couple maintained the town house in Adam Street. For summer breaks, they had a seaside retreat in Queen's Park, Brighton, a development inspired by Regent's Park in London. Here, as they joined those strolling on the promenade, Robert would change his uniform for a striped blazer and boater whilst Helen's only concession to the sunshine was a parasol. They owned at least two properties in Camberwell, which is now within Greater London but was then part of Surrey, and three cottages in the Handcross area, but again, these would not have produced anywhere near the sort of wealth they accumulated.

When they decided to lease the house in Adam Street in 1846, they replaced it with the purchase of numbers 8 & 9 St George's Place, keeping one for their own use and leasing the other. Six years before her death, Helen, who was now living in another of their properties in Earl's Terrace, had both houses demolished and rebuilt. In doing so she had the aspect changed by moving the front to the other side of the building where they became 15 & 17 Knightsbridge. The first occupant of No. 17 was Byron's son-in-law, the Earl of Lovelace, whilst No. 15 was later let to the Baden-Powell family. Both properties have now been combined and in the final year of the twentieth century became home to the Libyan embassy.

From what we can gather, it seems their marriage was a singularly happy one and life in Handcross was idyllic. Helen took a real interest in the garden and often got her hands dirty working alongside the gardener, particularly in the vegetable garden. Perhaps it reminded her of her childhood and her time in Castlebar.

Their support of the church and various local charities made them very popular in the community and although they remained socially active during their time in the country, it was by no means as frenetic as the London scene. Dinner parties for six to eight people or music evenings and parlour games in the drawing room, with reciprocal visits to the other country houses in the area two or three times a month was the extent of it.

There was great joy followed by great sadness when shortly after her twenty-third birthday Helen gave birth to a baby boy who, woefully, lived for less than forty-eight hours. The rest of that year was a very sorrowful time in the Blake household. In the following spring, however, she appeared to get a 'second wind' and threw herself back into the social scene with renewed vigour.

In the spring of 1824 Helen was one of a handful of women present when the couple attended a meeting in the City of London Tavern on Bishopsgate. Archbishop of Canterbury, Dr Charles Manners-Sutton, presided over the meeting at which Sir William Hillary announced the founding of the Royal National Institution for the Preservation of Life from Shipwreck, later to become the RNLI. We will never know, but perhaps it was this meeting that prompted her to support the institution so generously at the end of her life.

It was unusual for ladies to frequent such establishments but in this case, the tavern itself was also unusual. Built on the Tontine principal (a forerunner of crowd funding) it was huge, with a frontage measuring eighty feet wide and seventy feet high. It was recognised throughout the capital for its sumptuous food prepared by a team of up to forty chefs and cooks led by Craig Francis who had spent two years working with Antonin Carême – known as *Le Roi des Chefs et les Chef des Rois*, or 'The King of Chefs and the Chef of Kings' – when he was Chef de Cuisine of the Prince Regent.

The ballroom on the top floor held many banquets, including Robert's regimental dinner, for up to three hundred *feasters*, "exclusively of accommodating one hundred and fifty ladies as spectators in the galleries at each end". The basement was home to barrels of porter, pipes of port, butts of sherry, plus the finest of wines from Cape Colony (South Africa), Hungary and France including twelve hundred bottles of champagne and between six and seven hundred dozen claret. It also housed as much as two tons of live turtles, over a ton of which was consumed at one dinner in 1808.

This was a time when the poor struggled to find enough food to keep them alive whilst gluttony was rife amongst the upper classes. At one banquet given by the Mayor of York in honour of Prince Albert, Chef Alexis Soyer prepared what became known as the 'hundred guinea dish'. Five turtle heads and no less than three hundred poultry and birds including snipe, larks and ortolans were amongst the ingredients. To put this into perspective, one hundred guineas is the equivalent of over ten thousand pounds in 2018 terms.

It was at the RNLI meeting the couple first met Sir William Wilberforce, widely credited with being responsible for the abolition of slavery, with whom they forged a close friendship over the next few years. They were amongst those invited to attend his funeral in Westminster Abbey at the beginning of August 1833.

Helen learned to ride on their extensive grounds and used her new found skill to explore the beautiful countryside of Sussex with Robert. Although both were members of Lord St Leonards' Tilgate Hunt, she did not take an active part in the chase.

Like most of the upper classes (referred to in such terms, Helen said she often had to pinch herself to make sure it was not just a dream) they were keen followers of horse racing and would often attend meetings on nearby Epsom Downs, including the famed Derby. They were in the owners' enclosure in 1826 when their friend and regular house guest George Wyndham, Earl of Egremont, had the winning horse, *Lap Dog*.

The majority of 1832 was spent in Handcross, avoiding London where there was an outbreak of cholera which, having spread from the East End, was responsible for the deaths of over three thousand people. By the end of the year it had spread throughout the country killing almost fifty-five thousand.

Prize fighting, although illegal, was very popular with the British establishment and supported by the very highest echelons of society, including the Prince Regent (the future King George IV). It was definitely the place to be seen for the wealthy and the social climbers of the day, and the sense of danger appealed to Helen.

The last fight they attended was in May 1833 when Irish champion Simon Byrne, the *Emerald Gem*, fought James *Deaf* Burke for the English championship. The match is said to have lasted an astonishing three hours and sixteen minutes with ninety-nine rounds. Burke won the match and Byrne died three days later.

The Adelphi theatre was little more than a stone's throw from their Adam Street house and they were also regulars at the

Theatre Royal and Sadler's Wells, where Helen is said to have 'laughed heartily' at the comedian and clown Joseph Grimaldi.

Invitations abounded making them frequent guests at many of London's major events such as Trooping the Colour and the Royal Academy Summer Exhibition, where they were part of a select group invited to a private viewing before the public were admitted. In 1830 they were guests of their friend Sir John Key at a sumptuous banquet held in London's Guildhall following his inauguration as Lord Mayor of London.

26

Beware, so long as you live, of judging
men by their outward appearance.
– Jean de la Fontaine

Robert returned to his military career in 1822, joining
the Army of City of Westminster which, aside from
soldiering, served to widen their social circle and
opened many doors, particularly in government corridors.
Throughout his career, he appears to have served in regiments
that were absent from major conflicts such as the 1812 War in
the USA or the Hundred Days War in France; in fact, there is
no record of him ever being engaged in battle.

This would appear to indicate that he may not have 'walked
the walk', but he certainly 'talked the talk' and was meticulous
about his appearance. He was a regular visitor to the military
outfitters in Savile Row and his civilian suits, rarely worn, were
made by master tailor Thomas Hawkes at 17 Piccadilly.

Life was good but it was not without controversy and Robert
was engaged in more than one court battle over wills, including
his Mother's. The Dowager Lady Blake had died in March 1827

leaving the bulk of her estate to Robert's sister, Ann Stag, and and he sought, unsuccessfully, to have the will overturned in both the Ecclesiastical Court and the Prerogative Court claiming it was a forgery.

Though his efforts were to no avail, three years later he was back in court. This time he was being summonsed for non-payment of twelve pounds sixteen shillings and four pence in costs. The sum involved in the original case was a not inconsiderable six thousand pounds, which perhaps he needed to fund his purchase of yet another commission. His final promotion was on 10th January 1837, the year Queen Victoria ascended to the throne, when he became a full General before retiring later in the same year.

Tuesday 21st September 1841 saw the opening of the final section of the London to Brighton railway, with Robert and Helen amongst the invited passengers on the inaugural service from Haywards Heath, close to Handcross. There was great excitement amongst those on board when, less than ten minutes into the journey, they crossed the River Ouse by means of a ninety-six feet high, quarter-of-a-mile long viaduct, which provided commanding views over the surrounding countryside. With a stop at the new Hassocks Gate station en route, they were in Brighton a little over forty minutes later, a journey that would normally have taken them anything up to three hours in their horse drawn carriage.

The following year was an unhappy one for the couple and their wealthy acquaintances with the introduction by Robert Peel's government of the Income Tax Act 1842, designed to halt a growing deficit in the budget. It was the first time income tax had been payable in peace time. The rate was seven pence in the pound (2.9%) on all income over one hundred and fifty pounds per annum.

One of the many times they attended events in the presence of Prince Albert was in 1844, when he opened the exclusive British and Foreign Institute, which they both later joined as life members. The Institute was founded by adventurer and writer James Silk and provided yet another opportunity for Robert and Helen to mix with the cream of society. Fellow members included Rip Van Winkle author Washington Irving, a sprinkling of Dukes and Earls, Knights of the Realm, Members of Parliament, Bishops and Admirals.

Life membership for a couple cost seventy guineas for those residing in London within seven miles of the General Post Office, close to St Paul's Cathedral, which included Adam Street. Robert quite cleverly gave his address as Handcross House, a distance of more than twenty one miles which qualified them for country membership at a much lower twenty-five guineas (over three thousand pounds in 2018).

The fact that the life members included a number of clergymen prepared to pay up to six and a half thousand pounds in 2018 terms, would appear to indicate that the financial arrangements of the church were very different in those days.

The institute's premises, on Hanover Square, provided the ideal venue for a lavish party in September to celebrate Robert and Helen's silver wedding anniversary, attended by 'anybody who was anybody'. Just six years later, in the year of the Great Exhibition, Robert was struck down with paralysis on New Year's Day, although it is not known to what extent.

In the ensuing weeks he deteriorated rapidly, developing a fever, chest pains and a consistent dry cough; he was also having great difficulty breathing, even when he was lying down. There was nothing his doctor could do for him and on Thursday 7th February 1850, with Helen at his bedside, he died at home in Handcross House at the age of seventy-four.

Cause of death was established as 'paralysis leading to effusion into chest' – what today is known as a pleural effusion, or fluid on the lungs. Initially buried locally in the graveyard of Slaugham Church, Robert's body was moved twelve months later and reinterred in a vault Helen had prepared for him in the church graveyard in Norham, a small village just three miles from Twizel Castle.

According to Sir Michael Blake, 3rd Baronet of Tilmouth Park and grand-nephew of Robert, the vault was closed in 1915 and nothing is left of it now except four yew trees and a marking stone. The ruins of the castle have now been designated as a scheduled ancient monument and a Grade II listed building, meaning they are protected by law.

There was some considerable consternation concerning his will, written twenty years earlier, when it was found he had left his entire estate to Helen, specifically excluding all and any of the Blake family from any part of his estate. The poor Irish country girl was now an extremely wealthy widow.

Ten years later Robert's brother, Sir Francis, died a widower and, as a Thank You to Helen who had helped to bring up his illegitimate son, Frederick, left her a sizeable portion of his estate, adding to her ever increasing wealth. Francis also had a, none too popular, connection to Ireland when, as a Colonel in the British army, he was engaged in various skirmishes with Wexfordmen during the rebellion of 1798.

The couple had been happily married for over thirty years and Robert's death hit Helen very hard. Although she remained in Sussex for a little over two years after his burial she rarely ventured outside the house during that time except to travel to Norham with his coffin, and to attend church on their wedding anniversary.

In March 1852, leaving housekeeper Rosie May and her husband to take care of the property, she moved out of their beloved Handcross House and into their original town house at 19 Adam Street where the tenant's lease had recently expired, taking at least one of her servants, seventeen year old Catherine Baily, with her.

Later that year she bought a smaller and more manageable house at 4 Earls Terrace in Kensington from a Mr Bella, where her neighbours included writers George du Maurier and Walter Pater. 'Smaller and more manageable' is relative of course. Unquestionably smaller than Handcross House and Adam Street, it none the less occupied five floors, and boasted all 'mod cons' including gas lighting, a mains water supply and a water closet. In this instance, 'mod cons' is also a relative term; like every part of London, the water supply was intermittent at best and was very often severely polluted leading to the common practice of paying servants 'beer money' in addition to their wages – it was safer to drink beer than water!

The house was connected to the public sewers which flowed directly into the Thames and were believed to be the cause of cholera outbreaks that resulted in over thirty thousand deaths. The final straw was the so-called Great Stink of 1858, which caused a foul smell that permeated throughout London, including Parliament.

"The intense heat had driven our legislators from those portions of their building which overlook the river. A few members, indeed, bent on investigating the matter to its very depth, ventured into the library, but were instantaneously driven to retreat, each man with a handkerchief to his nose".

Parliament's first response was to dip the curtains in a mixture of chloride and lime to hide the stench but when that did not work the members quickly approved a major overhaul of the city's sewerage system.

Although now living in one of the most fashionable, and most expensive, parts of the capital (in the first decade of the 21st century, Earls Terrace was reported as being the most expensive street in London), Helen appears to have retreated from public life and withdrawn from all social activity.

It is not known if this was entirely through choice, or if invitations for an elderly widow were fewer than those for a vibrant young couple or a General who, resplendent in his full dress uniform, would add a touch of glamour to any event. Instead, she found new pursuits which she believed befitted her new role as a widow.

Prior to her move to London, she had disposed of her carriage and dismissed her coachman. Now, in the summer she would frequently take a hansom cab to Hyde Park and sit beside the Serpentine, idling away the hours just watching the ducks on the water, the people strolling by, and the horses exercising on Rotten Row.

As she continued to build her fortune she became ever more possessive of it and her frugality was evident in every aspect of her life. She had reduced her household staff to what she considered to be the absolute minimum of three and although she still took a lukewarm bath once or twice a month, washed her hair in diluted ammonia every few months and had her undergarments washed regularly, she paid less attention to the condition of the house. Her bedroom and the drawing room were reasonably well kept but elsewhere the house was filthy. The worst of the smell was obscured by the liberal use of ambergris scent; made from a sperm whale's intestines.

On 27th September each year Helen marked their wedding anniversary by attending church at St Martin-in-the-Fields in Trafalgar Square. She would instruct the Hansom cab to wait for her until the service was over, and then proceed to the former Mivart's Hotel for lunch. Having amalgamated with the smaller Claridge's Hotel next door, the name had now been changed to the one which has since become a byword for luxury.

It was a routine she varied only once. In 1869 she marked what would have been their golden wedding anniversary by travelling to Norham and attending a service in St Cuthbert's. She travelled alone by coach, reversing the route the couple had taken on their journey from Edinburgh fifty years earlier. By this time she was quite frail and had made the journey against her doctor's advice. It took a great deal out of her and on her return to London she was confined to bed for a month.

In the years before her death she would often take the recently opened underground Metropolitan District Railway from South Kensington to Westminster. There she sat in the new ladies gallery in the House of Commons, watching parliamentary proceedings through the iron grills that served the dual purpose of preventing any falls, and keeping the ladies away from the main body of the building.

During those visits she is also known to have strolled on the newly built Westminster Bridge, completed in May 1862 by Thames Ironworks, coincidentally the company that some years later would be responsible for building the lifeboat bearing her name.

Helen continued to add to her property portfolio with various purchases after Robert's death. On Sunday 13th July 1862 her agent, Thomas Mason, travelled from Coldstream, across the Scottish border, to attend a sale on her behalf at the Queen's Hotel in Newcastle, the hotel where forty-five years earlier Sir Humphry Davy had been wined and dined to celebrate his invention of the miner's safety lamp. On sale were the Twizel and Riffington estates, which had belonged to Robert's brother, Sir Francis.

Bidding started at thirty thousand pounds (the equivalent of three and a half million in 2018), eventually ending at thirty-five thousand after Mason outbid David Robertson who owned an estate on the other side of the River Tweed.

The lonely widow had been unwell for some years when, on Saturday 23rd September 1876, she ate some contaminated salmon which caused massive vomiting. Although not diagnosed as such, this was probably scombroid food poisoning.

Contaminated fish, and many other foods, was not uncommon in the Victorian era and one noted cookery writer of the time even suggested that pyroligneous acid, or wood vinegar, could be used to sweeten tainted fish, "when the taint is but slight". When the fish is in a worse state she suggested that chloride of soda, a form of bleach, would have more effect because of its powerful anti-putrescent properties. The famous HP Sauce, invented later in the century, was said to have

Typical 19ᵗʰ century cottage in the West of Ireland

FROM THERE TO HERE

4 Earls Terrace (in the 21ˢᵗ century)

gained popularity because of its ability to hide the taste of spoiled food.

As she became more and more exhausted from the vomiting, Helen could feel the energy draining from her body and it became clear to her the end was near. Her will had been drafted some three years earlier but had never been signed so her manservant, James Burke, was instructed to summon Mr King, her solicitor, from his office in Cannon Street.

It would be another twelve months before the telephone was introduced to London so Burke had to make a round trip of almost twelve miles in a hansom cab through the crowded and chaotic streets of the city and, unfortunately, Mr King did not arrive until about an hour after she had died. He went through all the papers in the house to see if any other will existed but was unable to find one, meaning she had died intestate.

The Crown would now take possession of her entire estate, valued in the region of one hundred and forty thousand pounds (equivalent to almost sixteen million in 2018).

Exactly one week later she was buried, in accordance with her wishes, alongside her husband in Norham, where the funeral service was conducted by Rev. Joseph Waite. There is no record of who attended the funeral or what it entailed but at a cost of £163.10.5 (sixteen and a half thousand pounds in 2018 values) it must have been a fairly lavish affair.

CHAPTER

27

Greed is a bottomless pit which exhausts the
person without ever reaching satisfaction.
– Erich Fromm

With such a vast sum of money involved, it did not take long before the claims started pouring in from a miscellaneous assortment of people in every corner of the globe, all proclaiming their relationship to Helen. There were supposed aunts, uncles, nephews, nieces, cousins; in fact everything except parents and siblings and although none of these were successful, each one added to the growing legend, and probably encouraged others to try their hand.

Over the years the claims slowly fizzled out but the mystery of Helen and her money never really went away. Indeed, it is often said that there may still be Sheridans somewhere in Ireland who are related and could, therefore, be entitled to a share of the legendary 'Blake Millions'. All they have to do is what nobody else has managed so far. Provide compelling documentary evidence.

The press had a field day with theories, assumptions, specula-
tions and, in some cases, pure guesses. One of the earliest reports
came in June 1877 from Joseph Cockerill, London correspondent for a number of American papers including the *Cincinnati
Enquirer* where he wrote: "On a recent visit to her late residence,
which is a curiosity, she having been both a miser and a collector
of eccentricities, I had occasion to be impressed that there is a
branch of her family in Ohio or Maryland". He also stated that
she, "… seems to have lived a solitary and squalid life midst
wealthy surroundings".

Quite how he came to visit to her house, and how such a visit
nine months after her death would have revealed this information, is something of a mystery in itself and the writer offered
no explanation for his assertions.

With over five hundred miles between Ohio and Maryland,
he appears to have been clutching at straws in order to make
the story relevant to his readers and no proof has ever been
forthcoming about a branch of her family in either state, or any
other part of the USA.

A few months later the same correspondent wrote another
piece in which he claimed to have received "over one hundred
and thirty-six letters" (one hundred and thirty-seven perhaps?)
"from claimants in Illinois, Indiana, Montana, California,
Maryland, Pennsylvania, Ohio, New Jersey, New York and
Washington DC". Perhaps in the belief that people will believe
whatever they are told, he also incorrectly stated that Helen was
eighty when she died.

For some time prior to her death her frugality had been
obvious to all and sundry so there was indeed some truth in
the statement about her being miserly. Perhaps this goes some

way to explain Helen's apparent lack of contact with anybody in Ireland during her six decades in London.

Embracing her new life, it would appear she put her past well and truly behind her, forgetting about her origins and about those she had left behind. Such neglect would have been especially sad during the Great Famine when an insignificant portion of her wealth could have made the difference between life and death for her family and relations who, like everybody else in the country, would have been enduring tremendous hardship and deprivation.

In November 1884, Waterford born MP Thomas Sexton raised questions in the House of Commons concerning a 'card' that had been found amongst Helen's papers in which she described herself as, "the daughter of William L Sheridan Esq. of Baltimore, USA and Galway, Ireland" (very different to the story she told Robert when they first met). Sexton wanted to know why a claimant to her estate, William P Sheridan of Galway, had failed to satisfy the authorities of his relationship to Helen, but was told the matter had been decided judicially and Parliament could not interfere.

There were, and still are, cynics who believe the reason this, and many of the other claims, was rejected by the Treasury had more to do with the huge sum that had been added to their coffers than the lack of evidence provided by the claimants.

Huge pressure was heaped on the Treasury to provide details and explanations surrounding the rebuttal of so many claims. Perhaps to counter this and appease the dissenters, it was decided that some grants should be made from Helen's estate, reflecting bequests made in her unsigned will.

Just over a year after his initial question in the House of Commons, Sexton obtained a parliamentary return showing the names of organisations and people to whom those grants had been made and on St Patrick's Day 1886, exactly sixty-seven years since Helen had first seen Robert in the dining room in Castlebar, various newspapers published details of the grants (shown opposite).

The sums involved may appear small, until you realise that one hundred pounds in 1876 is the equivalent of over eleven thousand in 2018. Edward Langford, who received five hundred pounds, was an old friend of Robert and Helen who had lived close to them in Sussex before moving to Norwood (now in South London). In 1850 Helen called on him to make arrangements for Robert's funeral and had then relied on him to sort out her affairs in the ensuing months.

Both Edward and his wife, Marian Isabella, remained on close terms with Helen who again summoned them by telegram when she realised she was dying. Mr King, the solicitor, asked the couple to remain in the house in Earl's Terrace to ensure the safety of her jewellery and other valuables.

They stayed there for three months "… at the cost of great inconvenience to themselves and amidst much discomfort at the first owing to the state of the house". The preceding quote is from a claim the Edwards' later made for the ground rents of the properties in St George's Place, which they claimed Helen had promised to them on a number of occasions. The claim was dismissed.

William and Charlotte Rovery were tenants in one of the cottages near Handcross and it must be assumed the legacy was for some service they had carried out for the Blakes. As so-called peasants, one hundred pounds would have been an enormous amount of money to them.

PAYMENTS MADE FROM HELEN BLAKE'S ESTATE

The O'Connor Don MP	£2,000.00.0
Lewis Llewelyn Dillwyn MP	£2,000.00.0
Edward Edwards Langford	£ 500.00.0
Henrietta Louise Browne	£ 500.00.0
Hon John Paul & Anne Methuen	£ 100.00.0
Sophia & George William Cave	£ 100.00.0
Executors of Rev W M Ellison	£ 100.00.0
William & Charlotte Rovery	£ 100.00.0
Rev James Stewart	£ 125.00.0
William Stewart	£ 125.00.0
Mary Stewart	£ 125.00.0
Annie Stewart	£ 125.00.0
Royal National Lifeboat Institution	£6,400.00.0
Royal Society for Protection of Life from Fire	£1,000.00.0
Trinity College,	
Blake Natural History Scholarship	£3,000.00.0
St George's Hospital, Knightsbridge	£ 100.00.0
Shipwrecked Fishermen & Mariners RBS	£1,000.00.0
Annuity of £50 for Miss Hudson	£ 275.12.6

To the following railway companies for benefit of Irish railway employees, £2,000, divided among these companies, according to the number of members in their benefit societies: Great Northern Railway Company of Ireland, Dublin Wicklow and Wexford Railway Company, Midland Great Western of Ireland Railway Company, Great Southern and Western Railway Company Ireland, Waterford and Limerick Railway Company, Belfast and Northern Counties Railway.

The Miss Hudson, who was provided with an annuity, was eighty year old Eliza Hester Hudson, a tenant in one of Helen's houses in Camberwell (then in Surrey and now a London borough) who had apparently known her as a friend for almost half a century.

There is no record of who the other recipients were, with two exceptions, the inclusion of which raised a number of questions in the press. Why were the largest individual legacies left to two Members of Parliament? What was their connection to the Blake family? Both gentlemen claimed they had never seen or heard of Helen and the first knowledge they had of her was by way of formal communication from the Treasury, informing them of their huge windfall, valued at over two hundred thousand pounds each in 2018.

The reputation of politicians in the nineteenth century was little different to that of today so it came as no surprise to anybody to hear that their lack of knowledge did not prevent them from accepting the money.

Was it possible they had also performed some service for the Blakes in the past, something that may have helped the couple in the acquisition of their wealth? Or was it simply, as some speculated at the time, that Helen developed an admiration of the gentlemen in question as she filled her hours watching debates in Parliament? Whilst either answer is feasible, it is a question to which we will never know the answer.

The O'Connor Don (Charles Owen O'Connor) who was the Member of Parliament for Roscommon, about forty miles from Claremorris, had inherited his title as head of the O'Connor clan and was said to have been a descendant of the High Kings of Ireland. After losing his seat in 1880 he stood, unsuccessfully, as a candidate for Wexford.

Lewis Llewelyn Dillwyn was the MP for Swansea. Prior to the 1892 election, after thirty seven years in Parliament, he was deselected by his local constituency in favour of an anti-Irish Home Rule candidate; he died two weeks later. Both men were members of Gladstone's ruling Liberal party.

Whilst it is no proof, the fact that fifty eight percent of the total went to Ireland – the money for the RNLI was to provide two lifeboats to be stationed in Ireland – does appear to indicate that her origins were indeed in the Emerald Isle.

It is not clear why thirty eight percent went to maritime charities but again it is an indication, this time that she may have had some connection with the sea or with coastal communities. Claremorris and Castlebar were only twenty miles or so from the sea and she would certainly have been aware of boating tragedies in the area; she may even have known people who were lost at sea.

If, as claimed in Leo O'Toole's book, she was born at sea, that would certainly be a good reason, but with no firm evidence, like everything else connected with Helen, all we can do is speculate as to her motives.

It soon became evident that many of the journalists writing about Helen subscribed to the old adage that you should 'never let the truth get in the way of a good story'. The *Melbourne Age*, in August 1896 claimed that Helen's sister married an Irish policeman and then emigrated to Australia where he rose to be a Member of Parliament. No name was given.

The same paper also incorrectly reported that the Right Honourable W. E. Gladstone had received one thousand pounds from Helen's will. Various American papers described Robert as a Scottish Captain who had met Helen in Westmeath and arranged for her to be sent away to school before marrying her some years later.

In 1888, the *Maitland Mercury*, another Australian newspaper, stated that after his marriage Robert was disowned by the Blake family. It went on to publish a much repeated story which suggested Robert left the army as a result of the alleged family disagreement and the couple moved to Mansfield, Ohio where they established a large millinery business. It seems the journalist who initiated this story was unaware that Mansfield was little more than a settlement at the time which would have struggled to support a millinery, or any other, business capable of generating anywhere near the wealth the couple amassed.

Without saying how or where, another newspaper, The *San Francisco Call*, made a wild claim that Robert had amassed his fortune in California. Neither paper produced any evidence of their claims, which is not really surprising as they are completely at odds with both his official military records and land registry entries, which show he remained in England until his death. As mentioned earlier, yet another report declares him to have been a shipping magnate with two of his ships named *Blake* and *Sheridan*.

June 1903 saw a claim from Edward Gleeson, proprietor of the Monster Clothing Store in Adelaide who "had not the slightest doubt" that Mrs Blake was his grandmother's sister as he had "… often heard his grandmother speak of her" (what more proof could anyone possibly require?).

Reported in *The Advertiser*, the article went on to say "Mrs Blake's maiden name was Anne Sheridan" and that Robert was a lieutenant when they eloped. At least they were correct about the couple eloping so on this occasion one out of three will have to suffice!

In the same year, Melbourne solicitor Thomas W Lloyd wrote to various newspapers in Australia and New Zealand warning readers about letters from fraudsters offering to help them make a claim on the estate. This was no wild assertion as he stated that shortly after Helen's death he was instructed in connection with the estate but found there was no next-of-kin.

He omitted to mention by whom he had been instructed, but he did go on to say the Blakes had emigrated to the USA where they had a millinery business, with Robert returning to England when he knew he was dying – after first making a will leaving everything to Helen – and passed away shortly after his homecoming.

Lloyd also repeated the earlier claim that Gladstone had benefitted from Helen's will. With such glaring errors, and obvious lack of research, it is hardly surprising he was unable to help whoever had been foolish enough to instruct him in the first place.

The *Pittsburgh Press* was one of a number of newspapers that told the story of a retired Indian civil servant by the name of J. D. B. Gribble – a member of the East Indian Service Club in St James' Square, no less – who would be looking for heirs, assisted in his investigations by his private secretary J. K. Lamont, a member of the "Scotch College of Heralds". (James Keir Lamont was a Scottish Officer of Arms at the Court of the Lord Lyon where he became Bute Pursuivant in June 1899. He was deprived of office on 18 May 1901 following what appears to be bankruptcy and went on to become Assistant Librarian at Aberdeen University. He died in Bournemouth in 1931, aged sixty two.)

Having spent some time in Ireland searching parish registers without success, Gribble decided to venture forth to America saying he was "going to all this trouble mainly for the fun of the thing", his interest having been piqued by the long standing mystery. He also mentioned an old friend he had met in India who thought he too had a right to a share and requested him to look into it on his behalf.

In the following year another civil servant with the British Colonial Office in India, Mr Quirke, returned to England to make a claim on behalf of an ex-soldier in the Indian army named Sheridan, and a year later a German woman claimed she was entitled to a share of the estate after being informed of her unexpected good fortune by a clairvoyant. Perhaps the clairvoyant should have foreseen the need for documentary evidence before sending her on a wild goose chase.

CHAPTER

28

Be able to notice all the confusion between
fact and opinion that appears in the news.
— Marilyn vos Savant

In the UK, there was resurgence in interest in Helen's estate in May 1909 when Frederick Blake, the illegitimate son of Sir Francis whom Helen had helped to raise, died at his home in Crawley just a few miles from Handcross. Having served as an officer in the British army, he was invalided out with severe sunstroke some years earlier. Like Helen, he had died intestate with his estate of forty three thousand pounds, equivalent to around five million in 2018, going to the Crown.

During the same year, the *Western People* newspaper in Ireland claimed that six years before her death, Helen had travelled to Galway to see her two sisters, whose husbands' names could unfortunately not be traced, and fell ill on her return journey. According to the report, she stayed for two months in Daly's Hotel, Tuam, where the coach had briefly stopped during her flight from Castlebar fifty years earlier.

Resuming her journey, she was apparently accompanied as far as Chester by a gentleman to whom she gave "an account of her birth, parentage and romantic career". Regrettably the paper did not share that account, or the gentleman's name, with its readers.

The same paper also reported a spurious declaration from Michael Feeney, a schoolteacher in Claremorris. He claimed to have found documents relating to Helen and her family in the Public Records Office, which established 'beyond doubt' the claims of two families of Sheridans in County Mayo who were descended from the brothers of Helen's father. Perhaps some doubt crept in later as nothing further was heard from Mr Feeney.

A London lawyer named McEvoy announced in the press that he was going to New York in 1912 to search for Pat Kileen, supposedly "somewhere in Kansas or Chicago". McEvoy said he was confident Pat's evidence would establish Helen's identity and validate the claim of an unnamed Mayo woman.

There are no reports as to whether Mr McEvoy crossed the Atlantic for his mammoth eighty-two thousand square mile search for an Irishman called Pat and, perhaps unsurprisingly, there are no records of any claim being submitted by him.

Towards the end of the same year ninety-four year old Frances Mead died a pauper in the Hackney workhouse in East London, where she had been an inmate for eight years, even though newspapers of the day stated unequivocally that she was entitled to a share of the millions. It appears the one thing which prevented any of these claims succeeding, like so many others before and since, was the fact that they were unable to provide any evidence of their relationship to Helen.

Helen was still in the news as late as 1982 when the *Irish Independent* ran an article over two days recounting her life and the many stories surrounding it. At that time fifty-three year old Dublin businessman Eamonn Sheridan was vainly researching his genealogical roots believing Helen was from a branch of the Sheridan family in Ballyheelan, County Westmeath, from which he and his eleven siblings were descended.

He had little hope of proving anything, however, due to an amazing touch of irony. One of his deceased relatives was reportedly part of the IRA group that, in 1921, set fire to Dublin's Four Courts building which housed the Public Records Office, reputedly destroying half the birth records of the country, including Helen's. If this is true, it would indicate that she was born into the Church of Ireland as Catholic birth records were not kept there.

One of the latest known claims materialised in 1932, over fifty-five years after Helen's death, and like so many before it came from Australia. On this occasion a firm of Adelaide solicitors were representing the Loxton family in River Murray, and their aunt, Margaret Muldoon, in Victoria. Mr A. C. Davis, who was handling the case for Badger & Badger Solicitors, was interviewed by *The Mail* which stated, "that all the evidence he had collected from England during the past four years appeared to establish the rights of the Australians to the fortune".

This claim included the contention that Helen had sailed to Australia "and on the voyage Capt. Blake became enamoured of her. The two eventually married and returned to England". A quick look at Robert and Helen's marriage certificate would have been enough to debunk this particular story so it is fortunate Mr Davis' said his evidence 'appeared' to establish their rights.

He badgered on for some time but needless to say, like so many before it, the claim was unsuccessful. This time the reason was not lack of evidence but the fact that, in nineteenth century parlance, it was utter poppycock!

Perhaps the Australians enjoyed a bit of poppycock because a couple of years previously, the *Catholic Press*, the self-proclaimed 'leading Catholic paper of Australia', published an entertaining piece of fantasy under the guise of fact. According to the article Robert was born in Knockfune, Co. Tipperary where he developed his skills as a marksman and hunter, keeping the family table well supplied with such delicacies as wild geese, plover and deer.

After obtaining a commission in the British Army, it went on, "the young Irishman so distinguished himself in the wars of the early nineteenth century that he rose rapidly in the service, finally retiring with the rank of Brigadier-General". The only thing in the whole article which could be described as factual was his name. I just hope the writer went to confession.

It is perhaps understandable that there were so many claims from the Antipodes and, although there were undoubtedly plenty of 'chancers', it would be quite reasonable to accept that many of them were made in good faith by people who genuinely believed they were relatives. During the first half of the nineteenth century, some forty thousand Irish men and women were transported to Australia and amongst those unfortunates there would unquestionably have been a good sprinkling of Sheridans.

Ireland has never been known for small families so it is quite conceivable that for every individual who was transported, there was an extended family of anything up to forty or fifty left behind, including a few Helens and Ellens and Eileens.

These would obviously have been talked about by the original 'convicts' as they reminisced with their children and grandchildren about life back home, and many of those stories would have quickly been brought back into focus as soon as details of the unclaimed millions emerged.

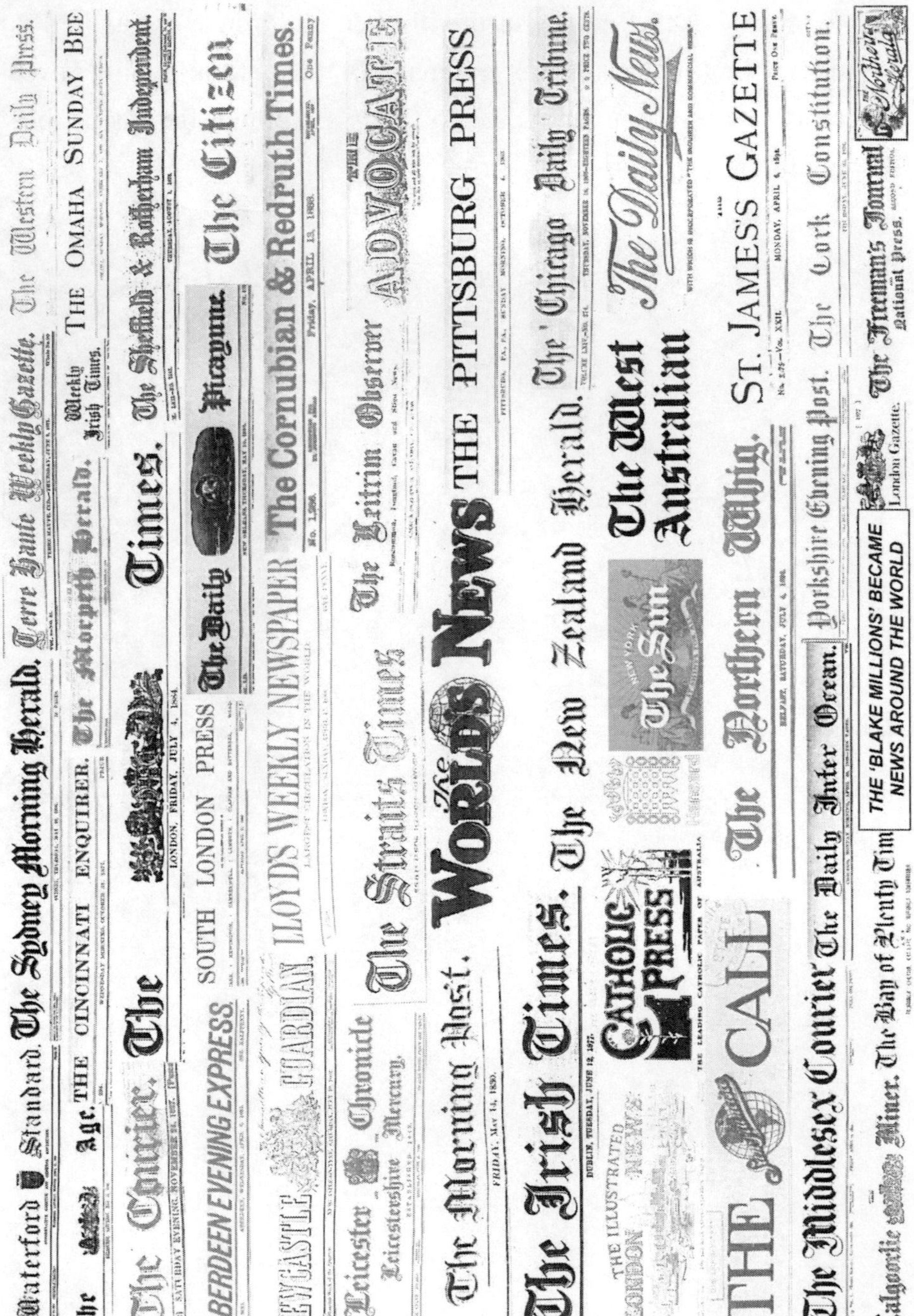

THE 'BLAKE MILLIONS' BECAME NEWS AROUND THE WORLD

chapter

29

Beware lest you lose the substance
by grasping at the shadow.
– Aesop

A merica had its fair share of claimants from both descendants of those who had fled the famine half a century earlier, crossing the Atlantic to make the new world their new home, and pure treasure hunters.

Lawrence Corcoran and his wife were undoubtedly dazzled by dollar signs after being informed that Mrs Corcoran was heiress to a large sum. The bearer of this good news appears to have been a Mr Gun of Kentish Town in London whom the press described as "an agent concerned in the case".

At the time, there were a number of so-called agents who were advertising in American papers for heirs to a host of British estates where people had died intestate and, whilst not wishing to unjustifiably besmirch the gentleman's good name, it is entirely possible that Mr Gun may have fallen into that category.

The advertisements were designed to attract responses from gullible readers who would then be told they had a claim, and be requested to send a retainer – in fact they were the forerunners to the email scams of today. The fraudsters played on the vulnerability of the poor; those on the bottom rung of society's ladder who would grasp at any hope of climbing up.

Mrs Corcoran said she discovered she was a first cousin of Helen, who was born in Longford, and went on to repeat the old story that Helen and Robert had established a millinery business in Ohio. The hapless couple were apparently in very poor circumstances and such news would obviously have been like manna from heaven to them. Reports say they "converted much of their meagre possessions into cash" and travelled from their California home to New Jersey where "detailed information was obtained which the Corcorans think will establish their claim".

Logically there is no reason why genuine information relating to Irish births or marriages would be available in New Jersey. It is far more likely it was home to an associate of the scammer who provided documents that would not be checked too carefully, or queried, by somebody who was clutching at straws. Sadly for the Corcorans, no claim was ever lodged.

In October 1910 farmer Tom Devery from Hepler in Kansas made an arrangement with merchant's wife, Mrs John Landers from Hiattville, ten miles away in Bourbon County, and two other apparent heirs. Between them they engaged the services of attorney J. H. Crain to pursue their claims.

Crain filed the claim with the treasury solicitor in London in advance of providing the necessary information to prove the claim's validity. Such proof, however, was never forthcoming and Mr Crain became the bearer of bad news, informing the claimants they were not related to Helen.

The Fort Scott Tribune said "Mr Devery has taken the matter nicely and has not decided to commit suicide". A strangely unusual comment to make, but very good to hear.

Three weeks later emerged the very sad story of a seventy year old Irish American farmer, Daniel Sheridan, who travelled to England to prosecute his claim, believing himself to be Helen's cousin. The wonderfully titled *Prattville Progress* in Alabama, and a number of other newspapers around the country, published the story of how, having crossed the Atlantic in 1885 he had been unable to find the evidence he needed to satisfy the treasury of the authenticity of his claim.

His family in Illinois were constantly writing to him believing he had forsaken them after inheriting Helen's fortune, when the sad fact was that he had run out of money and persuaded a lady to provide him with board and lodging in anticipation of his claim succeeding. When it became clear there would be no inheritance he was quickly evicted by his landlady and for a while was admitted to a workhouse.

Sometime later he discharged himself and wrote to his son Joseph saying he was going to Ireland to see someone who knew him as a boy. That was the last his family heard from him. Instead of crossing the Irish Sea, it appears he wandered the streets of London, homeless and helpless, until 6th December 1896 when he was taken to Lambeth Infirmary where he died three days later. With no address for him, the authorities had no way of informing his family and it was fourteen years before they discovered what had happened to him.

A little under nine months after Helen's death, the *Terre Haute Gazette* in Indiana printed a story that was baffling in the extreme. It starts with two brothers, Joseph and Richard Blake, who migrated to America from England with Lord Baltimore, who was the Proprietary Governor of Maryland.

Arriving in the province, as it then was, they settled on opposite shores of Chesapeake Bay, "early in the last century". This last comment would indicate they arrived in America sometime between 1700 and 1750, anything from fifty to a hundred years before Helen was born.

The article goes on to list the various children of Richard, and on down the family tree until reaching his eight great-great-grandchildren whose father, a doctor, had moved to, and now lived in, Terre Haute. After this it declares, "There remains therefore little doubt that the Maryland family are in the proper line of descent".

To the uninitiated there might seem to be a gap in their logic as there is no mention of where Helen fits into the picture. Be that as it may, however, one of the family, Joseph Blake II who was an attorney, set about establishing the claim and, "it is not impossible that he may go to England as the representative of the American heirs".

The paper estimated the number of heirs could be as many as six or seven thousand with each one entitled to around one hundred dollars. The writer concluded with a line from the 1839 play *Solon Shingle*, which said, "A hundred dollars in a pile is a heap of money".

Matthew Gilchrist who lived in the tiny township of Baldwin, about six miles from Pittsburgh, in 1885 declared himself as a second cousin of Helen who he said was born in Longford. His claim joined the ever growing pile labelled 'unsuccessful'.

Eighteen years later his widow, Margaret, read about the planned visit to America by the retired Indian civil servant Mr

Gribble and his private secretary from the "Scotch College of Heralds" in an attempt to find the true heirs. The report said that "he has made up his mind that before he will return to India he will have probed the mystery to the bottom, and either proved the claims of someone to be correct, or else proved that they are all false".

Perhaps they were unaware of his retirement and the fact that he would not be returning to India when they wrote that piece. Conveniently forgetting that the previous claim had failed, and hoping the treasury had done the same, Mrs Gilchrist decided she was one of those true heirs entitled to be rich, and together with the Hutten family from New York and the Nugent family in Chicago, she arranged to meet Mr Gribble. There are no details of what was discussed at the meeting, but no claim was lodged.

Just after the outbreak of the Second World War, *The Courier-Journal* in Louisville received a rather touching letter from Jessie Jane Caskey who pronounced, "I'm one of the heirs to a great fortune, the Blake Millions". Obviously no ambiguity there and she was clear that she knew all the facts, including that her Great-Grandfather Blake was an officer in King George's War (the American phase of the war of Austrian Succession).

On closer inspection, however, it did appear that a couple of facts had eluded the lady. Firstly, Robert never served in any war, and secondly her Great-Grandfather, whoever he might have been, was unlikely to have been even a twinkle in his parents' eyes when the war she referred to was fought two hundred years previously.

The largest claim in terms of numbers, most drawn out in terms of time, possibly the most ridiculous, and certainly the best publicised, came from the Boston area of Massachusetts.

The origins of the claim dated back to 1878, just a couple of years after Helen's death, when William Leonard, a supposed cousin, travelled to Ireland looking for evidence to back up his claim. Although he had secured the services of lawyers to assist him, the search ground to a halt when he started running out of money, and he returned to Boston empty handed.

William died a few years later, but that was not the end of it. In 1900, his daughter, Mary Murtha, and other members of the extended family decided to research the family tree and hired a genealogist, Oswald Bateman, who went to Europe in search of records. Having apparently uncovered some details, he too had to return to Boston when money started running short.

Perhaps this was another case of being dazzled by the dollar signs because within a couple of years the group were on the move again; this time they hired Henry S Lyons who after an initial investigation decided there was too much work involved, and called it a day.

He may have called it a day, but *they* had not called it off. In 1914, around the same time the *Helen Blake* crew were stranded on the Keeraghs, they surfaced again. This time they went to the top, hiring leading Boston attorney Thomas Mahoney who was also described as "a student of Irish affairs".

Tom arrived in England towards the end of July, just a few days before the outbreak of the First World War and after appointing an agent in London, made a hasty return to the USA.

Nothing else happened until the end of the war in 1918 at which time Mahoney turned over his files to fellow attorney and friend, Francis P Nicholls who retained a Dublin agent but, again, produced no results.

30

Never give in, never give in,
never, never, never, never.
– Winston Churchill

Like a phoenix rising from the ashes, after lying dormant for seven years, the Leonard, or Murtha, case surfaced again in 1925. At this point, enter the saviour – or the villain – Mr C W F Scott LLB.

Quite how the gentleman arrived on the scene is somewhat unclear, but his explanation as to why he had taken the case was very clear: "Fired by glowing accounts of the Blake Millions, touched by the romance of the Sheridan family, lured by adventure and with the failure of others to spur me on, I was prevailed upon by that ardent band of believers to take over the Blake case and try to win for them the untold riches that had been lying in the British treasury for almost fifty years".

Whatever virtues he may have had, I think we can say with some degree of certainty that modesty was not one of them, something which became evident again some years later when he self-published a book detailing his activities and efforts to prosecute the claim on behalf of the thirty-eight Bostonians.

In this publication he declared that he had made no attempt to render it "acceptable to the mere novel reader"; he was obviously too good for mere mortals. He also pointed out that "after all the garbled reports and hearsay accounts that have been going around, the truth of the Blake Millions is now being told for the first time". This was about the fifth or sixth occasion on which the truth was being told for the first time, in one publication or another.

In total Scott claims to have given it six and a half years of his undivided attention and spent some $485,000 (around seven million in 2018 terms) of his own money, having taken the case on a 'no win no fee' basis.

His first step was to collect affidavits from the claimants, all of which followed the same line recalling conversations with parents and grandparents, and affirming their belief that they were related to Helen. To a layman they looked very much like garbled accounts and hearsay. Armed with a brief case full of affidavits, the address of Hoey & Denning Solicitors in Dublin (who apparently had all the papers from the previous attempts), and "boundless enthusiasm", Scott left New York on 21st November for the first of thirty Atlantic crossings to seek out documentary evidence.

Arriving in London he immediately appointed a firm of solicitors to examine court records etc., inexplicably selecting Booth, Wade, Lomas-Walker & Colbeck who were based in Leeds – over two hundred miles, and a four or five hour train journey, from the Capital. Across the Irish Sea he discovered Hoey & Denning had already handed over all the papers to

Anna McHugh, the sister of yet another attorney who had been involved in the earlier attempts.

Back to square one and a few more Atlantic crossings before he eventually found a baptismal record for Elinor Sheridan, daughter of Richard and Sarah (Cassidy) in Donabate, Dublin. Success at last but with one small hitch – the baptism took place in July 1785 meaning Helen would have been thirty-two rather than nineteen when she married, and ninety-one when she died. Never one to be thrown off track by such anomalies, the young man continued his endeavours with renewed vigour.

Armed with this 'evidence', three years after taking over the case, it was time to up the ante and obtain the opinion of Counsel. Mr A. H. Droop, a member of The Honourable Society of Lincoln's Inn – one of the world's most prestigious professional bodies of judges and lawyers – was instructed and set about reviewing the case in preparation for a claim.

One month later Mr Droop produced his lengthy opinion, point one of which stated, "In my opinion there are no documents at present before me to suggest that the claimants have any chance of substantiating that Helen Blake was the same person as the Helen Sheridan baptised in 1785". Point two said, "In my opinion a claim against the Treasury is barred by Section 13 of the Law of Property Amendment Act, 1860 …"

Later on he suggests that "Unless a prima facie case on the facts as to kinship can be made out I do not think the Attorney General will give his fiat to a Petition of Right". (Rarely used today, the word *fiat* is from the Latin for 'let it be done' and is effectively a binding edict issued by a person in authority.)

To the layman this does not sound too hopeful but Mr Scott was obviously no layman, and saw it very differently, saying

"Mr Droop's opinion clearly justified our proceeding with the case …" He returned to Mr Droop six months later with further evidence including "an old letter and death notice". Droop's response was that it would be useless to go further with the case and once again to the layman this sounds like the end of the road.

Again Mr Scott saw it differently, however, and wrote that, "Following the receipt of Mr Droop's opinion there was nothing else to do but comply with strict professional etiquette; pay counsel's fees and secure all documents which had been left with him for examination before seeking new counsel". This really was taking 'never say die' to a whole new level!

The new counsel was Mr A. C. Edgar who studied all the papers before presenting his opinion, quoting numerous cases and legal precedents. He did mention a couple of things which were simple to understand, the first being "the evidence before me is substantially that of Mary Murtha (deceased) and Ellen Mary Leonard reproducing hearsay information given to them by their father, grandmother and step-grandmother". He went on to say, "… this evidence does not tally with the present claim; moreover the claims in support of which it was adduced have already been rejected by the Court".

Not one to be put off by mere facts, Scott went ahead with the petition in October 1929 and at the beginning of March 1930 he accompanied three elderly ladies as they boarded the Cunard liner *Aquitania* and set sail for England. The *New York Sun* said one of the ladies "admitted her identity" but in answer to questions she just said "I – we can't really tell you anything. You see, Mr Scott's taking care of everything. You'll have to see Mr Scott". Unusually however, Scott had no statement to make

THREE BOOKS

– all with a different opinion as to Helen's origins.

"and said so vigorously". It appears he was upset by a somewhat less than complementary report about him in the same paper two days earlier.

When the petition went before the court, a demurrer, or objection, was lodged: "Sir William Allen Jowitt Knight, His Majesty's Attorney-General, on behalf of our Lord the King gives the Court here to understand and be informed that the Petition of Right is bad in substance and in law ..." He went on to say, "... several averments and statements contained in the said Petition are not nor is any of them true in substance or in fact". Pretty damning comments, perhaps it really was time to call it a day but ... enter counsel number three.

This time Scott went to the top of the tree, engaging Mr H. B. Vaisey KC, and Doctor of Civil Law, Vicar General of the Province of York and Chancellor of the Dioceses of York, Carlisle, Derby and Wakefield, who was later to become an eminent judge. With Edgar as junior counsel they eventually made it to court at the end of February 1931 where the case was heard by Mr Justice Maugham who listened to all the arguments and studied all the evidence before reserving judgement.

A month later he handed down an eleven page decision dismissing the petition. Vaisey advised that there were no grounds for appeal so at long last, that really was that. Or was it? Scott met with various other members of the legal profession including former Home Secretary and prominent solicitor Viscount Brentford, who died before having an opportunity to review the papers.

In his 1933 book, *The Blake Millions*, Scott says, "The status of the case at the present time is that negotiations are underway with an eminent counsel for another opinion". Ten out of ten for effort, rather less for common sense.

His high profile, and love of publicity, was now coming back to haunt him with questions being asked in the press. Using the designatory letters LL.B after his name suggested he was a lawyer, although at least one newspaper report claimed there was no record of him ever qualifying as such.

How could a young man, as the press described him, afford to live for six or seven years without generating any income? Where did he get the equivalent of seven million dollars to invest in the case? This was the era of prohibition with mobsters always looking for ways to launder their money. Was he involved with them, and does that explain why he was so desperate to recoup the money?

It seems the man who started out claiming he would solve a mystery, ended up becoming one.

31

There are some frauds so well conducted that it
would be stupidity not to be deceived by them.
– Charles Caleb Colton

Although unsuccessful, many of the claimants were genuine people who clearly believed, or wanted to believe, they were entitled to a share of Helen's fortune. There were a number of others, however, who were simply chancing their luck, some who went to great lengths to persuade the authorities of their legitimacy (even though they could not prove it), and still others, with criminal intent, who fell into the category of fraudsters.

One of the more amusing claims was reported in the *Sheffield and Rotherham Independent* in August 1878. It came from Amelia Mary Tudor Radclyffe who, according to the paper, "had the notion that she was the Countess of Derwentwater, and that she was entitled to all sorts of estates in Cumberland, Westmoreland and Durham". She was also quite a character who in 1860 declared herself to be the great-granddaughter of the third Earl of Derwentwater, and laid claim to his estate using the name Lady Matilda Radclyffe.

Hearing of Helen's death, she presented a petition to the Master of the Rolls saying she was also entitled to her estate but, without even a shred of evidence to support her assertion, the case was dismissed. Like Helen, Amelia was something of an enigma in that nobody really knew who she was. One contemporary writer suggested she could be a lady's maid from Dover, another that she was a West Country servant girl trying her luck and yet another that she may have descended illegitimately from the Radclyffes of Dilson Castle in Northumberland.

Whatever the truth regarding her ancestry, she was certainly a colourful character who provided plenty of material for journalists, and an equal amount of entertainment for their readers. On one occasion, taking a steamer from Jersey City to Liverpool her luggage included "two old cane-seated chairs, one with two legs; two broken children's cribs, one with no rocker; three rickety deckchairs, with varnish scraped off; six cases of mysteriously packed bottles, supposed to be ale" and almost one hundred other items of equal interest!

She never gave up her pursuit of the original claim and her continuing eccentricities ensured she remained in the public eye until her death in 1880 at the age of forty-nine.

Equally amusing were the multiple claims of Thomas O'Neill, a Belfast salesman who worked on the principle 'if at first you don't succeed, try, try and try again'. He was quick off the mark following Helen's death and during a twelve month period between 1877 and 1878 produced three affidavits, followed by a fourth nineteen years later, in 1897.

In the first three he claimed his deceased father-in-law Richard Kirwan was her next-of-kin, describing him as a first cousin whose mother was Helen's aunt, and this time it was not just hearsay, Thomas had seen the evidence with his own eyes. This evidence, one of the mainstays of his claim, was a photograph of Helen, which he was unable to produce, taken fifteen or twenty years before her death, in which he stated "the chin and mouth strikingly resemble" and "the forehead and eyes are also like" those of the late Richard Kirwan. Incredibly, with such clear evidence, this claim was also rejected.

No point in going over old ground so in his fourth claim he forgot about his father-in law and moved on to produce his definitive history of the Sheridans. It was fascinating. Two hundred years ago they owned a considerable fishing fleet and were "esteemed for their probity and honour" in addition to being prominent smugglers. Following the Irish Rebellion of 1798 they "deprived the hangman" by smuggling many of the leaders to France, including Hamilton Rowan, a founding member of the Dublin Society of United Irishmen.

Thomas claimed Rowan owed his life to the Sheridans and, "Perhaps it is in revenge for depriving them of their prey that the English have deprived the heirs of the same Sheridan of their property".

The rambling narrative goes on to say Helen was baptised in 1785, married a parchment manufacturer named Walsh, took over his business when he died, met a military officer who "paid attention to her", sold the business and suddenly left Dublin around 1814 leaving behind her son for whom "she never showed affection".

Now came the *pièce de résistance*; O'Neill stated he had seen a photograph of Helen taken about twenty years before her death which "showed a most remarkable resemblance to the Sheridans". Perhaps there is some point in going over old ground after all, provided you make a few changes! It was an interesting story and the lads in the office probably had fun reading it, but without a shred of evidence to back up any of his contentions, it was filed alongside the previous petitions.

Given the sums involved, it was inevitable that the publicity given to Helen's death would attract a few shady characters. One claim, in 1903, that was unmistakeably fraudulent also deserves inclusion in the 'amusing' category. The claim, based on an entry in a parish register in Ireland dated 1820 was made by an elderly man purporting to be Helen's son, alleging he was born a few weeks after her marriage (naughty Helen!). Apparently this was in county Dublin, but although no details have ever been disclosed as to which parish was involved, the entry did indeed record the birth of a son to Robert and Helen Blake.

This would have been the 'Holy Grail' had it been true but instead it turned out to be a particularly clumsy effort that had plainly not been given a great deal of thought. The biggest give away was the fact that the date of the new entry was completely out of chronological order with those around it, making it stand out like as sore thumb. When examined by solicitor E. J. Ward of Tozer & Co in Chancery Lane, it did not take long for him to discover the original entry had been scratched out with a knife and a fictitious one written over it.

Coincidentally, the same solicitor was used when seventy-five year old John Doyle from Long Island in New York swore his affidavit. He was born in Ferns, County Wexford and stated "I have been informed and believe that my mother was a first cousin of Helen Blake". The wording of this would suggest that he was yet another victim of the so-called agents who were scouring the country for gullible prey.

Probably the most audacious, and blatantly fraudulent, claim of all came from Joseph Hollis Yates, a thirty-five year old solicitor with a practice in Dale Street, close to the docks in Liverpool and only a mile or so from the hotel where Robert and Helen stayed on their first night in England.

In 1896 he approached Michael Sheridan who lived in the city and informed him that he was the heir to what had by now become known as the Blake Millions. (A few years earlier, an unrelated Martin Sheridan of Carey Street in Liverpool had lodged an unsuccessful claim). Michael could hardly believe his luck, readily signing a contract that would allow Yates to pursue his claim in return for a share of the proceeds. The hunt was on.

Taking his research seriously, Yates made a number of trips to the West of Ireland and on one of them he *found* an old Bible in a second hand bookshop with a note signed by a Martin Sheridan, "My daughter Helen has run away with a young officer staying in Dublin Castle, and he has married her privately in Scotland".

Following this remarkable breakthrough, the solicitor's success went even further on his next trip when, by what he called "an amazing bit of luck", he *discovered* an old fob watch with the inscription, "From Helen Blake to her dear nephew, Patrick Sheridan 1866". With this kind of evidence, it looked as though Michael (and Yates) could indeed be in line for a huge windfall.

Everything was going according to plan, until a Liverpool jeweller came forward. He told the police that a short time previously a man – whom he later identified as Yates – had asked him to engrave an old watch with the identical words that were on the one the solicitor *discovered* in Ireland. The jeweller said he initially inscribed the date as 1896 (the current year) but when Yates saw this he was furious and insisted he change it to 1866.

Yates was arrested on a charge of fraud, following which a number of interesting discoveries were made. In his office was a collection of old Bibles, many of them containing entries designed to bolster the claim. It was also found he had purchased from a Birmingham undertaker two coffin plates bearing fake inscriptions and these were subsequently recovered from a graveyard where they had been buried to 'age'. There were even a number of 'old' gravestones being manufactured, each bearing an inscription that would further enhance the validity of the claim. At Liverpool assizes, Yates was found guilty of fraud and sentenced to penal servitude for life.

At least three claimants alleged that Helen was the daughter of Richard Sheridan and Sarah Cassidy of Donabate in county Dublin. Ship broker James McAllister of Egremont in Cheshire stated he was her nephew, seventy-nine year old widow Ann Harford of Rush in County Dublin claimed to be her aunt and John Browne of Galway who was "about seventy-five years of age" declared himself to be her cousin and "only next of kin".

At around the same time, Richard Sheridan of Ohio, USA, said his father was James Sheridan and his granduncle, William Sheridan, "had a daughter Helen who I often heard and verily believe married a man in the army of the name Blake, afterwards General Blake". His belief, verily or otherwise, did not sway the Treasury.

Three years later, William Patrick Sheridan of Galway maintained he was the only surviving son of James Sheridan "who was the lawful second brother of James Lawrence Sheridan who was married to a person named Bridget Hession". He also "verily believed" they had a daughter Helen, to whom he would have been first cousin, "and no other issue". He stated that he had been advised he was heir at law.

It was all getting very messy and in 1905 the *Irish Independent* became the latest publication to announce it was going to put an end to all the rumours and false claims, once and for all. On 25th April, page seven carried an eleven hundred word article which, it promised, "gives the true facts in connection with this extraordinary case". It went on to say that, "out of a mist of inventions and mis-statements the following unquestionable facts emerge".

Sadly, the 'facts' listed were far from unquestionable and the article is an excellent example of how things grew out of all proportion in the press. The first 'facts' stated Helen or Nelly Sheridan was born about 1800 in the village of Brize or Barnagreggaun in County Mayo. Other than being unsure of her name, uncertain of the village where she was born and unclear about the year in which she was born, the foregoing statement would appear to be one hundred percent accurate.

The article does state there are no records of Helen's birth, and after hundreds of unsuccessful searches over the past century and a half it would be fair to accept that as unquestionably true. It also points out there is no record of her marriage, which is unquestionably untrue. "A search in every registry office in the kingdom" obviously had excluded the major city of Glasgow. The statement that she died "23 years ago" (1882) would appear to indicate their research was something less than thorough.

Further into the article is a quote from Patrick Walsh who 'remembered' her going to England when she was about twenty-six, whilst Mary Cunningham also remembered her emigrating at around that time, and further recalled a letter sent to Helen's brother with details of the wedding and the honeymoon. These recollections are at odds with the marriage certificate clearly showing she married in 1819.

The journalist claims that the record of Helen's death "is the prosy point of an otherwise unconventional story". He may well be correct but it is unlikely that anyone would ever accuse his writing of being prosy, or unimaginative; in fact he must have had a very vivid imagination. There is mention of Robert being gazetted General in 1807 (the actual date was 10th January 1837), anecdotal evidence from what he condescendingly refers to as "two migratory Mayo peasants" and a claim "proved up to the hilt" that Mayo farmer Edward Godwin was the "real next of kin".

The writer finishes by saying, "our informants place before the public facts that have been revealed by long and patient investigation". Quite who the informants were, or where those facts were placed, is not clear and even after long and patient scrutiny of the article, none of the "unquestionably true facts" emerge.

A metaphorical spanner was thrown in the works in 1933 with the publication of a booklet entitled '*The Blake Millions or Helen Sheridan (The Wonder of the World)*'. In this, the anonymous author using the nom de plume of A Rustic, states emphatically, "Helen Sheridan was born in Carnin, Co Cavan, and of that there can be no doubt".

He further maintained that, "No other place in Ireland or outside it can produce credentials approaching those of Carnin". Unfortunately, he failed to produce any of those credentials, or anything else, other than hearsay, to justify his contention.

Although his overly flowery writing contains numerous anecdotes, it also contains a number of obvious errors including one that said Robert was a Lieutenant-Colonel when he met Helen. As we know from British army records, he was a Lieutenant-General at that time.

He goes on to say the Blakes entertained future Prime Minister William Gladstone and many more of England's greatest men in their residence, at 5 Kensington Gardens. Whilst the first part of that statement may well be true, there are no records to show that any such house ever existed.

On the subject of money, Mr 'Rustic' suggests that Helen's fortune belongs to the people of Carnin, but fails to explain why. He does make a good point, however, concerning the Free State Treaty, or Anglo-Irish Treaty, of December 1921. This treaty was, effectively, a transfer of Irish citizens to Irish rule under which all funds, the collective property of those citizens, was to be credited to the Free State current account with the British Government. Should this have included the Blake millions as he suggested? That is debateable, especially bearing in mind that the transfer of Helen's estate to the British treasury happened over forty years before the treaty was signed, and there is no absolute proof she was Irish.

As stated earlier, the Crown did honour the bequests in Helen's will, including six thousand four hundred pounds to build two lifeboats for Ireland, and the RNLI determined that one of those should go to Fethard. The first of the three different boats bearing her name and stationed in the specially built boat house arrived ten years after her death and was replaced in 1897 after eleven years' service. The third *Helen Blake,* the one involved in the tragedy was built at the Thames Ironworks boatyard in London under the supervision of a Mr Rube, and went into service in November 1905.

The other lifeboat funded by Helen's bequest was the *General R Dudley Blake,* which went to Blackrock in County Louth and was famously used on the insignia of the RNLI.

Almost a century and a half later Helen's money remains with the Crown and whilst her story is all but forgotten in the UK and elsewhere, her legacy will live on in the form of a replica Helen Blake being built by a community group and which, like the original, will established itself as an important part of the community in Fethard on Sea.

After copious research through books, reports and newspapers, there are still only a few things we know with absolute certainty: her husband to be was a Lieutenant-General when they met, they married in Scotland in 1819 when she gave her age as nineteen, she lived in London and the home counties, she was very wealthy, and she died in 1876, aged seventy-six, without leaving a will.

Truly, an enigma wrapped in a mystery.

Thank You

Writing is usually described as a solitary occupation, and for very good reason – there are many hundreds of hours spent alone in front of a computer screen, in libraries, museums and on location. The other side of the coin, however, is that there are also many hours spent listening to stories and talking to people without whose help a book like this would never see the light of day.

At the top of that list is Fethard on Sea historian Liam Ryan who is an absolute fountain of knowledge and generous enough to go out of his way to share it. Tom Neville and Declan Hearne shared their matchless memories of the village, recalling dates and names as if they were yesterday. Hayley Whiting, the RNLI Heritage Archive & Research Manager, provided information about the lifeboats, Tom Tangney, partner at Knight Frank in Kensington, provided details of Helen's house in Earl's Terrace and Paul Murray of Warwick & Warwick auctioneers shared his expertise on medals and awards. Arild Einar Syvertsen and Leo O'Toole allowed me access to their books, Brian Cleare permitted me to use his wonderful paintings and Phil Coulter granted permission to use a verse from his song, *Home From The Sea*. Johanne Powell translated *Mexico*'s log book from Norwegian while Chiara Hendry and Trevor & Margaret Winstanley translated medical terms into plain English. Jeremy Davis of Weather Routing Inc found details of weather conditions experienced by the *Mexico*.

Others to whom I am most grateful for their help are David Cronin who transformed pages of text into a book, photographer extraordinaire Steve Meyler, Sir Michael Blake 3rd Baronet of Tillmouth Park, Grainne Doran of Wexford County Archives, Shona Milton at the Brighton Museum, Ann Waters of Hook Heritage, Sylvia White of the Shipwrecked Mariners' Society, Raymond Foley for his cover design, fashion designer Kelly Clark, artists Jackie Edwards, Jason Ceannobháin, Leanne Mullen, Ivana Lavelle, Clive O'Sullivan, and, José Marques, George Crumpton's grandson Tom Crumpton, Pat Roche's granddaughter Statia Colfer, James Morrissey's grandson Tommy Morrissey, Richard Bird's nephew Larry Bird, Billy Doyle whose grandfather and uncle were on James Stevens, Des Peare of the Rosslare Maritime Museum, railway enthusiasts Nigel Wassell and Peter Davies, Eamonn Colfer, Paul McFarlane, Tracey Fraser, Charlie Colfer, Brian Matthews, Gary Chapman, Tom & Ann Nunan, Jack Butler, Paula Gouveia of Açoriano Oriental in the Azores, Andrew Power, John Hensman, Andrew Kiernan, Michael J Reidy of Claremorris, Les Craskill, Eibhlin Moynihan Wickham. Finally, thanks to my wife Carole who made a number of helpful suggestions, and my three amazing grandchildren for their constant inspiration.

BIBLIOGRAPHY

BOOKS

John Doyle, The Helen Blake, the last Fethard life-boat, *1970*

Liam Ryan, Awful Tragedy of the Helen Blake Lifeboat, *2010*

A Rustic, Blake Millions or Helen Sheridan (The Wonder of the World), *1933*

Leo O'Toole, Cailíns Road To The Rich Man's Wealth, *2009*

Samuel Lewis, Topographical Dictionary of Ireland, *1837*

Arild Einar Syvertsen, Skipshistorier fra de Syv Hav, *H. Aschehoug & Co., 2011*

Liza Picard, Victorian London, *Orion Books Ltd, 2006*

C W F Scott, The Blake Millions, *1933*

Billy Colfer, The Hook Peninsula, *Cork University Press, 2004*

On The Hook, 1995, 1997, 2003, 2006, 2008

Celia Fiennes, Through England on a Side Saddle, *1888*

Ernie Shepherd, Wexford Harbour Commissioners, *2018*

John Maddock, Rosslare Harbour Sea & Ships, Harbour Pub., 1996

John Maddock, Rosslare Harbour Sea & Ships, Harbour Pub., 1996

Sebastian Junger, The Perfect Storm, W W Norton & Co, 1997

DOCUMENTS & REPORTS

The Legal Guide, 6 August 1842

Hansard, 3 July 1884, 14 November 1884

Census of Ireland 1901 / 1911

US Department of Agriculture Weather Bureau, December 1913

United States Weather Bureau, 20 February 1914

Meteorological Office Monthly Weather Report, February 1914

Wexford Harbour Commissioners minutes 3, 4 & 16 March 1914

RNLI Report by Captain Rowley, 9 April 1914

Wexford County Council minutes, 15 April, 6 May 1914

RNLI Lifeboat Journal, 1 May 1914

Board of Trade Report No 172, 2 May 1914

Dáil Éireann Oireachtas Report, 23 October 1929

British History Online pages 21-28

Dáil Éireann Oireachtas Report, 23 October 1929

Topographical Dictionary of Ireland, Samuel Lewis, 1937

British History Online pages 21-28

History of the RNLI

Electrifying Rural Ireland, ESB Archives

Life in 1916 Ireland, Central Statistics Office, March 2016

Great Britain Historical GIS, University of Portsmouth, 2017

NEWSPAPERS & MAGAZINES

The Quarterly Review, England, December 1844

The Illustrated London News, England, 3 March 1850

London Courier, Scotland, 24 May 1827

The Morning Post, England, 14 May 1830

Newcastle Guardian, England, 19 July 1862

The London Gazette, England, 11 May 1877

Terre Haute Weekly Gazette, USA, 7 June 1877

The Irish Times, 12 June 1877,
    11 April 1878, 17 March 1886, 12 May 1906,
    23, 25, 27 & 28 February 1914,
    4, 5, 10, 11, 13, 14, 16, 23 & 25 March 1914,
    22 April 1914, 27 July 1914, 27 January 1915,
    17 February 1916, 12 February 1930, 16 April 1937,
    22 February 1954, 25 October 1954

The Kumara Times, New Zealand, 27 June 1877

The Cincinnati Enquirer, USA, 31 October 1877, 15 September 1929

The Morpeth Herald, England, 23 March 1878

Weekly Irish Times, 13 April 1878, 4 September 1909

The Sheffield & Rotherham Independent, England, 1 August 1878

Evening Herald, Ireland, 17 December 1882,
    7 August 1909, 26 February 1930

The Times, England, 4 July 1884, 23 & 26 February 1914, 14 March 1914

The Freeman's Journal, Ireland, 4 July 1884, 15 November 1884,
    17 March 1886, 15 August 1896, 7 August 1909

The Swindon Advertiser, England, 3 April 1886

The Age, Australia, 15 May 1886, 15 August 1896

Waterford Standard, Ireland, 21 April 1888

The Maitland Mercury, Australia, 29 April 1888

The Cornubian & Redruth Times, England, 13 April 1888
Lloyds Weekly Newspaper, England, 15 April 1888
South London Press, England, 21 April 1888
The Daily Inter Ocean, USA, 30 April 1888
The Daily Picayune, USA, 10 May 1888
Tyrone Constitution, Ireland, 11 May 1888
Te Aroha News, New Zealand, 10 October 1888
Yorkshire Evening Post, England, 19 March 1891
Gloucester Citizen, England, 10 April 1897, 25 March 1931
St James's Gazette, England, 6 April 1891, 27 May 1903
Aberdeen Evening Express, Scotland, 8 April 1891
The Middlesex Courier, England, 10 April 1891
The Hawke's Bay Herald, New Zealand, 5 September 1891
The Western Daily Press, England, 17 December 1892
Dublin Evening Telegraph, 20 January 1894
United Ireland, 27 January 1894
The Thames Advertiser, New Zealand, 7 June 1896
The Cork Constitution, Ireland, 25 June 1896
Leicester Chronicle, England, 27 June 1896
The Northern Whig, Ireland, 4 July 1896, 2
    3, 25 & 26 February 1914, 27 July 1914
Kerry Weekly Reporter, Ireland, 11 July 1896
The Drogheda Independent, Ireland, 11 July 1896
Irish Standard, USA, 18 July 1896
Taranaki Herald, New Zealand, 21 August 1896
The Otago Daily Times, New Zealand, 24 August 1896
Newcastle Morning Herald, Australia, 29 August 1896
The Mercury, Australia, 2 August 1897
Gloucestershire Echo, England, 20 May 1903
Dundee Evening Post, Scotland, 28 May 1903
The Kalgoorlie Miner, Australia, 29 May 1903
The Advertiser, Australia, 3 June 1903
The Daily News, Australia, 2 June 1903
The Thames Star, New Zealand, 3 July 1903
The Evening Journal, Australia, 4 July 1903
The Colac Herald, Australia, 10 July 1903
The Ballarat Star, Australia, 10 July 1903
The Evening Star, New Zealand, 11 July 1903,

21 October 1909, 21 October 1921

The Star, New Zealand, 16 July 1903

The Marlborough Express, New Zealand, 16 July 1903

West Gippsland Gazette, Australia, 21 July 1903, 13 August 1912

The Northern Star, Australia, 22 July 1903

The Clarence River Advocate, Australia, 7 August 1903

The Manaluata Times, New Zealand, 10 August 1903

The Morning Bulletin, Australia, 3 September 1903

The Pittsburgh Press, USA, 4 October 1903

The Nenagh Guardian, Ireland, 11 June 1904

The Advocate, Australia, 6 August 1904

The San Francisco Call, 27 August 1904, 15 September 1904,
    24 March 1905

Baltimore Sun, USA, 8 March 1905

Irish Independent, 25 April 1905, 3 November 1905, 18 January 1909,
    4 August 1909, 21 August 1909, 6 September 1982

The Los Angeles Times, 26 March 1905

The Dundalk Examiner, Ireland, 3 June 1905

Times Democrat, USA, 16 August 1905, 8 January 1906

New York Tribune, 16 November 1905

Chicago Daily Tribune, 16 November 1905,
    14 September 1909, 28 September 1973

Waterford Standard, Ireland, 22 November 1905,
    28 February 1914, 13 February 1937, 17 April 1937,
    24 June 1939, 23 August 1941, 18 December 1948

Tampa Tribune, USA, 6 January 1906

Pensacola Journal, USA, 7 January 1906,
    21, 23, 26 & 29 May 1909, 22 February 1914

The Express & Telegraph, Australia, 9 May 1906

The Evening Journal, Australia, 9 May 1906

The West Australian, 10 May 1906

The West Coast Times, New Zealand, 10 May 1906

The Sydney Morning Herald, 10 May 1906, 31 December 1927

The Chronicle, Australia, 12 May 1906

The New Zealand Herald, 23 June 1906, 31 December 1927,
    18 September 1909, 16 May 1931

The Berwickshire News, Scotland, 20 January 1909, 16 June 1925

The Western People, Ireland, 23 January 1909

The Wicklow News-Letter, Ireland, 23 January 1909

Berwick & County Gazette, England, 23 January 1909

The Omaha Sunday Bee, USA, 7 February 1909

The Londonderry Sentinel, Ireland, 5 August 1909

Roscommon Messenger, Ireland, 7 August 1909

Sunday Independent, Ireland, 8 August 1909

Belfast Telegraph, 9 August 1909

Larne Times, Ireland, 14 August 1909

The Tuam Herald, Ireland, 14 August 1909, 4 May 1929

The Ballymena Weekly Telegraph, Ireland,14 August 1909,
    14 August 1931

The Evening Star, USA, 23 August 1909

The Derry Journal, Ireland, 23 August 1909

The Washington Post, USA 14 September 1909

Times Dispatch, USA, 14 September 1909

Catholic Press, Australia, 23 September 1909, 24 April 1930

Southern Cross, Australia, 24 September 1909

The Star, Australia, 9 October 1909

The World's News, Australia, 9 October 1909,
    30 April 1930, 13 May 1931

The Winnipeg Tribune, Canada, 26 April 1910,
    7 April 1928, 1 March 1930

The Cork Examiner, Ireland, 18 August 1910, 25 May 1914

Salt Lake Herald Republican, USA, 29 September 1910

The Fort Scott Tribune, USA, 5 October 1910, 2 January 1911

Plymouth Tribune, USA, 6 October 1910

Wood County Reporter, USA, 6 October 1910

The Tensas Gazette, USA, 7 October 1910

The New Era, USA, 7 October 1910

Middle Park Times, USA, 7 October 1910

The Evening Item, USA, 8 October 1910

Spanish Fork Press, USA, 13 October 1910

The Sheboygan Daily Press, USA, 21 October 1910

The Prattville Progress, USA, 27 October 1910

Connaught Times, Ireland, 23 December 1911

The Brooklyn Daily Eagle, USA, 7 January 1912, 17 June 1928

Cheltenham Chronicle, England, 1 June 1912

The Weekly Freeman, Ireland, 8 June 1912,

28 February 1914, 7 March 1914, 25 April 1914, 24 July 1915

Vancouver Daily World, 22 June 1912

The San Francisco Chronicle, 23 June 1912

The Darling Downs Gazette, Australia, 8 July 1912

Bemidji Daily Pioneer, 6 February 1914

Cape Weekly Tribune, USA, 6 February 1914

Bridgeport Evening Farmer, USA, 21 February 1914

Seattle Star, USA, 21 February 1914

The New York Sun, 21 February 1914, 28 February 1930

Washington Herald, USA, 22 & 25 February 1914, 2 & 11 March 1914,
    22 September 1933

Manchester Guardian, England, 23 February 1914

Belfast Newsletter, 23, 24 & 26 February 1914,
    3 & 7 March 1914, 22 April 1914, 25 July 1914

Daily Gate City, USA, 23 February 1914,

Dublin Daily Express, 24, 25, 26 & 28 February 1914,
    5, 6, 9, 10, 12, 13, 14, 16 & 30 March 1914, 22 April 1914,
    12 & 15 June 1914, 27 July 1914, 27 January 1915

Ballymena Observer, Ireland, 27 February 1914

Hampshire Advertiser, England, 28 February 1914

The Free Press, Ireland, 28 February 1914

Wilmar Tribune, USA, 4 March 1914

Yorkshire Post, England, 25 March 1914

Sheffield Independent, England, 3 April 1914

Larne Telegraph, Ireland, 16 May 1914

The Daily News, Australia, 6 April 1921

The Anglo-Celt, Ireland, 17 February 1923

The Brisbane Courier, Australia, 31 December 1927

The Sunday Times, Australia, 8 January 1928

The Cairns Post, Australia, 5 March 1928

The Northern Herald, Australia, 7 March 1928

Orlando Morning Sentinel, USA, 17 March 1928

The Advocate, USA, 19 May 1928

The Register, Australia, 29 May 1928

The Observer, Australia, 2 June 1928

The Muncie Evening Press, USA, 30 June 1928

Madera Daily Tribune, USA, 11 July 1928

The Saturday Journal, Canada, 30 June 1928

Derby Daily Telegraph, England, 12 September 1928

The Meath Chronicle, Ireland, 8 December 1928,
26 October 1929, 25 July 2009

The Leitrim Observer, Ireland, 2 May 1929, 7 September 1929

Kerry News, Ireland, 4 October 1929

The Leeds Mercury, England, 15 October 1929

Aberdeen Press & Journal, Scotland, 30 October 1929

Connaught Telegraph, Ireland, 2 November 1929

Ellesmere Guardian, New Zealand, 6 December 1929

Allentown Morning Call, USA, 2 March 1930, 13 July 1930

Sunday Star, USA, 2 March 1930

Nashua Telegraph, USA, 26 February 1931

Yorkshire Evening Post, England, 26 February 1931

The Straits Times, Singapore, 27 February 1931

Nottingham Evening Post, England, 25 March 1931

The Evening News, USA, 26 March 1931

The Ottawa Evening Journal, Canada, 18 April 1931

Windsor & Richmond Gazette, Australia, 8 May 1931

The Mail, Australia, 9 January 1932

The Courier-Journal, USA, 14 September 1940

Dublin Evening Mail, 14 July 1956